Kōtoku Shūsui
Portrait of a Japanese Radical

Kōtoku Shūsui in 1909

Kōtoku Shūsui
Portrait of a Japanese Radical

F. G. NOTEHELFER

Assistant Professor, Department of History,
University of California, Los Angeles

CAMBRIDGE
AT THE UNIVERSITY PRESS
1971

Published by the Syndics of the Cambridge University Press
Bentley House, 200 Euston Road, London N.W.1
American Branch: 32 East 57th Street, New York, N.Y.10022

Library of Congress Catalogue Card Number: 76–134620

ISBN: 0 521 07989 6

Printed in Great Britain by
Alden & Mowbray Ltd
at the Alden Press, Oxford

To my mother and father

Contents

Plates

Acknowledgments

The following study is based on my doctoral dissertation which was presented at Princeton University in 1968. It gives me pleasure to be able to express my thanks to the many friends who made this book possible.

My interest in Meiji Christianity, a sub-theme readily detectable in the early chapters of the book, was first stimulated by my parents, the Rev. and Mrs J. Karl Notehelfer, who devoted much of their lives to missionary work in Japan. It was under the careful guidance of Professor Edwin O. Reischauer, who encouraged my formal study of the Japanese language, and my Harvard tutors, Akira Iriye and Albert Craig, that I received my start as a student of modern Japanese history. Their genuine interest in my work and the generosity with which they shared their ideas with me will always be remembered with gratitude.

As a graduate student at Princeton University I was especially fortunate to be able to work with Professor Marius B. Jansen. It was under his direction that I first became interested in the Meiji socialist movement and in the career of Kōtoku Shūsui. The care with which he followed every stage of my research, not to mention the many valuable suggestions he made in the preparation of the manuscript, leave me deeply in his debt. I always found him to be both an ideal scholar and a warm personal friend.

My thanks also go to Professor Tetsuo Najita, who read the manuscript in its entirety and made a number of useful suggestions. Many individuals, both in the United States and in Japan, helped me to acquire the materials without which this study would not have been possible. To each of them I would like to extend my personal thanks. I am also indebted to various Japanese scholars who aided my research in Japan in 1964-5. Here I would like to thank Professor Maruyama Masao of Tokyo University, Mr Nishida Taketoshi of Tokyo University's Library of Meiji Newspapers and Magazines, Professor Shiota Shōbei of Toritsu University and Professor Takeda Kiyoko Cho of International Christian University. I also wish to thank Hirao Michio for a delightful visit to Kōchi and for his assistance with materials in the Kōchi Ken Library. Upon my return to Princeton I was aided greatly by Haga Toru of Tokyo University, who was kind enough to go over some of my translations with me and clarified a number of difficult points in Kōtoku's language – any errors that remain are of course solely my responsibility. I also wish to thank Professor Sugii Mutsurō of Doshisha University for many an interesting afternoon in Princeton which we wiled away over long cups of coffee discussing the problems of Meiji history.

I am most grateful to Princeton University, the Foreign Area Fellowship Program, the Inter-University Center for Japanese Language Studies in Tokyo, and the University of California at Los Angeles for the financial support that made this book possible.

Finally I would like to thank my wife for her loyal support and all the help she gave me while this study was in progress.

F.G.N.

Introduction

For a period of over three decades from 1911 to Japan's defeat in World War II the name Kōtoku Shūsui connoted danger. Designated the chief plotter in the 1910 conspiracy to assassinate the Meiji Emperor, Kōtoku was condemned on the charge of High Treason and executed early in 1911. In the years that followed his name came to symbolize the type of person who indulged in 'dangerous thoughts' to the detriment of the national polity and for a whole generation of Japanese the name Kōtoku Shūsui meant 'traitor'.

In the postwar years this judgment was greatly altered. With Japan's defeat in war, the man who opposed militarism and nationalism at the time of Japan's conflict with Russia in 1904 now came to be regarded as a great visionary. The man who actually predicted the conflict with America as the inevitable outworking of Japanese imperialism as early as 1906 now took on the cloak of the outstanding political theoretician of his time. The man who saw in Socialism and Anarchism the political wave of the future now came to stand as a symbol of unflinching self-sacrifice and unmitigated opposition to an 'absolute' government that destroyed human dignity and freedom. In short, for those on the political left searching for a tradition, Kōtoku Shūsui became the ideal symbol of the 'true patriot' who had sacrificed his life as the first martyr of the movement.

In dealing with Kōtoku one is inevitably faced with the problem of where the real man ends and where the symbol begins. Nor is this problem new. As early as 1911, at the time of the High Treason Trial, Kōtoku was already imbued with symbolic significance for the intellectuals of the day.

In a famous speech at the First Higher School in Tokyo in which he addressed many of Japan's future leaders a few weeks after Kōtoku's death, Tokutomi Roka, the well known Meiji novelist, described him as a re-embodiment of the Restoration _shishi_: a follower of Yoshida Shōin and the other late Tokugawa revolutionaries, who like them had seen the 'vision of a new heaven and a new earth' and had been willing to sacrifice himself to the 'uttermost for mankind'.[1] Nagai Kafū, another writer critical of Meiji society, regarded Kōtoku as a symbol of the intellectual who had Westernized himself for the sake of the nation, only to discover that personal and national

[1] Tokutomi Roka, 'Muhon ron', _Hiyūmanizumu_, vol. 17 of _Gendai Nihon shisō taikei_ (Tokyo, 1964).

goals were no longer one, and that in the conflict between state and individual, the individual would have to give way.[1] Ishikawa Takuboku, a passionate young poet, saw in him a symbol of resistance to the 'increasingly oppressive, saber-rattling government leaders', who, he was convinced, would outlaw all 'thinking' in the future.[2]

Subsequent generations followed in the steps of Tokutomi, Nagai, and Ishikawa. If much of Kōtoku's career remained shrouded in secrecy in the 1920s and 1930s, a situation which was not augmented by the censorship of the late Taisho and early Showa years, this did not prevent him from continuing to serve as a symbol for both the right and the left.

Following World War II the previous dearth of materials was suddenly replaced by a wealth of documentation. As manuscripts, long closeted out of the reach of government 'spies' and censors, suddenly saw the light of day, a Kōtoku 'boom' resulted. Personal accounts of friends, family, and political associates shed new light on Kōtoku's background and personality, and the publication of a good part of his writings, including his letters and diaries, did much to enlighten the public.

But greater knowledge did not alter Kōtoku's role as symbol. The biographies based on new materials remained the products of ideological commitment, and not objective scholarship. The picture of Kōtoku which emerged was that of a political visionary far ahead of his times, both in values and ideas, who staunchly opposed the encroachments of an increasingly autocratic state.

While it is possible to picture Kōtoku as a revolutionary in the tradition of the *shishi* loyalist, the samurai who played such an important part in the Meiji Restoration, a closer examination of his life and thought cannot help but lead one to question the extent to which Kōtoku conformed to the image of the modern revolutionary suggested by postwar Japanese historians.

What the following study attempts to delineate is the difficulty with which the modern Japanese intellectual broke with his tradition. Here I would agree with Robert Bellah that in a modernizing society in which the process of modernization is not the product of its own 'internal logic', but is carried out as a result of outside pressures, as was the case in Meiji Japan, the individual is all too often not innerly ready to give up traditional patterns of social behavior and traditional ways of thinking. And yet, under the pressures of a modern society, he is constantly forced to give them up. The result is tension and anxiety. On the other hand, even when the intellectual is able

[1] Nagai Kafū, 'Hanabi', *Nagai Kafū zenshū* (*Chūō Kōron* ed., Tokyo, 1949), vol. XII.
[2] Iwaki Yukinori, *Ishikawa Takuboku den* (Tokyo, 1961), p. 212.

to break with the past and does accept foreign intellectual or ideological systems those systems are frequently subjected to premises and limitations that expressed themselves in the former intellectual order. The values of the past limit choices. In some areas the tradition may aid the adoption of new ideas, in others, and here I would include particularly those areas in which new ideas most directly challenge older values, new choices become extremely difficult if not impossible.

As a product of the *shishi* tradition, there was inherent in Kōtoku a potential for revolutionary action. There was even a potential for revolutionary thought. But such action, and such thought, had their roots within traditional, not modern, values. The manner in which these traditional values were restructured to meet the requirements of a new society, and the effect that such a restructuring process had on the thinker, remain the central problems towards which the following study of Kōtoku Shūsui's life and thought is directed.

CHAPTER 1

The Tosa years 1871–88

T

WENTY-FIVE MILES from the southwest tip of the island of Shikoku, slightly inland and facing the broad Bay of Tosa to the east, lies the small Kōchi Ken city of Nakamura. It was here on September 22, 1871 that Kōtoku Denjirō was born.[1]

Even today Nakamura nestles in one of the more isolated corners of Japan and cannot be reached by rail. Its people still speak a dialect markedly different from the *Tosa-ben* usually spoken in Kōchi Ken, and among its citizens there are many who remain proud of the fact that Nakamura was originally laid out in imitation of the Kyoto capital and once housed a retired emperor and one of Kyoto's noble families.[2]

Until 1689 Nakamura maintained itself as a small castle town and served as the headquarters for approximately four hundred warriors. In 1689 the head of the Nakamura fief was asked to serve on the Tokugawa Junior Council. Seeking to avoid the ruinous expenses of such an office, he declined. The Tokugawa bakufu did not take insubordination lightly and was thorough in its punitive measures. These included not only the destruction of the local castle, the confiscation of the lord's mansions in Edo, the elimination of his retainers' incomes, and the confiscation of the han's finances for several years, but went so far as to destroy the warriors' dwellings, thereby forcing them to scatter and make their living as ordinary merchants or artisans. A local history described the town's plight 'as though a fire had ravaged it'.[3]

With the destruction of the Nakamura fief, the town of Nakamura became little more than the center of a rural area under the control of Tosa han. As might be expected, the changes which took place in Nakamura in 1689

[1] Shiota Shōbei, *Kōtoku Shūsui no nikki to shokan* (Tokyo, 1965; hereafter cited as *Nikki to shokan*), p. 466. This date is according to the lunar calendar. Shūsui (autumn flood) later became Denjirō's pseudonym.

[2] Shakai keizai rōdō kenkyūjo, *Kōtoku Shūsui hyōden* (Tokyo, 1948), p. 127. This work contains an article by Denjirō's cousin, Okazaki Teru, titled 'Itoko Shūsui no omoide', in which she mentions that at the time of the Shōkyū War (1219–21) Nakamura housed the retired emperor, Tsuchimikado while during the Ōnin War (1467–77) the Ichijō family settled there.

[3] Nakamura Chō Yakuba, *Nakamura chō shi* (Kōchi, 1950), p. 32. This curious incident is also mentioned in Marius B. Jansen, *Sakamoto Ryōma and the Meiji Restoration* (Princeton, 1961), p. 27.

4

seriously affected the power structure of the community. With the removal of the samurai, new families were able to rise to positions of local leadership, that is to say, into the ranks of headmen (*shōya*) and elders (*toshiyori*). The Kōtokus were one such family.

The history of the Kōtoku family is closely related to the developments which took place within Nakamura. It is particularly interesting for the mobility it reflects in the latter half of the Tokugawa period.

Kōtoku Denjirō's ancestors can be traced back to the Kyoto court where they served as diviners. In 1738 Kōtoku Atsutane was sent from Osaka to Nakamura to become the adopted son in the home of Kaheiji, the local dealer in herbs and medicines. There were advantages for a diviner's family which had developed an interest in traditional medicine in such an alliance since it expedited the procurement of the raw materials necessary for its trade. At the same time the Tosa merchant gained the security of a steady outlet for his produce. The Nakamura merchant, Kaheiji, had the further advantage of using the Kōtoku name which meant increased prestige in the local community.

The five generations of the Kōtoku family which preceded Denjirō as Nakamura shopkeepers proved themselves to be able businessmen and the family's fortunes rose steadily. By 1840 Denjirō's great grandfather, Atsuchika, was granted an honorary position equivalent to that of elder, and his son, Atsumichi, became a town elder of headman rank with the right to carry a sword. Kōtoku Denjirō's father, Atsuaki, was granted the title of councilor (*machi otona*) in 1851 with the stipulation that this rank was to become hereditary. In 1871 further laurels were added to the family name when Denjirō's father was granted the right to carry a sword by the new Meiji government. Later in the same year, after the abolition of the han and the formation of the prefectures, he was placed in charge of four villages.[1]

While headmen and elders represented the bottom link of han control and were responsible for local administration, they were not samurai but commoners chosen from the leading village or town families. Their power and authority, though considerable, did not extend to the *gōshi*, or 'country samurai', who stood at the apex of rural Tosa society.[2] It was natural,

[1] Nishio Yōtarō, *Kōtoku Shūsui* (Tokyo, 1966), p. 5. Also mentioned in Kōtoku Tomiji's chronology, *Nikki to shokan*, p. 464.

[2] A good description of the *shōya* and *gōshi* can be found in Marius B. Jansen, *Sakamoto Ryōma*, pp. 26ff. Jansen mentions that *gōshi* were immune from *shōya* jurisdiction and that this was the source of considerable conflict. The *gōshi*, while outranking the *shōya*, had no direct administrative authority. Both groups were tied to the land, however, and thus had common interests in protecting their holdings against the encroachments of han administrators.

therefore, that headmen and elder families wanted to break into the *gōshi* rank. Since *gōshi* titles were offered as rewards for land reclamation by the han administration, headmen and elder families often used their offices to acquire the capital necessary for such projects.[1]

With its gradual rise in status, the Kōtoku family identified more and more strongly with the values of the warrior class and made every effort to educate itself in the samurai tradition. This was particularly true of Denjirō's father who was renowned for his scholarly abilities, having studied with the Confucian scholar and Tosa loyalist, Yasuoka Ryōsuke.[2] It can also be seen in the 1857 marriage of Atsuaki to the daughter of Ōno Ryōsuke, a prominent doctor in the Nakamura area whose family was of *gōshi* rank. This mixture of commoner and country samurai backgrounds was later responsible for the peculiar tension and conflict of values which Denjirō faced as a youth.

Ōno Ryōsuke's daughter, Tajiko, was unusually small of stature, and it was in an attempt to spare her the strenuous life of the country samurai's wife that her father arranged for her the match with the more affluent merchant family. Despite her size, Tajiko bore Atsuaki five children – two daughters and three sons – of which Denjirō was the youngest.[3]

Atsuaki was an easy-going man who preferred his books to his abacus, and it is to this trait that the financial difficulties which befell the family after his death are usually attributed.[4] There is probably some truth to this accusation, but the family's financial difficulties were as much the fault of the rapid social and economic changes that attended the Meiji Restoration as they were of Atsuaki's character. Indeed, there is evidence which suggests that Atsuaki possessed considerable foresight and saw the Restoration as a period offering new possibilities. The family had already added sake-brewing to its traditional herb and medicine (*tawaraya*) enterprise, and Atsuaki now tried to make the transition from these to the new field of mining.[5]

Atsuaki's early death in 1872 jeopardized his family's financial position since there was no one to carry on the merchant enterprise. Moreover, just at the moment when the Kōtokus seemed to be making a successful transition

[1] *Ibid.* p. 29.

[2] Morooka Chiyoko, *Otto Kōtoku Shūsui no omoide* (Tokyo, 1946), p. 9.

[3] Despite the three sons which were born into the family, Denjirō soon became the sole heir of the family line. Kakyūta, the oldest son, died in childhood, and Kameji the second boy, was adopted into an uncle's family.

[4] Morooka Chiyoko, *Otto Kōtoku Shūsui no omoide*, p. 9.

[5] In the immediate post-Restoration period one of Atsuaki's relatives, Kuwabara Kaihei, a former Tosa loyalist who served as an official in the Bonin Islands, came into possession of a copper mine in the province of Iyo. In order to develop this mine he approached his relatives for capital and Atsuaki appears to have invested heavily in the venture; *ibid.*

from feudal to modern Japan, their personal link with the Meiji administration, which was vital to this transition, was broken. The result of this tragedy left them in much the same position as many Nakamura ex-samurai (*shizoku*) families who also suffered from a loss of status and income. Having always associated closely with *gōshi* families, it was only natural for Denjirō's family to identify with the warrior's cause in the immediate post-Restoration years.[1]

At first Tajiko appears to have made an effort to run both the household and shop, but it soon became apparent that she was neither mentally nor physically qualified for such a task. To help manage the business, Atsuaki's older brother Kachiyuemon and his wife moved into the Kōtoku home; and Kameji, Denjirō's older brother, became the adopted son of this childless couple. Denjirō, though still an infant, now became the sole heir of his branch of the family, but because of his age the family took in the former clerk (*bantō*) as an adopted son.[2]

Komatarō, the clerk, turned out to be an able administrator and his talents were soon recognized by the Dōkyūsha, a business organization designed to alleviate the distress of the local samurai by engaging in the production and sale of such items as camphor, paper, sake, sugar, and tea, as well as copper ores, native to the area. The Dōkyūsha was modeled on the broader Tosa han organization, the Kaiseikan, which Gotō Shōjirō started in 1865 for the purpose of expanding Tosa trade and production.[3] By the early seventies the Kaiseikan had fallen into the hands of Iwasaki Yatarō, who was busy converting its enterprises into the Mitsubishi Company. The Dōkyūsha was loosely affiliated with the Kaiseikan, and later with the Iwasaki interests. During its most prosperous years it was managed by Komatarō and used the Kōtoku home as its business headquarters.[4]

As the headquarters of the Dōkyūsha, the Kōtoku home became the meeting place for many of the former samurai of the Nakamura area. Faced

---

[1] It should be kept in mind that many *gōshi* and *shōya* went on to become the landlords of Meiji Japan and did well in the Restoration, Marius B. Jansen, *Sakamoto Ryōma*, p. 374.

[2] Nishio Yōtarō, *Kōtoku Shūsui*, p. 7. After Denjirō's death in 1911 the clerk, Komatarō, carried on the family line in Nakamura.

[3] The functions of the Kaiseikan are described by Marius B. Jansen as follows: 'Opened in the spring of 1865, this bureau was designed to centralize and direct all han enterprise in Tosa. Departments were set aside for naval development, for a medical school in which English and French were taught, an industrial department which would promote the production of camphor, paper, sugar, tea, and other domestic products, a mining division to seek out and exploit reserves of gold, silver, copper, iron, lead, and lime, a division to promote the whaling industry, and a purchasing agency to market such goods and to purchase needed foreign ships, machines, weapons, and books, with offices in Nagasaki and, later, in Osaka', Jansen, *Sakamoto Ryōma*, p. 246.

[4] *Kōtoku Shūsui hyōden*, pp. 133–5. By the late 1880s the Dōkyūsha's profits were falling and the organization atrophied.

with the complexities of adjusting to a new way of life the former samurai were often frustrated, and it is not difficult to imagine the discontent that must have been aired at the meetings of these men, particularly in the mid-seventies when samurai throughout the country turned to violence and open rebellion. Thus, it was in the home of a commoner which had been converted into a mutual aid society for displaced warriors that the young boy Denjirō was raised. The ferment of this dying class confronted with the threats and challenges of a new age constituted his childhood environment; in many ways this ferment became a part of his life and thought.

Denjirō was a weak child. His family, consequently, showed some concern over his ability to withstand the rigors of a Nakamura childhood. He was particularly susceptible to stomach ailments which troubled him for the rest of his life. Despite his physical weakness, however, he displayed great intellectual gifts: the story is told that he learned to write characters before he was weaned.[1] This no doubt constituted an exaggeration based on his subsequent achievements, but it is a fact that he entered elementary school at the age of five in 1876 and made extremely rapid progress to the delight and surprise of his elders.[2]

During his early years Denjirō was a solitary child preferring to spend his time deep within the old, dark family home, entertaining himself with his own pranks and with the books and pictures of his father and grandfather.[3] The more he learned to read, the more he secluded himself among his father's books. His mother later commented that while the wooden clogs of the other children were constantly worn out and in need of repair, Denjirō's always remained brand new.[4]

Although Denjirō's mother interpreted his withdrawal as indicative of 'intellectual pursuits' and consequently as a sign that he would follow in the footsteps of his father, the real reason for Denjirō's seclusion may well have lain in his fear of the other children with whom he came into contact at school and in the neighborhood. A bright and extremely sensitive child, Denjirō's abilities seem to have alienated him from his classmates and companions even at an early age. As he recalled in his diary some years later: 'In elementary school I really suffered under the hatred of several of my classmates who were jealous of my grades. I was bashful and said little, being discontented deep within.'[5]

---

[1] Nishio Yōtarō, *Kōtoku Shūsui*, p. 8. Also mentioned in his cousin Teru's recollections, *Kōtoku Shūsui hyōden*, p. 126. His wife, Chiyoko, mentions he could read at the age of three or four. Morooka Chiyoko, *Otto Kōtoku Shūsui no omoide*, p. 35.
[2] *Ibid.*   [3] *Ibid.* p. 30.   [4] *Ibid.* p. 29.   [5] *Nikki to shokan*, p. 19.

One point in particular left Denjirō vulnerable to the criticism of the neighborhood children and made him want to withdraw from their circle. This had to do with his family background. Kōtoku Denjirō's family had achieved considerable status in the town of Nakamura, but in the end it had never broken into the country samurai class. Despite the fact that Denjirō's mother came from a well-known *gōshi* family, and that his home served as the business office for the Dōkyūsha, a *shizoku* organization, Denjirō was only the son of a townsman. The children with whom he associated came almost exclusively from former warrior families. Unable to compete with him at school, they mercilessly asserted their superiority by calling him a '*machi no ko*' or 'townie'.[1]

Having been ostracized from the inner circle of the local *shizoku* children, Denjirō set out to master them at their own values. He determined that despite his background as the son of a townsman he would become a better samurai than the children of the neighborhood. Consequently, in the immediate post-Restoration years, when many a *shizoku* child was casting about for new values in an attempt to integrate itself into the new Meiji world, Kōtoku Denjirō, due to the peculiarities of his environment and family background, found himself identifying with the values of the past. Although this was done largely out of the need to assert his own personality in an effort to counteract the ridicule of his youthful companions, the effects of this early identity can be traced throughout his life.

In 1876, while the Dōkyūsha debated the best means of preserving the financial integrity of the local samurai, discontented warriors elsewhere took up arms against the central government. One of these uprisings erupted in Kumamoto, where arch-conservatives attacked government offices and troops.[2] Although a minor uprising, when compared with the full-scale Satsuma Rebellion of the following year, the effects of the Kumamoto insurrection were keenly felt in Nakamura, for the chief victim of the disturbance, the governor of Kumamoto prefecture, Yasuoka Ryōsuke, was one of Nakamura's native sons. The loss of this well-known loyalist and scholar was particularly poignant for the Kōtoku family, for Ryōsuke had been Atsuaki's teacher. In the wake of the tragedy Ryōsuke's widow returned to

---

[1] *Kōtoku Shūsui hyōden*, p. 132.

[2] The Kumamoto uprising is usually known as the Shinpūren Ran, a name taken from the Shinpūren, or 'Clique of the Divine Wind', which consisted of malcontented samurai who were dissatisfied with the reforms carried out by the Restoration. At midnight on October 24, 1876, 170 members of this band attacked both the prefectural government offices and the Kumamoto garrison. The uprising was put down almost immediately, but in the fighting the head of the garrison, Taneda Masaaki, and the governor, Yasuoka Ryōsuke, were killed. Fujii Jintarō, *Outline of Japanese History in the Meiji Era* (Tokyo, 1958), pp. 111–12.

Nakamura bringing with her some of the leading *shizoku* families which had joined the government at the time of the Restoration.[1]

The return to Nakamura of the Yasuoka, Ōno, and Kuwabara families was of great significance for the young boy Denjirō, because it resulted in contact with children whose parents had taken a direct part in the political activities of the early Meiji period, and who kept themselves well informed of developments in the capital through members of the family still in government service. It was among the children of these families that Denjirō found some of his lifelong friends, particularly Yasuoka Hideo, Ryōsuke's youngest son, who later went on to become the editor of the *Jiji Shimpō*, one of Meiji Japan's leading newspapers. It is to Hideo's detailed recollections of his youth that we owe much of our knowledge of Denjirō's development.[2]

In the years that followed, the Yasuoka home became a great attraction for the neighborhood children in general and Kōtoku Denjirō in particular. It provided a pleasant atmosphere and many curious items from the capital and other far-off places. Among these were books, pictures, and magazines, as well as the newspapers which arrived regularly from Tokyo and later delighted both Hideo and Denjirō. The children also enjoyed plays, and in the production of these often involved the entire household including the maids.[3]

Hideo later remembered the Denjirō of those days as follows:

With the passing of time I made various friends. Among these was the boy K, who was a year older than I, and whose family was somehow related to mine. He was the most strikingly brilliant of all my many friends, and one probably ought to refer to him as a child prodigy or a wonder boy. I too did well at school and was a little advanced, I think, but not at all like K. In elementary and middle school I always took him as my model and followed in his footsteps agreeing almost entirely with everything he did and said.[4]

Later Hideo recalled with the same sense of awe that Denjirō was reading, at the age of 'six or seven', books which others hesitated to take up at 'twelve or thirteen'.[5]

The rapidity of Denjirō's progress made it possible for him to graduate from the lower division of the elementary school at the age of eight. At the

[1] *Kōtoku Shūsui hyōden*, p. 134.
[2] These were published in a series of articles which appeared in the *Jiji Shimpō* during June, 1922.
[3] Nishio Yōtarō, *Kōtoku Shūsui*, p. 11.
[4] Nankyoku Rōsei (Yasuoka Hideo's pseudonym), 'Kumo no kage', *Jiji Shimpō*, June 3, 1922, p. 5. Denjirō is referred to as 'K' throughout. Hideo and Denjirō were second cousins.
[5] *Ibid.*

same time he entered the private academy of the scholar, Kido Mei,[1] where he began his training in the Chinese classics by reading the *Classic of Filial Piety*.

The warmth of the Yasuoka home, the interesting games and plays which became a part of the lives of the children who gathered there, the admiration and friendship of boys like Hideo and Yokota Kinba, a son of the Yasuoka's neighbors – all these helped to draw Denjirō into a more active social role. Gradually he began to realize that, despite his background as the son of a townsman, there was a place of natural leadership for him among the sons of the former samurai.

At the same time, Denjirō's education, particularly his education in the Chinese classics at Kido Mei's private school, tended to reinforce the Confucian values which were still very much a part of the former warrior class. Denjirō's position within the group rested largely on the recognition by his companions of his superior intellectual talents, this qualification for leadership being itself a part of the Confucian tradition which made intelligence, rather than physical charisma, the requisite of the ideal leader. Thus Denjirō realized from an early age that his position within the group rested upon his intellectual prowess, that in order to maintain his position as leader he could not allow anyone to better him at school. Fortunately, there were few who could compete with him. Even Yasuoka Hideo was clearly outdistanced.

The association of status with intellectual prowess which Denjirō learned as a child was to lead to later complications. This association was much more a part of late Tokugawa society in which the ruling elite shared the Confucian values upon which it was based than it was a part of the mid-to-late Meiji years in which Denjirō matured. In fact, while late Tokugawa society paid a great deal of lip service to the idea that government was to be the responsibility of the educated man and supported education on what appears to have been an extensive scale, actual power all too often remained in the hands of those who were entitled to it through heredity. It was only during the *bakumatsu* years, when the country was faced with a crisis which did not lend itself to traditional solutions, that ability began to replace heredity as the main qualification for a successful career in the political world.

[1] Kido Mei (1835–1916) was the leading Confucian scholar of the Hata district during the bakumatsu period. After studying Kokugaku with Iwagaki Gesshū in Kyoto he returned to Nakamura and joined Higuchi Shinkichi and Yasuoka Ryōsuke in organizing Hata loyalists. Appalled by the bakufu's failure to take stronger measures against Western encroachments, these men not only emphasized self-strengthening (Kido is said to have cast 38 cannon), but eventually called for the destruction of the Tokugawa government and the restoration of Imperial authority. Among Kido's close friends were such Restoration *shishi* as Yanagawa Seigan of Edo and Tominaga Yūrin of Chōshū. After the Restoration Kido devoted himself to education in Nakamura and Kōchi. Nakamura Chō Yakuba, *Nakamura chō shi*, p. 259.

With the Restoration's destruction of the entire hereditary status structure, the idea that ability polished through education constituted the path to success – which for anyone trained in Confucian values meant a role in government – was unleashed with a force that contributed much to the rapidity of the Meiji changes and was responsible for the peculiar dynamism found in the early Meiji students both at home and abroad. Now the brilliant student was in demand, and during the formative years, while the new government was establishing itself, the demand was almost unlimited. The early Meiji years therefore fulfilled the Confucian ideal that the educated man's responsibility was government. But it was not long before government positions were less plentiful, while the ranks of the educated – those who had been quick to realize the new Meiji success formula – swelled. Such a situation could only lead to discontent on the part of the latecomer.

In 1881 Denjirō turned ten and entered the Nakamura branch of the Kōchi Middle School. This was an important year in national politics for it marked the promise of a constitution by the Meiji leaders, as well as the founding of the Jiyūtō, or Liberal Party, which became the main voice for those desiring more extensive popular rights.

It was at this time that Hideo and Denjirō became avid readers of the *Eiri Jiyū Shimbun* and the *Marumaru Chinbun* (newspapers that supported the Liberal Party) which Hideo's brother Yūkichi, a student in Fukuzawa Yukichi's Keio University, regularly sent from Tokyo. Hideo later wrote that he understood little of what these papers contained and read them largely in imitation of Denjirō. About his friend he observed: 'But when it came to reading newspapers K's eyes were far in advance of mine. When he was eleven or twelve he was talking about "liberty" and "popular rights", and even started a newspaper of his own.'[1]

Even though Denjirō was an avid reader of the *Eiri Jiyū Shimbun* and may have discussed 'liberty' and 'popular rights', his original sympathies did not lie with the Jiyūtō and its program. The Nakamura environment was basically conservative. The citizens of the town, proud of their identification with the Imperial cause in the Restoration struggles, were not about to support a party which was rumored to favor a republican form of government. Denjirō and Hideo shared this sentiment.

About the town Hideo wrote: 'Tosa was the birthplace of Count Itagaki, the founder of the Jiyūtō, and at the time of this party's flourishing served as the home of the Popular Rights Movement. My home town, and nearly

[1] Nankyoku Rōsei (Yasuoka Hideo), 'Kumo no kage', *Jiji Shimpō*, June 3, 1922.

everyone in the surrounding territory, belonged to the opposition Teiseitō,[1] however, and consequently became the base for Tosa reactionaries.'[2]

About Denjirō he added: 'K had also been raised in this kind of environment and talked about constitutional monarchy and gradualism when he first discussed politics, but before long he was speaking about popular rights. This was probably the result of his reading the *Eiri Jiyū Shimbun* and various other newspapers and magazines which came to my house.'[3]

Among the works which appeared in the *Eiri Jiyū Shimbun* in the early eighties was Miyazaki Muryū's *Kishushu* (*The Devil's Cry*) which was based in part on Stepniak's *Underground Russia*, and which like much of the nihilist literature to appear in the paper stressed the necessity for resistance to oppression.[4] Such novels fascinated Denjirō who was not without his own views on 'oppression' and 'resistance'. They also aroused in him the desire to take up the Jiyūtō cause in the basically conservative Nakamura setting.

At first Denjirō's decision to support the Jiyūtō appears to have alienated him even from his friend Hideo, who recalled: 'At the start K's hand-made newspaper also followed the ideas of the Teiseitō, but after a while it came out strongly in favor of liberalism. Since I myself was highly dissatisfied with K's shift of ideas and theory, I joined a group of elder youths who were influenced by politics and helped them to suppress K.'[5]

Before long the split between Denjirō and Hideo was healed, however, and, as Hideo noted, he was 'baptized into liberalism at the age of ten or eleven'.[6] In the months that followed, the two boys became the core of a group of young Jiyūtō supporters whose harassment of Chūseitō meetings became the consternation of their elders.[7]

Denjirō's rebelliousness was not ameliorated by a stiff reprimand from his uncle Kachiyuemon.[8] In fact, there is good cause to believe that his home life was partially responsible for his defiant behavior. A fatherless child, Denjirō

---

[1] While Hideo's recollections of Nakamura's conservative environment are correct, his reference here, and elsewhere, to the Teiseitō cannot be substantiated. Nakamura was a power base for Tani Kanjō's Chūseitō (sometimes mistakenly referred to as the Kokumintō), and it was this party which most Nakamura citizens supported in opposition to the Jiyūtō. Denjirō's uncles, Kachiyuemon and Ōno Tōichi, both supported this party. The latter was a personal friend of Tani's and served as a local organizer for the Chūseitō. For a discussion of the Chūseitō see Hirao Michio, *Shishaku Tani Kanjō den* (Tokyo, 1935), pp. 504-31.

[2] Nankyoku Rōsei (Yasuoka Hideo), 'Kumo no kage', *Jiji Shimpō*, June 4, 1922.   [3] *Ibid.*

[4] Nobutaka Ike, *The Beginnings of Political Democracy in Japan* (Baltimore, 1950), p. 122.

[5] Nankyoku Rōsei (Yasuoka Hideo), 'Kumo no kage', *Jiji Shimpō*, June 4, 1922.   [6] *Ibid.*

[7] Hideo and Denjirō organized their friends to descend upon the political gatherings of the opposition shouting 'Jiyūtō Banzai!' ('Long live the Jiyūtō!') while carrying large flags inscribed with Jiyūtō slogans. Morooka Chiyoko, *Otto Kōtoku Shūsui no omoide*, p. 49.

[8] Nishio Yōtarō, *Kōtoku Shūsui*, p. 16.

was permitted greater freedom than most children. This resulted in an independent personality. At the same time, all decisions of importance regarding his life were made not by his immediate family – that is his mother, Tajiko – but by his father's brother, Kachiyuemon. While tolerant, Kachiyuemon was not easily approached by the young boy, and Denjirō soon came to dislike him.[1] His uncle, meanwhile, came to regard Denjirō's actions as inexcusable. The lack of communication between uncle and nephew led to conflict and bitterness. Denjirō's diary, *Nochi no katami*, outlines some of the issues. 'When I entered middle school, the treatment I received earlier did not change significantly. It was at this time that I developed the idea of going away to study. Because my family refused to let me go, I spent my days aimlessly and in discontent.'[2]

Denjirō's desire to leave home to study elsewhere (elsewhere no doubt implying the city of Kōchi) was given further impetus in 1885 when the Nakamura branch of the Kōchi Middle School was destroyed by a storm. This natural disaster was to have far-reaching effects. In the first place, it meant that most of the *shizoku* children with whom Denjirō had grown up suddenly departed Nakamura for Kōchi. With the exodus of Hideo, Yokota Kinba, and the others, Denjirō was left a leader without followers. Overnight the Yasuoka home, once echoing with fun and laughter, became deserted and silent. Denjirō, whose uncle vetoed his repeated requests to be allowed to join his friends, was at a loss as to what to do. The destruction of the school totally demolished the arena in which he had learned to perform.

For Denjirō, who had come to associate status with intellectual achievements, the school environment was vital for the maintenance of his identity. His first reaction was to try to re-enter the elementary school. When this proved impossible, he gathered about him a group of similarly dislocated students in order to recreate the school environment by setting up a 'discussion group' in the Jizōji, one of Nakamura's deserted temples. The group that gathered at the Jizōji read the *Eiri Jiyū Shimbun*, debated politics, and affected the other symbols of adulthood and progressivism, namely, drinking bouts and the eating of beef.[3] Nor was it above making trouble when the opportunity presented itself, and this further increased his uncle's reluctance

---

[1] The depth of Kōtoku's antipathy towards his uncle is reflected in an incident recorded by his second wife, Chiyoko. In 1907, when she and Kōtoku returned to Nakamura for a few months of rest and recuperation, a friend gave them a puppy. Chiyoko asked Kōtoku what to name the dog. After a moment's hesitation Kōtoku replied with a sardonic smile, 'Kachiyuemon!' Chiyoko thought this very disrespectful and named the dog 'Chiyame' instead. But Kōtoku continued to insist that 'Kachiyuemon' was a more appropriate name. Morooka Chiyoko, *Otto Kōtoku Shūsui no omoide*, pp. 40–1.

[2] *Nikki to shokan*, p. 19. [3] Nishio Yōtarō, *Kōtoku Shūsui*, p. 19.

to allow him to go to Kōchi. In effect, Denjirō had become something of a juvenile delinquent and his uncle, worried by his conduct, wanted to keep him under the family's supervision.[1]

Cut off from his study of the Chinese classics, Denjirō directed his attention to the world of active politics. Knowing that Kachiyuemon supported the Chūseitō, Denjirō became more and more outspoken in his support of the Jiyūtō. In December 1885 he met his first 'great man of distinction' when Hayashi Yūzō, one of the Liberal Party politicians, visited Nakamura. Shortly thereafter, Itagaki Taisuke arrived on a hunting expedition, and Denjirō managed to obtain an invitation to a banquet honoring this 'leading light of liberty'. He was immensely pleased when those attending asked him to read a poem he had composed on Itagaki's behalf.

Denjirō's political protest against his uncle lasted until the spring of 1886 when his family finally permitted him to leave Nakamura for Kōchi. Most of his friends had already established themselves at the Kōchi Middle School and at Kido Mei's private academy, the Yuengijuku. Denjirō and Hideo both roomed at the academy, which Hideo remembered with a certain amount of disdain:

The scholar of Chinese studies from our home town, under whose wing we had been since childhood, in addition to his regular job at the Middle School, opened a private academy for Chinese studies and I boarded there. But since the academy was truly based on the academies of old, its food was really awful. Believing that anything could be done on a stomach full of roots and vegetables, it was established that meals and snacks consist of nothing besides pickles, and only on certain fixed days were such things as soups and fish served. I had always been spoiled at home and found this unbearable. Requesting special permission, I had two meals brought to me from the home of a standing committee member of the Prefectural Assembly who was from my home town.[2]

The quality of the Yuengijuku's food was notorious, and Denjirō with his

[1] The reason usually given for his family's actions is a 'lack of finances'. See Tanaka Sōgorō, *Kōtoku Shūsui: ikkakumeika no shisō to shōgai* (Tokyo, 1955), p. 33. Tanaka makes the point that Denjirō saw education as the only 'road to success', and that he became embittered with the social order when he realized that his family could not afford to send him to Kōchi. Like other of Kōtoku's biographers, he sees a causal link between the family's economic circumstances and Denjirō's interests in the Jiyūtō. It remains curious that there was no lack of finances six months later. Kido Mei's tuition was in fact minimal: 1 Yen or 17·6 lb of rice per year plus an entrance fee of 'a barrel of sake and two or three fish'. See Kōchi Kenritsu Toshokan, *Kōchi han kyōiku enkaku torishirabe* (Kōchi, 1932), p. 206. It is hard to believe that a *tawaraya-sake* brewer could not afford such fees. Perhaps Morooka Chiyoko's point that his family did not approve of his 'drinking bouts' as well as the company he kept and was consequently concerned about what he would do in Kōchi without their supervision, serves as a better explanation. Morooka Chiyoko, *Otto Kōtoku Shūsui no omoide*, p. 51.

[2] Nankyoku Rōsei (Yasuoka Hideo), 'Kumo no kage', *Jiji Shimpō*, June 10, 1922.

weak stomach suffered even more than Hideo. His complaint with the school was not with the food, however, but with the education, which he felt was overly restrictive and 'old-fashioned'. In his diary Denjirō had few good things to say about his teacher and the school:

The education of the Yuengijuku was extremely strict and meddlesome, which depressed the spirit of the boys. In fact, we were like prisoners, not allowed to leave the school with its filthy rooms and coarse food for even one hour a day. To bring newspapers and the like into the school was strictly forbidden. While our teacher probably performed distinguished service for the nation at the time of the Restoration and was high minded and well educated, he had now retired to his mountain-surrounded home town where he was growing senile and knew nothing about the world. His one remaining interest was classical Chinese history.[1]

For a boy who was used to reading about current events in the newspapers and spent much of his leisure time debating politics, life at the academy was somewhat cramping. The situation was not improved by the quality of the other students, who in his opinion were all 'little devils' absorbed only in carrying out their 'evil plots'.[2] Even Hideo was startled by the 'disgustingly antiquated ideas' of a majority of the students. The fault he was convinced lay with Kido Mei:

Standing before all the students of the academy he admonished us saying that each of us was to make the governing of the nation, the bringing of peace to the world (*chikoku heitenka*) his goal. He preached that we should cease all mischief and sniveling and aim instead at becoming great men of distinction. If he heard that we were debating over whether water or air were blue or white, he severely scolded us as if we were absorbed in some foolish sidetrack.[3]

In his effort to instill in his students the classical Confucian ideals – the governing of the nation and the bringing of peace to the world – Kido Mei was attempting to educate men concerned with statecraft. For him such men were individuals trained in principles and morals who were to devote themselves to the nation, and not just politicians representing factions and regional interests. Being deeply convinced that the purpose of education was to prepare men for government, he was naturally opposed to his students' interest in such areas as science.

On the other hand, perhaps it was only natural that his students considered their training in the Chinese classics rather dull when beyond the walls of the academy the city of Kōchi still seethed with the ferment of the Popular Rights Movement, and the echo of 'wooden swords and trumpets' could

---

[1] *Nikki to shokan*, pp. 19–20.   [2] *Ibid.* p. 19.
[3] Nankyoku Rōsei (Yasuoka Hideo), 'Kumo no kage', *Jiji Shimpō*, June 11, 1922.

be heard almost 'constantly'.[1] These were politically exciting days: what was the point of being locked away preparing for the future, even if this were to be a political future, when all one had to do was join one of the local parties and become involved directly? For Denjirō and Hideo, who had already played the role of political activists in Nakamura, the isolation imposed by the Yuengijuku was oppressive. As Denjirō later wrote in his diary: 'I could not stand to be a prisoner and schemed innumerable escapes from this cage. But in these attempts I was always opposed by my family, and nothing came of my efforts.'[2]

While Denjirō had few positive things to say about the Yuengijuku and its teacher in later years, his rejection of the school and its students must to some extent be attributed to later experiences that shaded his days there in tones that grew darker with time. If Denjirō did suffer as much at the academy as his diary, *Nochi no katami*, suggests, his suffering seems to have found little expression in his work. Hideo remembered him as well integrated into the school's routine:

The academy included a mixture of students, some of whom were seventeen or eighteen, but the most brilliant person was after all this boy [Denjirō]. From time to time there were poetry sessions, discussions of books, readings of books in turn, and debates over history. All of which were held in accordance with the teachers' orders. In these it was always K who far surpassed everyone else.[3]

After being at the Yuengijuku for only a short period of time, Denjirō had once more recaptured his position as the academic leader of the other children. This victory, too, was short-lived, however, for in 1886 Denjirō became seriously ill with pneumonia and was forced to leave the Yuengijuku. From May to August of that year he hovered on the verge of death. It was not until the following January that he was able to return to the academy. Having been ill for nearly a year, he had naturally fallen behind his fellow students.

For Denjirō a loss of his superior intellectual position meant a loss of the qualifications for leadership. It was on this point that he was particularly vulnerable. Once before, as mentioned earlier, when his friends had all moved to Kōchi and left him alone in Nakamura, Denjirō had faced a personal crisis. At that time the crisis had not been as serious for only the environment had changed, and he was able to react by re-creating the environment among the boys he collected at the Jizōji. This time the crisis

[1] *Ibid.*   [2] *Nikki to shokan*, p. 20.
[3] Nankyoku Rōsei (Yasuoka Hideo), 'Kumo no kage', *Jiji Shimpō*, June 11, 1922.

proved much more serious. Three years later Denjirō still smarted as he recalled:

My weak constitution was well known among my friends and acquaintances, and because of it I soon became ill and had to enter a private hospital where I lay close to death. In the six months that I was ill, I fell far behind my classmates in their studies. After returning home briefly I once more went to Kōchi and entered the Middle School. I now felt the full effects of my previous idleness. Discovering that the level of my studies had fallen far below those of my classmates, I was overcome with remorse and failed the yearly examinations.[1]

The cause of Denjirō's failure seems to have been not so much the fact that he was incompetent, but rather his brooding over the realization that he had lost his position of absolute superiority. His despondency led to his failing the annual examinations, and this in turn increased his personal crisis. As he later explained:

Not once since I entered school at the age of six had I tasted failure. Being unable to face my friends and acquaintances, and having previously regretted not being able to join my schoolmates who were leaving for the capital, I turned my back on the fact that I had no money for schooling and, reconciling myself to hunger, fled to Tokyo.[2]

Tokyo proved to be of little refuge for Denjirō. No sooner had he settled himself in Hayashi Kaneaki's Yūrakuchō Eigakkan and begun his study of English than the Peace Preservation Laws were promulgated.

The autumn of 1887, during which Denjirō arrived in the capital, found the city of Tokyo in turmoil over the question of treaty revision. The government under the Itō Cabinet was fearful of the increasing tempo of anti-government agitation and as a counter measure passed a series of laws that allowed it to expel from the capital individuals considered politically undesirable. On the twenty-seventh of December it ordered out of Tokyo over five hundred individuals considered in this category, among whom were many of the former leaders of the Popular Rights Movement, including Hayashi Yūzō, Denjirō's sponsor. Officially registered as a student under Hayashi, Denjirō's name was also on the list of those expelled, and like the others he was forced to leave Tokyo in great haste. Although a mere pawn in this struggle, Denjirō considered his expulsion from Tokyo a personal affront from Itō. Kōtoku never forgave Itō for this insult and carried a life-long hatred for the framer of the Constitution.[3]

---

[1] *Nikki to shokan*, p. 20.   [2] *Ibid.*

[3] For details regarding the *Hoan Jōrei* see Tanaka Sōgorō, *Kōtoku Shūsui: ikkakumeika no shisō to shōgai*, pp. 40ff.

The trek down the Tokaidō in the middle of winter was cold, and Denjirō, in financial straits as usual, went hungry. Like many of his expelled compatriots he hoped to settle in Osaka to continue his studies, but due to the intervention of his family he was compelled to return to Nakamura.

For Denjirō the forced return to Nakamura under the stigma of having been expelled from the capital was humiliating. Just five months earlier he had set out from Nakamura for the capital with the intention of proving his worth. Now he was back in disgrace. Like many a young Japanese educated in the early Meiji period, Denjirō pictured education as the road to success. Success, measured in Confucian terms, continued to mean a role in government. But for Denjirō each educational opportunity seemed to be terminated just at the moment when he started to make progress. Although the situations were different, the cumulative despair and frustration became more profound with each experience. Forced back to Nakamura, a place where he had already found it impossible to 'face' his friends and acquaintances, Denjirō went into a deep depression. The depth of his despair can be seen in the following lines from his diary: 'From spring to summer of that year I was eternally shut up in one room... At the same time I came to feel that there was absolutely no hope in my trying to make a name for myself through learning.'[1]

Denjirō's running away from Nakamura in the previous year without his family's permission tended to confirm his relatives' opinion that he was something of a troublemaker. His present state of turmoil elicited little sympathy on their part; instead, his aimless moping evoked their criticism and heightened his inner tension. He later recalled his family's reactions as follows: 'Seeing my aimlessness my family and relatives scolded me for my insolent departure of the previous year and criticized my lack of purpose for the future. As might be expected, only my mother sympathized with me, complaining as if to herself, "If only he had a father he wouldn't be so afraid of the world outside and would be able to study."'[2]

Of the content of Denjirō's mind during the six-month period he spent in retreat from the 'world outside' we know little except, as is indicated in the above statement, that he temporarily despaired of achieving anything through his studies and appears to have given up all hope for the future.

It is important to note in the formation of Denjirō's character that failure frequently led to almost total rejection, and that the solution to the problem always involved a change of environment and an attempt to master a completely new situation. Thus, Denjirō later wrote some bitter passages about

[1] *Nikki to shokan*, p. 21.   [2] *Ibid.*

the Yuengijuku, its teacher, and students, when, as facets of his personality were subsequently to reveal, he identified strongly with the values taught at this school. Or one might recall the period when his *shizoku* friends left him for Kōchi after the destruction of the Nakamura middle school. At that time he considered the main cause of his difficulties the fact that his family did not permit his going to Kōchi. Indirectly he felt himself deserted by the *shizoku* friends with whom he had been brought up. His reaction was to make trouble for his family and to organize a new group of children which backed the Jiyūtō in direct opposition to Nakamura *shizoku* values.

The cause of his most recent failure Denjirō attributed to the Itō Cabinet, and as such to the Japanese government which had expelled him from Tokyo and forced him back to his home town in disgrace. The reaction, which emerged from the depth of his personal crisis, was to reject not only the Japanese government, but Meiji Japan itself. Since there was no chance for him to make a name for himself in Japan in the way he had been taught, the only alternative was to leave Japan and prove himself abroad. Having been brought up in the Chinese tradition, Denjirō's mind naturally turned to the continent, and so in the summer of 1888 he once more left Nakamura, this time for Nagasaki, and what he hoped would be China.

Denjirō's hopes for reaching China were soon shattered by a lack of finances. Meanwhile the repeal of the ban under which he had been ousted from the capital made it possible for him to return to Tokyo. It was on his way to the capital, where he hoped to resume the study of English, that he encountered Nakae Chōmin in Osaka. Denjirō's meeting with Nakae brought to a close the Tosa years of his youth. Under Chōmin, Denjirō received the training he had hoped to find in Tokyo, and, in the years that followed, Chōmin's influence did much to mold the young man Denjirō into the journalist and political thinker, Shūsui.

CHAPTER 2

In search of power and glory, 1889–99

MEIJI JAPAN, which Kōtoku came to confront more directly in Osaka and Tokyo on his quest for 'power and glory', was a rapidly transforming society. Certainly by 1888 and 1889, the years in which Denjirō moved from rural Tosa to the national stage, the country had already undergone many of the major reforms that were subsequently to define the Meiji Restoration. Such fundamental changes as the abolition of the han and the establishment of a modern prefectural system, the elimination of feudal rights and privileges, the establishment of modern education, postal, and military systems, had been achieved in the 1870s. Not only had the youthful Meiji leadership successfully maintained its commitment to the priorities of internal development against dissent and open rebellion, but by the 1880s many of the false starts and contradictions of the government's early efforts at modernization were being resolved in favor of a sustained drive for national wealth and power.

The extent to which the early Meiji changes penetrated the relative isolation of Nakamura and Kōchi to influence and shape Denjirō's adolescent development has already been discussed. Kōtoku's restlessness and dissatisfaction with life in the countryside was in part spurred by his awareness of the extent to which the Meiji Restoration had shifted the balance of power and influence in favor of large urban centers. By the 1880s, youth with ambition looked to the cities for a better life. Kōtoku was no exception.

Much of the vigor of Meiji society expressed itself in the cities. Tokyo and Osaka, already among the world's largest urban centers during the Tokugawa period, had undergone further population explosions in the early Meiji decades as young people and former samurai from throughout the country came to the cities in search of educational opportunities and official employment. Tokyo had in effect become the great melting pot of Japanese cultural life. It was here that the government's efforts at Westernization were most symbolically visible. Railroads, electric lights, horse-drawn carriages, Western-style buildings, men in tails and top hats accompanied by gaily dressed women in bonnets and hoop skirts – all favorite subjects of the wood block artists of the day – were open expressions of Japan's new course. More subtle was the intellectual confrontation with the West that came in the city's foreign academies, language schools, book stores, and the innumerable 'lecture halls' that sprang up throughout the capital for the discussion and debate of everything from literature to politics. Discussion and debate, in fact, appear to have been the favorite pastimes of the age. Whether in the increasingly popular newspapers and magazines or in the bustling restaurants catering to the new taste for beer and beef, in formally organized learned societies or in the quiet of the traditional home over cups of warm sake, men addressed themselves with intensity to the issues of the day.

The passion for new ideas had hardly abated in twenty years since the Restoration. Instead, the small intellectual elite which had started the nation on the path to 'civilization and enlightenment' was now being supplanted by a vast new group of young people, who, as the first products of the new educational system and the idealistic followers of the Popular Rights Movement, combined a thirst for knowledge with a highly developed political consciousness. Most of the members of the new generation had been nurtured in the early Meiji penchant for self-improvement, and the large majority believed that sacrifice and hard work would result in official employment and personal success.

The dynamic quality of the new generation expressed itself in a tremendous outburst of creative energy in the late 1880s. A part of this outburst involved a major literary revival which led not only to a rediscovery of the writers of the past, but to a conscious effort to create a new literature that could stand on a par with the literature of the West. Out of this effort came Japan's first modern novel, *Ukigumo*, published in 1887 by the twenty-three-year-old author, Futabatei Shimei. Futabatei's success rested on his ability to take the strivings of Meiji youth and to articulate them creatively within a literary framework. In this effort he was joined by other young writers, particularly Tokutomi Sohō, who better than anyone else came to speak for the new generation. In 1886, as an unknown writer of twenty-four, Tokutomi published *Shōrai no Nihon* (*Future Japan*). Within a year the book had gone through four editions. In 1887 he brought out *Shin Nippon no Seinen* (*Youth of New Japan*) and the magazine *Kokumin no Tomo*. By the close of the decade *Kokumin no Tomo* had a regular circulation of over 10,000 and the name of its publisher was as well known among the reading public as the name of Fukuzawa Yukichi had been ten years earlier.

Tokutomi's meteoric rise to fame and the unprecedented success of his journal attested to the extent to which he mirrored the aspirations of the younger generation. Tokutomi's concern for the 'common people', his belief in the Meiji Restoration as an unfulfilled revolution that Meiji youth would have to complete through a spiritual revolution, his elevation of economic over military competition, his belief in the ultimate triumph of wealth over military might, and his uncompromising commitment to reform and to youth as the source of reform – all these appealed to the new generation. Kōtoku himself later looked back on the Minyūsha, the society Tokutomi founded in coordination with *Kokumin no Tomo*, as the 'second Meirokusha', and on the journal as the source of the 'new ideas of the age' from which the 'currents of socialism sprang'.[1] In his *History of Japanese Socialism*, which he co-authored with Ishikawa Sanshirō in 1907, Kōtoku praised the early Sohō for his ability to recognize the need for 'economic equality' as well as 'political equality', an awareness in which other advocates of popular rights and 'democracy' had shown themselves to be seriously lacking.[2]

To what extent Kōtoku's evaluation of Tokutomi was the product of retrospect remains difficult to determine. Although it is clear that he regularly read *Kokumin no Tomo* as a student in the home of Nakae Chōmin, we have little further evidence to suggest that he identified strongly with Tokutomi's ideas. This is not to say that Tokutomi's influence on Denjirō was negligible. Like others of his generation, Denjirō had come to see the essence of the Meiji experience as reform. He was idealistic and no doubt responded to Tokutomi's appeal to youth. He had every reason to appreciate Tokutomi's emphasis on historical change as the product of young people from the have-not classes. More important, Tokutomi could serve as a model. Success and recognition at the age of twenty-four was as much Denjirō's goal as it was the goal of other youthful readers of *Kokumin no Tomo*. It was only with time that he came to realize how elusive 'power and glory' could be.

Despite his restless ambition Kōtoku regarded his student days in the home of Nakae Chōmin as the most satisfying years of his life. By contrast to the 'senile' Kido Mei, who shunned Meiji politics for the world of 'Chinese history', Nakae was a political activist, and Denjirō found him warm and friendly. A close and lasting relationship soon developed between teacher and student.

A product of Tosa, an early student of Dutch and French and one-time interpreter for the French envoy, Leon Roches, Nakae had gone to France

[1] Ishikawa Sanshirō and Kōtoku Shūsui, *Nihon shakai shugi shi*, in *Meiji bunka zenshū*, vol. 21, Shakai hen (Tokyo, 1929), p. 345.
[2] *Ibid.* p. 348.

as a government student in the immediate post-Restoration years. There he had come under the influence of French liberal thought, particularly the ideas of Rousseau, whose *Social Contract* he translated into Japanese a few years after his return to Tokyo in the mid-seventies. A journalist of great skill, Nakae played an important role in the liberal journalism of the 1880s, briefly joining Saionji Kimmochi in the ill-fated but influential *Oriental Free Press*, and later heading a series of papers and magazines of his own. At the same time he became a leading spokesman and theoretician for the radical wing of the Popular Rights Movement, publishing such works as his treatise on statecraft, *San suijin keirin mondō*, and calling for the establishment of a parliamentary system of government. Although subsequently known as the 'father of Japanese materialism', Nakae skillfully blended idealism with realism. An interesting and complex thinker, he was frequently misunderstood by those around him – not least perhaps by his disciple, Kōtoku, who came to see him as a 'revolutionary' in the French tradition.[1]

By the late 1880s Nakae was open and outspoken in his criticism of the Itō Cabinet. One of the targets of the Peace Preservation Laws, he was expelled from the capital in 1887, and like many of his fellow critics settled in Osaka, where his home became the meeting place for a cross-section of those interested in liberal reform. As might have been expected, Denjirō, who had always hoped to sit at the feet of a 'leading light of liberty', was immensely pleased with his new post of 'door man' in the Nakae household.

Nakae's efforts to eke out a living through political journalism left him in constant financial difficulties. Meals, Denjirō recalled, frequently consisted of soups with bean curd and a few vegetables, and Chōmin's library, which was renowned for its Western-language materials, had slowly drifted into the hands of the second-hand book sellers.[2] Nearly everything else of value was impounded in the local pawnshops. The four-room house which served as a home not only for Chōmin, his wife, daughter, and maid, but in addition for four or five students, was further overcrowded by an unending stream of visitors who came to discuss business and politics, or just to 'talk', 'drink',

---

1 In 1890 Nakae successfully ran for the first national Diet, but when the Liberal Party gave in to government bribery and pressure he resigned his seat and returned to private life. After an unsuccessful business career which took him to Hokkaido, Nakae contracted cancer in 1900 and died the following year. Nakae's most important political work, *San suijin keirin mondō*, has been discussed by Nobutaka Ike in *The Beginnings of Political Democracy in Japan*, pp. 126ff. For a good biography see Hijikata Kazuo, *Nakae Chōmin* (Tokyo, 1959). The thought of Kōtoku and Nakae is compared by Hayashi Shigeru in *Kindai Nihon no shisōka tachi*, and by Ichii Saburō in *Tetsugaku teki bunseki*.

2 Kōtoku Shūsui, 'Chōmin sensei gyōjō ki', in Hirano Yoshitarō (ed.) *Kōtoku Shūsui, senshū*, vol. I, p. 87. (Hereafter cited as *Senshū*.)

or 'argue'.[1] For Chōmin, in contrast to the Denjirō of later years, poverty was a way of life, and as such was constantly subjected to his own unique sense of humor.[2]

Despite the poverty and overcrowded conditions, Denjirō found Chōmin's home congenial and soon settled himself into a regular routine of study. Chōmin recommended that he turn to the Chinese classics for 'style', and Denjirō immersed himself in Mencius and the T'ang poets.[3] In addition, he spent at least six hours a day reading the contemporary press. These studies were further augmented by his interests in the Japanese warrior tradition, and Denjirō tells us that he sought 'consolation' in the heroic tales of the past.[4] There is no evidence that Chōmin encouraged his student to interest himself in Western literature or in European political writings; instead, he seems to have considered it important that his young protégé ground himself thoroughly in the traditions of China and Japan before branching out to Western schools of thought.[5]

As Chōmin's student, Denjirō's interests appear to have been predominantly literary. This may well have been the result of his intellectual environment. The literary revival of the mid-1880s was now in full swing. Kōtoku shared his generation's renewed interest in the writers of the Tokugawa period. The plays of Chikamatsu and the novels of Bakin were among the works he explored in 1888, as were the *Taiheiki* and *Heike Monogatari*. At the same time, he read with excitement the new works of Tsubouchi Shōyō and Futabatei Shimei. Kōtoku's literary interests reflect his curious combination of concerns which united an idealized warrior past with social criticism and reform in the present. Under the circumstances, it was only a matter of time before the tension in values which separated *Ukigumo* from the *Taiheiki* would make itself felt in his life.

In the meantime, Kōtoku's taste for political activism seems to have declined. While Chōmin continued to be surrounded by political toughs and bullies, Denjirō made every effort to disassociate himself from this side of his environment. A conversation with his former mentor, Hayashi Yūzō, in the

[1] Nishio Yōtarō, *Kōtoku Shūsui*, p. 25.

[2] In contrast to Chōmin, Kōtoku's nephew remembered him as 'serious', 'silent', and completely lacking in humor at home. 'Not once did he crack a joke.' Kōtoku Yukie, 'Oji Shūsui no omoide', *Chūō Kōron*, vol. XLVIII, No. 4 (April, 1933), p. 163.

[3] *Nikki to shokan*, p. 10.   [4] *Ibid.* p. 11.

[5] Kōtoku later wrote that his readings in *San suijin keirin mondō* had inspired him to become a 'believer in the principles of democracy', and had led him to develop an interest in 'social problems'. *Heimin shimbun*, January 17, 1904. It is worth noting, however, that in an 1889 diary entry in which he lists thirty-four books which he read in the past eighteen months there is no mention of either *San suijin keirin mondō* or Chōmin's translation of Rousseau's *Social Contract*. *Nikki to shokan*, pp. 10ff.

summer of 1889 bears this out. Asked what life was like at the Nakaes, Denjirō replied that he usually spent the mornings doing chores and devoted the afternoons to reading newspapers and Chinese books. The evenings he gave over to foreign languages. When the conversation turned to politics, Denjirō told Hayashi that he no longer participated in political demonstrations. Hayashi warned him that he 'shouldn't read too many books', otherwise he might 'end up like Nakamura Keiu'.[1] Later one of Hayashi's companions tried to imply that Denjirō must be a political bully (sōshi) because he lived with Chōmin. Denjirō grew angry in response.[2]

Denjirō's attempt to dissociate himself from active participation in politics does not mean that he lost interest in the political world. It merely serves to point out that his early political interests had, in part, been spurred by a sense of rebellion and discontent; now that he had attained a measure of security in Chōmin's home, introspection and analysis calmly conducted in a dialogue with books and newspapers replaced the active rowdyism of former days.

The reactions of Chōmin's student to some of the important political events of the period tend to reinforce such a picture. On February 11, 1889, after nearly a decade of preparation, the Meiji Constitution was promulgated. This was an event of singular political significance and the contemporary press devoted a great deal of space to its coverage. But Denjirō was unimpressed. While he later recorded that his teacher 'frowned' and did not think much of the Constitution, Denjirō himself was more absorbed by the assassination of Mori Arinori, the Minister of Education, which occurred on the same day.

Only moments before the Constitution was made public, Mori was cut down by a young fanatic, Nishino Buntarō. His bodyguard immediately killed the assassin, but public sentiment, which had already turned against the Minister of Education for his alleged desecration of the Grand Shrines at Ise, sided with the assassin.[3] Denjirō, who was fond of heroic tales and may be said to have maintained a lifelong, if somewhat theoretical, fascination with the idea of assassination, immediately identified with Nishino and composed a funeral oration in his honor.[4]

[1] Conversation with Hayashi Yūzō recorded in Kōtoku's diary for July 7, 1889; Nikki to shokan, p. 27. Nakamura Keiu (1832–91) was one of the early 'reformers' of the Meiji period. The translator of Mill's On Liberty and a leading supporter of popular rights, he became increasingly conservative with age. Hayashi attributed this change to his overly scholarly temperament.

[2] Ibid. p. 348.

[3] Rumor had it that one day, while visiting the temples at Ise, Mori raised the sacred curtain with his cane in order to be able to look into the sanctuary. It was this insult to the Japanese gods that Nishino determined to revenge.

[4] The piece was called 'Cho Nishino Buntarō-kun bun', Nikki to shokan, pp. 5–7.

A part of this oration is worth quoting, for while it tells us little about Nishino, it gives us some insight into the Denjirō of these years. In his diary Denjirō wrote:

On the 11th of February 1889 my friend Nishino Buntarō was cut down. I did not even know you before, my friend. In fact, the first time I heard of you, Nishino, man of loyalty, was when I was informed of your death. Oh, how sad! You too have experienced this singular moment in the history of our nation when the Constitution was promulgated, national policy determined, and order established. What was it then that you suffered? What led you to commit to the point of the sword such a promising future, and caused you to reject as so much dust off the bottom of your feet the happiness and pleasure that you and your fellow countrymen should have eagerly sought under the glory of our Constitution?[1]

Again Denjirō poses the basic question of 'discontent' which permeates his autobiographical 'Fuhei no rireki' ('A Personal History of Discontent').[2] At the same time one senses Denjirō's strong identification with the *shishi* ideal of the man of action fully committed to national goals and willing at any point to sacrifice himself for the 'purification' of society. The values inherent in passages like the following were distinctly *bakumatsu* in origin:

Ah, I know what it was; this whole stormy scene which you played was truly the inevitable outworking of your innermost feelings of loyalty and sincerity which belong to the patriotism which you sought to but could not control... moreover, swallowing pain and refusing to look back upon the wretched clouds of sorrow with which you alone choked your family and parents at a time when their fellow countrymen were dancing with joy... *you turned your back on the obligations of more than twenty years of affectionate training, and planning this deed, swallowed your bitter tears and bid farewell for the last time.* [Italics added.][3]

An examination of Denjirō's early writings and the descriptions of him left by others confirms the view that Chōmin's student pictured himself as a warrior in the *shishi* tradition. A passage like the foregoing could be closely autobiographical, for Denjirō had himself turned his back on years of 'affectionate training', and by running away from home and subsequently being expelled from the capital had brought 'wretched clouds of sorrow' to his mother and family in Nakamura. It is interesting that Denjirō attributed Nishino's behavior to the 'inevitable outworking' of the 'feelings of loyalty and sincerity' which belonged to the 'patriotism' which he sought to but could not control.

Here Denjirō has his finger on an important problem that was not only extremely personal, but in many ways extended itself to a whole sector of

---

[1] *Ibid.* pp. 5–6.　　[2] See *ibid.* pp. 18ff.　　[3] *Nikki to shokan*, p. 6.

Meiji youth that had been brought up and trained in the warrior tradition. A young man like Denjirō had been taught from childhood that his ultimate purpose in life was to play a role in government. He had been encouraged to be ambitious, to exert himself, and to make every effort to achieve his goal. At the same time it had been impressed on him that the achievement of this goal was impossible without personal morality which implied filial piety and loyalty among other things. But filial piety and loyalty, which even in Tokugawa times constituted a source of tension, had now begun to move in separate directions. The call of loyalty and patriotism, the kind of call that drew a young man like Denjirō to the capital, often clashed with the wishes of his parents. While dedication to national goals provided a new kind of antitraditional individualism which made possible a certain amount of unfilial behavior, as was true in Denjirō's case, the problem of personal morality was not as easily solved and was responsible for some of the tensions which a person like Denjirō experienced. To begin with, the object of running away from home was to make a name for oneself and to serve the nation, presumably in some form of official position. And yet, to succeed in this quest personal morality was of prime importance. On the other hand, running away from home against the wishes of one's parents was clearly an immoral act. While success in the capital might ameliorate such conflict, the type of failure which Denjirō experienced heightened it.

The problem involved not only filial piety. The question of loyalty was equally vexing. Loyalty to one's lord had, after all, been one of the regulating principles of the Tokugawa warrior, but with the destruction of the feudal system there were no more lords to whom one could be loyal. For those who had committed themselves to the concept of loyalty the question now became: what new objects were worthy of loyalty and what did loyalty mean under new circumstances? While the framework in which a concept like loyalty operated changed, loyalty, as a moral value, seemed to possess a life of its own regardless of the object towards which it was directed. As Ebina Danjō, a Meiji samurai undergoing a similar period of discontent, wrote: 'I had within me a spiritual demand for loyalty which had been fostered for a long time...I wanted some kind of loyalty...I wanted something to revere ...I wanted again the morality of the Analects.'[1]

In his effort to rediscover the morality of the Analects, Ebina turned to Christianity. Others turned to the Emperor, nationalism and other causes. The restructuring of traditional ideas which took place in the Meiji period

[1] Ebina Danjō, *Kirisuto kyō gairon: waga shinkyō no yurai to keika* (Tokyo, 1937), pp. 53–4.

was not always easy, however, for the dislocation of values that accompanied the Restoration inevitably led to conflict and tension. That Kōtoku was himself subject to such conflict and tension is documented in his works. Living under similar clouds of discontent, a person like Ebina had been able to jettison his former moral system when it no longer proved adequate to meet his personality needs, and substitute for it a Christian system of ethics into which much of the former system could be restructured. Ebina's transition from the morality of the warrior to that of the Christian was a smooth and satisfying one which provided the requisites for transcending the discontent he felt as a young man. But Kōtoku rejected Ebina's kind of modernizing approach which involved a substitution of Christian for Confucian values. Instead, when threatened by flux and change, Kōtoku's response was to hold even more firmly and uncompromisingly to the values he had set out to emulate as a child. Kōtoku's maintenance response was basically the polar opposite of the restructuring response adopted by Ebina. Ebina had himself attempted the maintenance response before turning to Christianity, but this response had proved particularly unsatisfying because it did not permit the transcendence of the discontent he felt. Denjirō's unrest and constant discontent reveals a similar difficulty, but Kōtoku, in contrast to Ebina, possessed a tenacity and stubbornness that made it possible for him to adhere to a personally dissatisfying position for a much longer period of time.[1]

From the earlier quotation it seems clear that Denjirō was aware of the powerful force that Meiji nationalism played in the lives of the young; at the same time he seems vividly conscious of the difficulty involved in turning one's back on the 'obligations of more than twenty years'. The root of the problem lay in the fact that Denjirō was basically a product of the *gemeinschaft* society that prevailed in the Japanese village of the late Tokugawa and early Meiji years. The Confucian ethical system had been structured around the foundations of such a society, and for a person like Kōtoku the situation of being on the one hand pulled out of this environment by the 'inevitable' force of nationalism, while at the same time needing desperately to cling to the values of the old order, presented an immense dilemma.

But even in Nishino's case there were further problems that did not lend themselves to easy solutions. The *shishi* type of behavior which Denjirō attributed to Nishino – not to mention himself – was a form of conduct reserved for moments of national crisis, and yet, as Denjirō noted earlier, this was a period in which national policy had been determined and order

[1] For a discussion of Ebina Danjō's position see F. G. Notehelfer, 'Ebina Danjō: A Christian Samurai of the Meiji Period', *Papers on Japan*, vol. II, 1963.

established. What was the justification and cause of such behavior then? Denjirō was not certain when he wrote: 'I only wonder why it was that such a loyal and upright person was not able to bask in the benefits of the present dynasty on such a joyous occasion as the unprecedented grand ceremony of February 11, 1889. *Exactly who, or what is to blame – is it the times, or is it life?*' [Italics added.][1]

The question which Denjirō raises here is an extremely personal one. 'Is it the times, or is it life?' remained one of the pressing issues for Nakae's young student. The same question later continued to perplex the journalist and political activist Shūsui. Fundamentally, the question was one of discontent and its causes, and faced with the classical formulation of this problem, that is to say, is discontent the product of man's nature, or is it the product of the environment, Denjirō remained uncertain. Writing in his diary he noted:

Last night, lying under the quilts, I thought about the past and the future and my ideas ran as follows: Is discontent the product of the environment, or are there such individuals who because of their nature will be, or must be, discontented no matter what the environment. I have seen and heard of many of the first type. But then, I have also seen some who belong to the second category. To which does a person like myself actually belong? If discontent is the product of my nature, I wonder if I will experience nothing but greater pains no matter what the environment hereafter? If it is the product of the environment, will I always be a person confined only to an environment of discontent?[2]

In many ways the questions which perplexed Denjirō were the same as those with which his teacher had wrestled. Chōmin finally combined French liberalism with Zen Buddhism, solutions that tend to suggest that he continued to believe in both causes of 'discontent', but Denjirō, who failed to grasp the 'spiritual' side of his teacher, was to move in a different direction.

The values to which Chōmin's student committed himself were the values of the Tokugawa warrior. The highest individual qualities of the elite that had been entrusted with the task of leadership under the former system had been self-negation and self-denial. The sacrifice of the individual for the group, the willingness to live in poverty for the sake of ideals, to offer one's life for the cause of loyalty – all these were elements of the 'way of the warrior' to which Kōtoku aspired. But one must also remember that these were not the ideals of the Meiji world in which Kōtoku sought to make a name for himself. Instead of cooperation, the Meiji world was a world of increasing

1 'Cho Nishino Buntarō-kun bun', *Nikki to shokan*, p. 6.
2 *Nikki to shokan*, p. 22.

competition; instead of self-negation and self-denial, the Meiji world was a world of self-aggrandizement and egotism; instead of a world of idealism, it was a world of pragmatism; instead of emphasizing the world of the spiritual it emphasized the world of the material. The spirit of the age was perhaps best incorporated in the figure of Honda Noboru, one of the protagonists of Futabatei's *Ukigumo*. Shrewd, aggressive, and calculating, Honda represented that segment of Meiji youth which had come to realize that success was more the product of whom, not what, one knew and promotion in the new bureaucracy was more the product of flattery, pretense, and acquiescence than talent, diligence, and hard work. A sycophant of the first order, Honda combined a quest for material gain with a lack of ethical concern. For him success left no room for moral doubts. The ultimate question was not whether something was right, but whether it worked.[1]

In the eyes of Denjirō, who like Honda Noboru's opposite in *Ukigumo*, Bunzo, identified with the Confucian values of sincerity, honesty, and straightforwardness, the behavior of men like Honda represented degeneration and decline. The Restoration had immersed the entire nation in corruption; immorality, which was rampant in all sectors of public and private life, forecast the doom of the nation. Nor were the Honda Norobus the only culprits. A person like Mori Arinori, committed as he was to all-out Westernization, slighted the most sacred elements of the Japanese tradition without fear, revealing the extent to which even the top echelons of society had been corrupted. Under the circumstances, the assassination of Mori was a righteous act aimed at the purification of society.

In reading Kōtoku's early writings, one senses that he was not free from the crisis mentality of the early Meiji years. But for him the crisis was internal, not external. What was threatened was morality, not national sovereignty or territory.

Living in a world he saw as morally corrupt, Kōtoku found it all the more important to cling to the ideals of his youth. While Chōmin had been able to work out a compromise in which the ideal and real were balanced, Kōtoku was able to achieve a sense of purity only by compartmentalizing the one from the other. The separation of ideas and ideals from practical action and ambition was not uncommon for the Meiji intellectual, but for those who had been taught to value single-mindedness of purpose and the close relationship of knowledge (morality) to action, dichotomous lives often led to discontent and unrest. And yet, while others allowed their discontent to lead them to an

---

[1] For a discussion of the character contrasts of Futabatei's protagonists see Marleigh Grayer Ryan, *Japan's First Modern Novel: Ukigumo of Futabatei Shimei* (New York, 1967), pp. 170ff.

acceptance of new universal doctrines through which they managed to transcend those elements of the tradition and modern life that were responsible for their discontent – and by doing so became revolutionaries of a very different order – Kōtoku remained a staunch supporter of the past. As such he visualized his enemies not in the ties and restrictions of the former social order, but in the forces that were working to destroy that order.

In the autumn of 1889, Chōmin moved back to Tokyo and Denjirō accompanied the Nakaes to their new quarters in Ura-Jimbochō, which lay in the heart of Tokyo's publishing and second-hand book district. Although the Nakaes' home provided him with an environment of warmth and affection which he later looked back on with gratitude, Denjirō did not always succeed in overcoming the deep and dark moods that assailed him. Increasingly alienated and despondent, Kōtoku recorded in his diary early in 1890: 'I am as lonely as ever. What have I learned; what have I gained in the year that has passed? Last year the Constitution was granted; this year parliament is to open. The public rejoices. The people are glad. But what have I to do with all this? Time waits for no man.'[1] Momentous events were transpiring, but Kōtoku felt himself barred from participation.

Denjirō's discouragement was augmented by frequent periods of ill health that interrupted his studies with Chōmin, forcing him on several occasions to leave the capital in order to recuperate. Finances, too, were a problem, but by 1891 both his health and his family's economic position took a turn for the better, and he once more settled himself into his studies with renewed vigor.

Using the seven yen a month his family now sent him to set himself up in a boarding house, Denjirō commenced to live the life of the typical Meiji student. To be certain, seven yen a month meant few luxuries, but they did allow for some books, a few good bottles of wine, and trips to the cheaper houses in the Yoshiwara. In addition, Denjirō maintained his interest in literature and constantly frequented the lending libraries of the neighborhood. The independent life seems to have suited him well. His studies made rapid progress and he was able to graduate from the Kokumin Eigakkai, a school of English, towards the end of 1892.

Early in 1893 Denjirō went to live with Chōmin once more. Again the period of his stay in the Nakaes' home was cut short; this time by Chōmin, who in April of the same year left Tokyo for a position in Hokkaido. Shortly prior to Chōmin's departure, Denjirō secured a position with the *Jiyū*

[1] Diary entry for January 1, 1890. Kōtoku's pessimism frequently expressed itself at the New Year. *Nikki to shokan*, p. 46.

Shimbun as a translator. Chōmin, who had a number of friends on the staff of this influential paper, no doubt played a role in getting Denjirō the job. In his eyes the future of his young protégé lay in the world of literature and journalism.

On the evening before Chōmin's departure, Denjirō had a long talk with his teacher. Later he recalled that they discussed art, literature, and music as well as political and economic questions. Chōmin, Denjirō remembered, encouraged 'ambition', 'hope', and 'optimism'; at the same time, he reprimanded Denjirō for his 'brooding' and 'pessimism'.[1] It was also during this conversation that Chōmin suddenly said:

Now take that money lender who came this morning. He was tactless, evasive, and probably really harasses people, but it is an individual like him who becomes wealthy. The key to this world is vagueness, I tell you! You are much too concerned with reason and justice. So how would it be if I gave you the *gō* [pen name] 'Shunai'? [*Shunai* implies vagueness.]

Denjirō, thoroughly startled by his teacher's choice, replied: 'But you know I despise vagueness above everything else, couldn't I have another *gō*?' To which Chōmin countered laughing: 'Well, in that case how about the opposite of "Shunai" – "Shūsui"! That was my nickname, too, when I was young.'[2]

This exchange reflects some of the interesting differences between Nakae and Kōtoku. For while Nakae shared his student's commitment to such Confucian values as sincerity, honesty, single mindedness of purpose, and a concern for reason and justice, he did not share Kōtoku's disdain for the commercial world and commercial ethics. The realistic side of Nakae told him that business ethics, while far from Confucian, were very much a part of the Meiji reality, and that a person who wanted to succeed in the Meiji world would have to compromise with the system as it stood. It was the mechanism which balanced the real and the ideal in Chōmin's mind which was seriously lacking in Shūsui. What amused Chōmin was the fact that Denjirō combined an unlimited ambition with an unlimited refusal of the means through which that ambition could be fulfilled. Chōmin tried repeatedly to show his student that compromise was necessary if one were to live in the real world, but this was a side of his teacher that Kōtoku either could

---

[1] 'Chōmin Sensei gyōjō ki', *Senshū*, vol. I, pp. 88-9.

[2] 'Shūsui', literally 'autumn flood' (implying purity and straightforwardness), was taken from the title of the seventh chapter of the *Chuang Tzu*. The compound is said to have served as Chuang Tzu's nickname. Perhaps Chōmin saw something of the ancient Chinese mystic-moralist and social reformer in his student. The conversation between Chōmin and Denjirō can be found in 'Chōmin Sensei gyōjō ki', *Senshū*, vol. I, pp. 39-40.

not, or would not, understand. After suggesting various ways in which his student might make a success of himself, Chōmin summed Denjirō up with the following line: 'You are a literary man and were never cut out to be a bureaucrat!' To which Denjirō rejoined: 'That may be very true, but I still intend to become a minister of state.'[1]

Thus, while Chōmin saw the *Jiyū Shimbun* post he had acquired for his student as a chance to develop literary talents, Denjirō viewed his new job as a stepping-stone to political power. Nor was he alone in such aspirations. The choice of journalism as a career was a very prevalent one among the young men of the Meiji period who longed to play a role in government. Finding the road to office barred by the obstacles of wealth, influence, and education, these 'outsiders' looked to the highly mobile newspaper world as a means of battering down the barriers which separated them from power. Not only was the journalistic world of the mid-Meiji years new, exciting, and lively, it was consequently also the chief battleground in which many of the former warriors of *shishi* disposition traded their swords for brushes in a new attack on power and authority.

The twenty-three year old Kōtoku who joined the *Jiyū Shimbun* in 1893 was a complex individual. The discontent which he experienced may well have been a part of his 'nature'.[2] All evidence tends to confirm the picture of a troubled and moody young man given to moments of alcoholic escape and explosions of physical violence. At the same time, the world of ideas in which this young man lived was a world of neatly ordered beauty and ideals. This was a world upon which the hard realities and complexities of life were not allowed to encroach. Here was a world of safety in which the shabby young student living a life of frequent ill-health was instead the loyal and pure *shishi* devoted selflessly to the good of the nation. This compartmentalization of the real and the ideal could not but lead to conflict,[3] and with time the attack of the real world on the world of ideals was to become overwhelming. The seeds of trouble lay in Denjirō's combination of an uncompromising moral position with uncompromising ambition. Above all, he was in a hurry. Others like Tokutomi and Futabatei had made their reputations at twenty-three

---

[1] 'Chōmin Sensei', *Senshū*, vol. I, p. 89.

[2] Hyman Kublin has maintained that Kōtoku was 'probably neurotic'. *Asian Revolutionary: The Life of Sen Katayama* (Princeton, 1964), p. 153. Many of Kōtoku's actions suggest serious emotional instability.

[3] One senses in Kōtoku the need to maintain symbols in an age of increasing flux and change. As a result, Kōtoku was forced to take ideas such as anti-commercialism, self-denial, and a commitment to ideals, far beyond the implications these had held for the Tokugawa warrior. In doing so he contradicted basic elements of his personality which were not always committed to the same ends.

*

and twenty-four. For Kōtoku too much time had already been lost. Only haste, he was convinced, could make up for lost opportunity.

On the other hand, translating English articles and cables for the *Jiyū Shimbun* was slow, unrewarding, and 'excruciatingly painful'.[1] His new job, he soon discovered, was no way of setting the world in motion through the power of his brush. Impatient with his lack of advancement and overcome by the 'shame' of constant mistranslations, Denjirō once more allowed discontent to spill over into his private life. Koizumi Sakutarō, who roomed with him at the time, recalled these days as follows: 'Although he later reformed somewhat, in those days he was spirited and in his best form under the influence of a *sho* of sake. If anyone were around on such occasions he did not hesitate to argue or to come to blows, thus, often leaving me at my wit's ends.'[2] Unable to cope with the frustrations of his job, Shūsui turned to drink and dissipation, a formula that was to become a powerful habit.

On August 1, 1894, war broke out between Japan and China. While Shūsui later viewed the Sino-Japanese War as one of the great dividing lines in modern Japanese history, his personal involvement, even in its coverage, appears to have been minimal. There is certainly no shred of evidence that he took any kind of anti-war position; instead, like those in the commercial world whose actions he decried, Kōtoku saw the war as an unprecedented opportunity for fame and fortune.

Unforeseen to Kōtoku the war caused a shift in the Imperial Headquarters from Tokyo to Hiroshima. Overnight Hiroshima replaced Tokyo as the news center of Japan, and Kōtoku, stranded in Tokyo, was forced to watch the golden opportunity slip through his fingers. This was more than he could bear. 'If only he were in Hiroshima, they might recognize the power of his brush.'[3] Determined to resign from the *Jiyū Shimbun* in order to get to Hiroshima, Shūsui wrote of his intentions to Chōmin, who replied: 'Why, in comparison with Tokyo even the people of Osaka are slow and easy going; then how will you, with your impatience, ever reconcile yourself to a place like Hiroshima?'[4]

Kōtoku paid little heed to the advice of his teacher. Resigning from the *Jiyū Shimbun* in February, he moved to Hiroshima where he took a position

[1] Kōtoku discussed his difficulties in 'Honyaku no kushin'. See Tanaka Sōgorō, *Kōtoku Shūsui*, p. 92.
[2] Quoted by Arahata Kanson in 'Kōtoku Shūsui', *Sandai genron jin shū*, vol. VIII (Tokyo, 1963), p. 16.
[3] Asukai Masamichi, 'Kōtoku Shūsui', in *Hangyakusha no shōzō*, vol. XIII of *Nijū seiki o ugokashita hitobito* (Tokyo, 1963), p. 189.
[4] 'Chōmin Sensei', *Senshū*, vol. I, p. 42.

with one of the local papers. But again he was too late. The war, largely over by March, drew to its conclusion with the Treaty of Shimonoseki in April. The following month Kōtoku was back in Tokyo, disappointed, and forced to admit that Chōmin had been right.

Through the help of Koizumi Sakutarō, Kōtoku secured a new position with the *Chūō Shimbun* which he was to retain until the early months of 1898. As before, his job consisted of translating cables and articles. Still sensitive about his lack of preparation, he later recalled his difficulties:

Here as before I greatly humiliated myself through mistranslations of telegrams, and in addition I translated abstracts of American and British newspaper articles. These too were extremely troublesome...No matter whether one read the articles thoroughly or not, abstracting the important points was not something easily accomplished by the amateur. This was work that required considerable experience... During the years of the Sino-Japanese War and the Triple Intervention the problems of Far Eastern diplomacy and the intentions of the Great Powers were of unprecedented significance and could not be overlooked. After doing this work for a year or two, I was at last convinced that my ability to read newspapers and magazines had improved somewhat.[1]

During his early days with the *Chūō Shimbun* Shūsui boarded at the home of his uncle, Ōno Tōichi, in Azabu. Teru, his cousin, remembered him as having adopted a style of life which generally included studying until the wee hours of the morning and then sleeping away a good part of the day.[2] The evenings frequently included drinking bouts with Koizumi Sakutarō and Matsui Hakken, or trips to the Yoshiwara.[3] The money for these revels usually came from the pawnshops in the neighborhood, where it appears a majority of Kōtoku's possessions could always be located.[4]

In the autumn of 1895 Kōtoku's uncle suddenly died, and Shūsui, left to fend for himself, moved into a small rented house in the area, where he was joined by his mother. A few months later he married the daughter of a former samurai from the old Kurume fief in Fukuoka.

Kōtoku's first marriage represents a curious episode. The match seems to have been encouraged by his mother, who thought it time that her son settled down to a 'normal' way of life. The arrangements were handled by one of his friends, and Asako, his bride, seems to have been a gentle, well-mannered country girl. She was seventeen and Shūsui twenty-six at the time of their wedding in 1896.

---

[1] From 'Honyaku no kushin', in Tanaka Sōgorō, *Kōtoku Shūsui*, p. 96.
[2] Okazaki Teru, 'Itoko Shūsui no omoide', *Kōtoku Shūsui hyōden*, p. 140.
[3] *Ibid.* p. 138.
[4] Nishio Yōtarō, *Kōtoku Shūsui*, p. 45.

Asako, like Shūsui's mother, was the product of a traditional warrior home. She had little education, and while Tajiko became extremely fond of her daughter-in-law, Shūsui, who Koizumi tells us was something of a connoisseur of beautiful women, found her less enticing than the photograph the go-between had shown him. After three months Shūsui suggested to Asako that she take a trip home to visit her parents. Asako was overjoyed by what she took to be an act of generosity on his part, and Shūsui accompanied her to Ueno Station in high spirits. Several hours later he mailed her a letter of divorce.

Needless to say Shūsui's actions shocked both Asako and his mother.[1] In his handling of the situation one is faced with a side of his personality that was completely inept at handling human problems. One is also faced with his inability to reconcile ideals with reality, an inability which was to have considerable influence on the development of his thought, and one which Chōmin had diagnosed from the start. Koizumi Sakutarō, who probably knew Shūsui better than anyone else during this period, explained the divorce as the product of Shūsui's extremely idealized view of what a wife should be and what Asako was.[2] Unable to reconcile the ideal with the real, his only recourse lay in a heartless clean break.

Kōtoku's decision to rid himself of Asako appears cold and calculated. The 'tough-minded' image is somewhat faulty, however, for he was not a schemer. For him action was almost always the product of impulse and not contemplation. Perhaps Kinoshita Naoe was not far from the mark when he insisted that Kōtoku was fundamentally a 'poet' by nature.[3] The divorce was the product of great stress, and Shūsui described going through with it as difficult as 'swallowing boiling water'.[4] Sakai Toshihiko tells us that Shūsui was unable to post the letter until he had fortified himself with a large amount of sake.[5] Koizumi, for his part, always maintained that Shūsui's rash act left a lifelong scar.[6] Most of his biographers claim that this incident reflects his 'feudal' attitudes towards women and the institution of marriage. Such an assertion may not be incorrect, but it glosses over more fundamental personal problems.[7] Finally one cannot help but conclude that Kōtoku's handling of his first divorce seems bizarre by any standard.

[1] Okazaki Teru states that Shūsui's mother was in 'constant tears' after the divorce. 'Itoko Shūsui no omoide', *Kōtoku Shūsui hyōden*, p. 144.
[2] Koizumi Sakutarō, 'Sakai kun to Kōtoku Shūsui o kataru', *Chūō Kōron* (October, 1931), p. 185.
[3] Kinoshita Naoe, *Kami ningen jiyū* (Tokyo, 1934), p. 23.
[4] Nishio Yōtarō, *Kōtoku Shūsui*, p. 45.
[5] Koizumi Sakuratō, 'Sakai kun to Kōtoku Shūsui o kataru', p. 185.
[6] *Ibid.* p. 171.
[7] Kōtoku appears to have had serious psychological misgivings about marriage. On the wedding night of both his first two marriages he was known to have gone to the Yoshiwara, and later the

Early in 1896 Kōtoku was given his first start as a writer. Interestingly enough, the article that brought him to the attention of Ōoka Ikuzō, the publisher of the *Chūō Shimbun*, was a eulogy for the late empress dowager. The article, which was widely read and circulated, combined a beautiful style with deep 'loyalist' sentiment. Openly patriotic in tone, it suggested the extent to which the young journalist supported the Throne as well as the tradition.

If one examines Kōtoku's writings for the years 1895-7 one finds them somewhat deficient in focus. Perhaps this was due to the fact that his early pieces were, in keeping with his inner struggles, emotional outbursts rather than closely reasoned logical essays. In reading the early Kōtoku, as we shall see shortly, one is confronted not only with extreme intensity, but with the constant effort to relate the problems of the inner man to society at large. While this highly personalized approach to the problems of his environment reveals a good deal about the tensions within his personality, it renders precarious any dissection of a specific body of ideas to which he can be said to have adhered during these years.

It would be convenient to show a smooth progression of Kōtoku's thought from that of the left-wing leaders of the Jiyūtō like Nakae and Oi Kentarō, to that of modern socialism, as some Japanese scholars have attempted to do, but such an effort forces one to go beyond the available evidence. What is clear during these years is that Kōtoku was feeling his way between two poles of the Meiji intellectual environment of the 1890s. One of these poles consisted of the 'nationalism', or 'Japanism', of Miyake Setsurei, Kuga Katsunan, and the *Nihonjin* group; the other centered around the newly aroused interest in social problems which Kōtoku identified with the early Sohō and the magazine *Kokumin no Tomo*.[1]

Kōtoku had reason to be attracted to both groups. His participation in the literary revival of the late 1880s had aroused a new appreciation of Japanese history which coincided with the historicism of Miyake and Kuga. Like them he accepted the prevalent myth that the Restoration had been radical

responsibilities of being a husband weighed heavily on his shoulders. Feminine authority was difficult for Kōtoku to reject openly. This was particularly true in his mother's case. Having been brought up in a family consisting almost entirely of women (there is an excellent photograph of the young boy standing defiantly in the midst of the women that constituted the family in Teru's recollections - see plate 1), Shūsui was constantly torn between what he considered filial behavior towards the symbol of authority in his family - his mother - and the desire to get his own way. It is quite possible that without a strong male figure in the home with whom he could identify, or against whom he could identify, Kōtoku's masculine identity remained stunted.

[1] For a discussion of both groups see Kenneth Pyle, *The New Generation in Meiji Japan* (Stanford, 1969).

and popular, and that the gains of the people, which he saw largely in terms of legal equality, mobility, and political participation, had come to be threatened by the Meiji oligarchs, who, under Itō and Inoue Kowashi's leadership, had restored aristocracy and privilege through the peerage and bureaucracy. At the same time, he shared Miyake and Kuga's emphasis on the need to retain a sense of moral cohesion in the modernization process, and agreed that this should be done by bringing about a closer union between the throne and the people. Like them he opposed the brand of Westernization – his own term for it was 'Germanism' – of Itō and Inoue which aimed at the elevation of the state. This, he felt, stood in direct contradiction to the original Westernization of the Restoration which, under the direction of Fukuzawa Yukichi and the Popular Rights Movement, had addressed itself to the elevation of the people and not the state.[1]

Kōtoku's attraction to Tokutomi has already been mentioned. The early Sohō, he felt, had inherited the mantle of the original Westernizers. Like the advocates of the Popular Rights Movement, Tokutomi championed the cause of the common man, but in doing so, Kōtoku insisted, he had also gone a step further. The Popular Rights Movement had based itself on a theory of 'materialistic utilitarianism'. But Tokutomi had rejected this theory for the 'spiritualism of Christianity'. More important, Tokutomi had taken the concept of popular rights, which had been based on the idea of natural law, and had substituted for it the concept of 'social idealism', which rested on a belief in evolution and a utopian future. Finally, Kōtoku felt that Tokutomi had come to realize that political democracy, which he had at first envisioned as possible through a spiritual transformation of the people, could not be achieved without the establishment of economic equality. Such a realization, Kōtoku maintained, placed Tokutomi close to the fledgling socialist movement which was about to be given its start by Katayama Sen, Abe Isoo, Murai Tomoyoshi, and other Japanese Christians concerned with social reform.[2]

[1] Kōtoku's relationship to Miyake Setsurei and the *Nihonjin* group has all too often been overlooked by those who see him as a forerunner of the contemporary left. As late as 1903 Kōtoku was a regular contributor to *Nihonjin* and some of his most important articles appeared in its pages. His friendship with Miyake lasted until his death in 1911. An anarchist in prison on the charge of *lèse-majesté*, Kōtoku asked Miyake to write the foreword to his final work, *Kirisuto massatsu ron* (*Rubbing Out Christ*).

[2] Kōtoku's views of Miyake and Tokutomi were expressed in his *Nihon Shakai Shugi shi* (*History of Japanese Socialism*) published in 1907. In considering these views one must be cautious to take into consideration the ten-year gap which separates this work from the period under discussion. The years may have colored Kōtoku's analysis. For example, in 1907 Kōtoku criticized the Miyake group for having failed to make a clear distinction between its brand of nationalism, which Kōtoku regarded as popular and radical, and the conservative brand of nationalism propounded by the

Both the 'true conservatives', as Kōtoku referred to Miyake and his group, and those concerned with social problems were stimulated by the social and economic changes that followed in the wake of the Sino-Japanese War. For many Japanese intellectuals the Sino-Japanese War brought the curtain down on Japan's first stage of nation-building. The war with China had been almost unanimously supported by all sectors of the Japanese public, but with the conclusion of the war, and with the consolidation of the imperial state, there were those who questioned Japan's new course. Expansion abroad, they felt, was being carried out at the cost of much needed social reform at home. Increasing urbanization and the beginnings of an industrial system aroused an interest in the plight of the worker, as well as a sense of apprehension about the future growth of capitalism. Economic concerns were matched by ideological dissatisfactions. Nationalism, with its state-centered focus, was but one of these. Even more prominent was the concern that the old 'liberalism' of the Popular Rights Movement had buckled under government pressure and that the political parties, operating under a constitution which had been designed to share power as grudgingly as possible with the 'people', were all too frequently forced to compromise principles for influence. For those like Kōtoku who looked on politics not as the art of the possible, or as the best possible compromise, but from the Confucian view of the search for a policy beneficial to all, the parties stood for little more than symbols of corruption. Kōtoku probably expressed the feelings of others when he remarked to a friend: 'The age of Popular Rights is over. I am undertaking an investigation of socialism in order to raise a new standard.'[1]

What Kōtoku wanted was a new ideology to replace the rapidly fading ideals of the Popular Rights Movement. At the same time, his concerns were still largely spiritual and not economic. In his opinion the question of prime importance for the nation concerned 'morality' not 'wealth and power'.

Kōtoku's moral position is reflected in his early writings. One of the most interesting of these was an article titled, 'The Paralysis of the People' ('Kokumin no mahi'), which appeared in the *Chūō Shimbun* in 1897. In this article Kōtoku decried the state of the Japanese nation in the period follow-

government leaders. Such an analysis could come only after Kōtoku had himself rejected nationalism in the years leading to the Russo-Japanese War. In the wake of the Triple Intervention Tokutomi had, of course, shifted his position from popular reform to one which supported the military buildup directed by the government. But for Kōtoku there was only one Tokutomi, and that was the editor of the early *Kokumin no Tomo*. Kōtoku always looked to Sohō and the journal as the source of the Japanese socialist movement. For Kōtoku's views on the Seikyōsha and the Minyūsha, see Ishikawa Sanshirō and Kōtoku Shūsui, *Nihon Shakai Shugi shi* in *Meiji bunka zenshū*, vol. XXI (Shakai hen), pp. 347ff.

[1] Asukai Masamichi, *Hangyaku sha no shōzō*, p. 191.

ing the Sino-Japanese War. He took a particularly dim view of the 'people' who, he felt, had lost sight of the ideals that had been responsible for modern Japan's success. In the wake of the war the country seemed 'spiritually paralyzed':

Previously the sensitivity of our people was extremely keen and their passion can be said to have stood at a peak. They offered themselves gladly for the sake of humanity and justice, and thought lightly of death for the cause of loyalty and devotion. In doing so they appeared almost insane, but such insane individuals emerged one after another for the glory of the history of our land and represent one of the reasons we can be proud to be a country of superior men (*Chün tzu*). Look at our victory over Ch'ing China! In the strictest sense it can be attributed to the wisdom and bravery of the officers and men of our army and navy, but half of the credit must certainly go to the enthusiasm of the people.[1]

As Kōtoku saw it, the war had been fought for the sake of 'humanity' and 'justice'. It was for these ultimately 'moral' ends that the people had been willing to sacrifice themselves on the traditional altar of 'loyalty' and 'devotion'. However, by 1897 the early idealism of the people seemed all but dead:

Today, a mere three to five years later, what has become of such things as patriotism, bravery, and enthusiasm? The government is trampling down our constitutional system through the use of money; our representatives throw away their responsibilities and rush about seeking influence and personal gain; the honor of the victory which was the product of the people's sacrifices of their lives and possessions has been cast into the dust, and a civilized nation has been transformed into a land of barbarians. And yet, the people remain unconcerned and do not lament this degeneration. The government, under the guise of protecting industry, patronizes its own favored concerns in order to carry out its own will, but the people remain unconcerned and do not accuse the government of this injustice. Moreover, in trying to tide over a momentary difficulty, the government, without thinking about the great evil it will bequeath the nation for a century, borrows money from foreigners and is on the verge of entrusting national financial rights to outsiders, but the people remain indifferent and are almost completely unaware of this danger. The Prime Minister lacks virtue, public morality declines daily, and things have deteriorated to the point where there are even those who are evil enough to kill their husbands and parents. And yet, the people remain indifferent and do not grieve over this degeneration. The corruption of the political world, the economic unrest, and the daily increasing corruption of public morals, all these foretell the doom of our country. But the people remain indifferent, almost as if they were unaware of this danger. Truly one has to say that the paralysis of the people has reached an extreme.[2]

[1] 'Kokumin no mahi', *Senshū*, vol. II, p. 62.
[2] *Ibid.* pp. 63–4. It is worth noting that Kōtoku's position on the people closely parallels that of Yoshida Shōin, who wrote: 'If one thinks about the people today – they are all deceitful. Truly, the

The foregoing passage is typical of Kōtoku's polemics. It also reflects some of his traditional biases and fears of what was happening in the modernization process. A country which had once based itself on morality, whose citizens had gladly offered themselves selflessly for the sake of 'humanity' and 'justice', was being transformed into a land of 'barbarians', whose egotistical self-seeking and self-aggrandizement had so permeated the moral core of society that the future could only witness decline and destruction.

A few years later Kōtoku composed another article on the same theme in which he revealed in even more emphatic terms his dissatisfaction with the values of modern Japan. Writing in the *Yorozu Chōhō* on the subject, 'A People Without Ideals' ('Riso naki kokumin'), in 1900 he noted:

The reason why Japan has made such unprecedented progress in the last fifty years must certainly be attributed to the fact that her people have possessed lofty ideals which they have constantly followed and from which they refused by dint of courage and devotion to retreat or deviate. Depending on the time and place these ideals have differed in name and expression. At times they were expressed as *sonnō jōi* (revere the Emperor; expel the barbarians), as *kaikoku shinshu* (open country progressiveness), or as *minken jiyū* (popular rights and liberty), but a common thread running through all of these lofty ideals was the establishment of a great civilized nation in East Asia. Our countrymen risked both their lives and their possessions by becoming *rōnin*, rebels, members of political parties, and managers of industry and commerce. Moreover, out of loyalty to their ideas they bowed neither to force nor to authority and made no attempts to avoid personal hardships. Thus, they were able to create the glorious Meiji era. But what about today? Those of our people who were loyal to ideals are old and on the decline, what they do is no longer sufficient. The new group that follows them, that is today's young people, retain not a trace of their former lofty ideals...I know that it serves no purpose to censure the old who have one foot in the grave. It is just that I wonder with whom we are to manage the realm when our young people today are individuals completely devoid of doctrines and ideals, and live for no purpose...Seeing the complete destruction of the once idealistic Japan and its transformation into a land of materialism, I think there is little one can expect from the nation in the future.[1]

For Kōtoku the glory of the past was being besmirched by money and greed and, in addition, the government whose objective should be the welfare of the people had fallen into the hands of those who used it for their own selfish ends. Worst of all, no one seemed concerned; no one protested; no one

people are like drunkards, they understand nothing that is said.... They never become indignant over national affairs.' Quoted in Kosaka Masaaki (ed.), *Japanese Thought in the Meiji Era* (translated and adapted by David Abosch, Tokyo, 1958), p. 39.

[1] *Senshū*, vol. II, pp. 61-2. Kōtoku's picture of the 'people's' role in the past was of course an idealized one. Perhaps it shows more than anything else his own need for ideals that could give meaning to his existence.

seemed to object. The people had, in effect, lost their usefulness both as a political and a moral force. It was purposeless to rely on them and the institutions of parliament to save Japan from moral decline and ultimate destruction:

When people take an overdose of stimulants they become momentarily excited and then lapse into unconsciousness and lose all self-control. When they awake they feel as if they have been bewitched by foxes. Following the excitement of the Sino-Japanese War our people have fallen into a troubled sleep of exhaustion, and have reached a state where they are completely unaware of anything. In the meantime thieves are plundering their warehouses and robbers are about to rob them of their lives, but they remain paralyzed and unaware, dreaming idly of price rises in the stock market.[1]

In 'The Paralysis of the People' Kōtoku pictured the corruption and decline of society as the fault of the corrupt and degenerate individual. The hope of reform rested not in the masses, but in the handful of morally upright men of *shishi* disposition who were aware of the dangers and devoted themselves to the proper remedial measures. These individuals were to play the same important role that had once been carried out by men like Sakamoto Ryōma and Nakaoka Shintarō. Kōtoku therefore concluded 'The Paralysis of the People' with the following lines:

Thirty years ago, on the night of the assassins, Sakamoto Ryōma and Nakaoka Shintarō were cut down at an inn in Kyoto's Kiyamachi. Soon thereafter others were singing love songs under the same eaves, and Nakaoka with his hands on his wounds remarked indignantly, 'The world consists of many types, but it is the *shishi* alone who suffers while others enjoy themselves unconcerned.' Today I sympathize deeply with these words. Ah, if the people are not aroused from their stupor what will become of the future of the nation?[2]

It was through moralistic pieces like 'The Paralysis of the People' and his lighter and more amusing articles in the *Maru Maru Chinbun* that Kōtoku slowly became known to the public in 1897. Unfortunately, we know little about Kōtoku's private life for these years. It is not until the autumn of 1899 that we have another diary fragment which gives us some insight into the development of his character and personality. There were, however, a few events to which Kōtoku reacted strongly during these years. One of these was his response to the *Chūō Shimbun*'s decision to support Itō Hirobumi early in 1898.

In Kōtoku's eyes Itō represented that part of the Meiji state that he most despised. Itō's emphasis on German legalist ideas, his consolidation of the

---

[1] 'Kokumin no mahi', *Senshū*, vol. II, pp. 63-4.   [2] *Ibid.* p. 64.

oligarchs' power through the bureaucracy, peerage, and Privy Council, his role in drafting the Constitution with its limited popular participation, and his efforts to retain a firm control over the Emperor through the Imperial Household Ministry, not to mention his manipulations of the early Diets, all these Kōtoku saw as representing an effort to increase the power of the state and its ruling minority at the expense of the common man. While most of his fellow citizens accepted these changes without protest, Kōtoku found himself unwilling to 'bend his brush' for a man who ten years earlier had been responsible for his expulsion from Tokyo. With the *Chūō Shimbun* serving as Itō's official mouthpiece, Kōtoku, who felt that he had finally 'organized his ideas', decided to resign. He informed Nakae of his decision, and Chōmin replied with a letter in which he pointed out that it was all very well to speak of ideas and commitment, but that one also had to think of feeding and clothing oneself in this world. Occasionally it might be necessary to 'alter one's aspirations slightly', Chōmin wrote, 'how would it be if you made a few allowances?'[1] To Kōtoku, compromise always smelled of moral decay. Instead of accepting Chōmin's advice, he immediately resigned from the paper.

In February 1898, shortly after leaving the *Chūō Shimbun*, Kōtoku joined the staff of the *Yorozu Chōhō*. It was as a writer for this paper that he became well known both as a socialist and as a pacifist who tried vainly to quell the mounting tide for war with Russia.

As the months of 1898 sped by, Kōtoku's articles began to appear with increasing regularity in the *Yorozu Chōhō*. At the same time, the young journalist underwent a gradual intellectual transition. This transition reflected itself most clearly in the articles that Shūsui wrote towards the end of the year. The most interesting of these was a piece entitled, 'The Degeneration of Society: Its Causes and Cure' ('Shakai fuhai no genin to sono kyūji') which appeared in the *Yorozu Chōhō* in November.

In 'The Paralysis of the People' Kōtoku had attributed the degeneration and decline of society to the corrupt and immoral individual. Despite his lack of faith in the 'people', Kōtoku had hoped that they might be aroused from their lethargy and once more instilled with the flame of idealism. In 'The Degeneration of Society: Its Causes and Cure' he was more sceptical. Scathing in his denunciation of the people he wrote:

In recent years the people of our country rid themselves of their political, social, and economic morality, and have reached the extremes of depravity and corruption.

[1] 'Chōmin Sensei', *Senshū*, vol. I, p. 43.

Needless to say, their deeds forecast the annihilation of our country in the same way that Rome fell in the past, and Ch'ing China is falling today. Among the politicians, educators, religious leaders, and other polemicists of public affairs there are those who call for the strict enforcement of official discipline or the elevation of the Imperial Rescript on Education, while others lecture on humanism and philanthropy at first patriotically indignant and then overcome by tears. Although one might truly expect such efforts to have the power of arousing the people, they seem to be completely incapable of this because the people do not want to be aroused. Long ago they not only reconciled themselves to immorality and crime, but were satisfied with them, and gradually moved towards depravity and corruption. *The problem today is no longer how to arouse them from depravity and corruption, but how to save the country from ruin by preventing these.*[1] [Italics added.]

In 'The Degeneration of Society: Its Causes and Cure' Kōtoku continued to picture the cause of decline as the corrupt individual, but all hope of reforming this individual appears lost. Now legalistic measures are needed to prevent 'depravity' and 'corruption' in order to save the country from ruin. One is faced with a significant change here. In 'The Paralysis of the People' both the responsibility for moral decline and the hope for regeneration were centered in the individual. This is no longer the case in 'The Degeneration of Society: Its Causes and Cure'. While the individual is not divested of total responsibility, the environment comes in for an increasing share of the blame. As Kōtoku wrote:

If you want to lecture on the means of preventing degeneracy and corruption, you must first clarify the reasons for them. *The way I see it, today's degeneracy and corruption are not so much the faults of the corrupt or degenerate individual as they are the crime of the system of organization that prevails in society today and forces them* [the people] *to fall into these against their will.* It is man's nature to say and do anything, both good and evil, in his quest for happiness and pleasure, and this is one of the reasons for the active progress of society. To restrict, or to try to eliminate, this desire has always been difficult, and only a society based on a good system of social organization has been able of its own accord to restrict the means through which this desire might be fulfilled, or by directing it has been able to spur sound advances.[2] [Italics added.]

The foregoing passage reflects the extent to which Kōtoku had begun to shift the emphasis from the individual to the 'system of organization'. But at stake was an even greater shift.

One of the basic beliefs of the early Meiji period was the concept that the individual could play a role in shaping his society and environment. In the very open society of early Meiji Japan the individual was seen as a creative

[1] 'Shakai fuhai no genin to sono kyūji', *Shūsui bunshū*, pp. 3-4.   [2] *Ibid.* pp. 4-5.

force which molded the environment, and not as the victim of his surroundings. The symbol of the age was Carlyle's 'hero', and not the Buddhist concept of man ruled by karma. Kōtoku had been brought up with the belief that he too could become a 'hero'. He had, moreover, set himself in opposition to his environment by maintaining the values of the *shishi*, but even as a student of Nakae's he had questioned man's 'freedom'. As his own warrior values came to be threatened and corroded by a hostile environment, he became increasingly aware of his own lack of freedom.

On the other hand, a lack of freedom implied a lack of responsibility. As he observed:

In our country, too, the morality and reliability of the warrior, which were based on the so-called 'way of the warrior', were firmly and splendidly preserved before the Restoration. But after the Restoration they gradually became extinct. It is not that only the warriors who lived before the Restoration knew that they ought to value morality and reliability, and that those living after the Restoration did not know this, but it is a fact that if the organization of the society of that day had not been in accordance with the 'way of the warrior' it would not have been able to provide them with happiness and pleasure, and if today's organization of society were in accordance with it, it would not cause them to lose that happiness and pleasure.[1]

During the Tokugawa period the 'way of the warrior' had meant honor and success, as well as happiness and pleasure, but in the Meiji period this was no longer true. Surrounded by an environment of corruption, even the warrior who sought to maintain his virtue according to traditional values found himself tempted and forced to submit to the influence of his surroundings.[2]

Kōtoku's early writings suggest the extent to which he had already come to feel the tensions of trying to maintain the *shishi* ideal by 1898. For him the 'way of the warrior' no longer meant happiness and pleasure, but the op

---

[1] *Ibid.* p. 5.

[2] Kōtoku was not alone in experiencing the tensions of trying to live by the values of a previous age. Natsume Sōseki in his novel, *Sore kara*, has the young protagonist reflect on what may well have been a common malaise. 'His father', he observed, 'had received the moral upbringing usual for samurai before the Restoration. This upbringing taught a code of conduct utterly removed from the realities of day-to-day living, yet his father believed in it implicitly – and this despite the fact that he was forever being driven by the fierce demands of business life. Over the long years he had changed with these demands, and now he bore little resemblance to what he once was, though he was quite unaware of this. Indeed, he was always boasting that it was his strict warrior education that accounted for his success! But Daisuke thought differently. How could one fulfill the hourly demands of modern life and live by a feudal ethic! Even to try one must wage war against oneself.' (Quoted in T. C. Smith, *The Agrarian Origins of Modern Japan*, p. 206.) Kōtoku bridged the generations of Sōseki's father and son. As we shall see, he had even greater difficulty in maintaining the values of the father against the scrutiny and criticism of the son. Like Sōseki's hero he was increasingly at war against himself.

46

posite – discontent, deprivation, and unrest. Unwilling to take personal responsibility for his difficulties, he began to emphasize the role of the environment. If the fault lay in the environment, the solution rested in its transformation:

> If one wants to prevent today's degeneration and corruption, one must first of all fundamentally reform the organization of society. If one wants the people to support the 'way of the warrior', one must build a society in which the 'way of the warrior' means honor and success, as well as happiness and pleasure, for one can hardly expect the people to support the 'way of the warrior' as long as they live under a social system in which this means dishonor, ridicule, and ruin.[1]

Despite his increasing emphasis on the role of the environment, which premised the power of impersonal forces, Kōtoku continued to see reform as the product of 'righteous individuals' who 'plotted for the sake of the nation'.[2] Moreover, despite mounting difficulties, Kōtoku continued to see himself as such a reformer.

The tensions which expressed themselves in 'The Degeneration of Society: Its Causes and Cure' mounted in the following year. For Kōtoku, 1899 combined a fury of political activity with increasing psychological difficulties.[3] His personal problems were further aggravated by his second marriage which did not begin on a note of promise.

Kōtoku's second wife was the daughter of Morooka Masatane, a late Tokugawa Kokugakusha (scholar of national studies) of some renown.[4] The match was arranged by Nakae, in whose eyes, Chiyoko, with her talent for foreign languages and her accomplishments in the traditional arts of painting and *waka* poetry, seemed the right person for the 'literary' Shūsui. As a result of her pedigree and education Chiyoko must have presented something of a prize and Shūsui appears to have been enthusiastic.

Koizumi Sakutarō, who served as Kōtoku's confidant during his unsuccessful first marriage, sensed trouble as soon as he heard about the proposed match. He immediately asked him whether he had seen the girl, and if she

---

[1] *Ibid.* p. 8.

[2] *Ibid.* p. 9.

[3] In October Kōtoku became a member of the League for the Promotion of Universal Suffrage, and a month later he became secretary of the Shikoku League for the Reduction of Taxes. At the same time he met regularly with such politicians as Okazaki Kunisuke, Inukai Tsuyoshi, Tani Kanjō, and Goda Fukutarō. Nishio Yōtarō, *Kōtoku Shūsui*, pp. 63ff.

[4] Morooka Masatane came from Uwajima in Iyo. He had been active in the *bakumatsu* loyalist movement, and for a time was placed under house arrest in Shinshū. After the Restoration he held various government posts dealing with shrines and temples until he passed away in January 1899 a few months before the marriage of his second daughter, Chiyoko, to Shūsui.

were beautiful.[1] Kōtoku replied that she 'appeared to be beautiful', to which Koizumi countered by asking what he meant by 'appeared?' Had he, or had he not, seen her at the *miai*? Kōtoku confessed that it had been dark, but insisted that her figure, seen from the back as she got up to leave the room, had been that of a beauty. Koizumi was exasperated by Kōtoku's reply, called him a 'fool', and asked him if he wanted to commit the same blunder twice.[2]

On the evening of the wedding day Kōtoku appeared at Koizumi's rooming house in 'feverish haste' and 'dragged' him out to a restaurant. There he started drinking heavily.[3] Soon he suggested a trip to the Yoshiwara. When Koizumi asked him whether this was not his wedding day, Kōtoku replied that it had been a great failure, and that as Koizumi had predicted he had made the same mistake a second time. Kōtoku proposed that he should spend two or three days in the Yoshiwara, this would probably so shock his wife that she would run away and return to her home, thus annulling the marriage. The more he drank the wilder his talk became. Koizumi, aware of Kōtoku's close ties to his mother, pointed out the distress he had caused her by his curt handling of the previous divorce. He insisted, moreover, that carrying out what Kōtoku proposed lay beyond the range of 'unfilial' behavior.[4] Despite Koizumi's pleading, Kōtoku headed for the Yoshiwara. The next morning he calmly announced to his wife and mother where he had spent the night.[5]

Such behavior was not conducive to harmonious relations at home and, despite Kōtoku's stress on humanism and moral purity in his writings, one is frequently left with the impression of a man seriously lacking in human warmth. While there existed a great deal of involvement with mankind on the intellectual plane, in real life there was almost a fear of involvement. This facet of Kōtoku's personality is borne out by his diary for the latter half of 1899. On September 4, for example, Sakai Toshihiko stopped in at Kōtoku's home to let him know that his child was critically ill. Shūsui noted in his diary:

This morning Furukawa [Sakai Toshihiko] dropped in. He wanted to let me know that their dear child was ill and in the Tokyo hospital. It would be better for those who are of no use to the world, who are incurably ill, or for whom recovery means a world of uselessness and imbecility, to die an early death. On this point the beauty of suicide can also be seen in More's *Utopia* and other works. I would rather resign

---

[1] Koizumi Sakutarō, 'Sakai kun to Kōtoku Shūsui o kataru', *Chūō Kōron*, October 1931, p. 175.
[2] *Ibid.*   [3] *Ibid.*   [4] *Ibid.*
[5] Setouchi Harumi, 'Kanno Sugako', *Chūō Kōron*, vol. LXXX, no. 9 (September, 1965), p. 292. Kōtoku is reported to have announced: 'Yoshiwara de tomatte kita.'

myself to the death of my child than have it recover from its illness an imbecile, whose life of unhappiness and suffering I would have to watch.[1]

For Kōtoku only the ideal, the perfect, the beautiful, was worthy of involvement. The imbecile child, like the imperfect woman, constituted more than he could bear. Nor were these feelings limited to women and children, for the same entry continues: 'We also discussed the question of whether it was right to encourage someone who has tuberculosis to commit suicide.'[2]

The 'someone' of this passage bears a close resemblance to Saitō Ryoku-u, the novelist on the staff of the *Yorozu Chōhō*, who later died of tuberculosis. Kōtoku was fond of Saitō and visited him regularly at his home. Moreover, there is no evidence that he ever suggested suicide to his friend, but once again one senses Kōtoku's inability to live in a world of ambiguity, pain, and imperfection. Curiously enough, Sakai and Kōtoku's discussion next turned to Kidd's theory of evolution and the survival of the fittest, a theory which Kōtoku quickly rejected because, as he put it, 'it leaves love and benevolence out of its arguments'.[3]

One cannot help but wonder on occasion what Kōtoku meant by 'love' and 'benevolence', but it seems clear that these, like harmony, purity, single-mindedness of purpose, filial piety, and other concepts that had come to him out of the Confucian tradition, were abstractions that rarely reflected themselves in his daily actions. But the compartmentalization of the real and the ideal, and the protection of the one from the other, became increasingly difficult. Kōtoku's diary, *Jijiroku*, clearly documents the problem. In it one can see that the attack on the world of ideals came from many sides.

Kōtoku rejected the theory of evolution and the concept of the survival of the fittest on the grounds that these doctrines did not take into account love and benevolence. They furthermore contradicted the world of harmony in which he believed. On the other hand, scenes like the following were obviously disturbing. On the fourteenth of September Kōtoku and Saitō Ryoku-u went to the Hōonji garden to view the flowering bush clover. They stopped at a tea house overlooking a pond and the conversation turned to the theory of evolution.

While leaning on the rail that surrounded the pond Ryoku-u said he wanted to show me an example of the struggle for existence and started throwing wheat bran on the water to attract the carp. The carp of this pond differ both in size and number from those found in the Asakusa Kōen and at Kudan, and when they rose to the surface the entire water became red. They are not usually like this during

---

[1] *Nikki to shokan*, p. 64.　　[2] *Ibid.*　　[3] *Ibid.*

49

the plum and wisteria seasons when they are well fed and satiated, but at this time of year there are few who feed them, and the way they fought for the wheat bran was horrible. Truly as a result of the struggle for existence and the survival of the fittest, all, whether large or small, will be destroyed.[1]

If passages like this reflect the pressures of the real world on the realm of ideas, there are others which tend to show that the pressures of the real world were also extending themselves into Kōtoku's domestic life.

As a young man Kōtoku had always prided himself on his scorn for money, which was part of the image of the ideal warrior to which he aspired. Years earlier, as a student of Nakae's, Kōtoku had met Ōmiwa Chōbei, the head of the Osaka City Council. Ōmiwa tried to impress on the young man the fact that the Meiji world was a world of money, and that learning how to use the abacus was the wisest investment a young man could make. Denjirō had been incensed at Ōmiwa's suggestion and had called him a 'maggot' and his ideas 'the heights of baseness' that could be produced by 'evil Osaka gentlemen'.[2] But in the autumn of 1899 money, or the lack thereof, came to be more and more a burden. Financial want led not only to domestic unrest, it also prevented political mobility. Finally Kōtoku found himself forced to admit that Ōmiwa had not been completely wrong. Complaining about his difficulties in his diary, he wrote:

The life of poverty I have just outlined is truly due to the fact that I stepped out into the world full of youthful ardor and without an understanding of the value of money. I tried to rely in everything on chivalrous ambition and turned my back on everything that was vulgar. But today, due to the fact that I have a wife and a certain amount of honor, no, in order to acquire honor, in order to carry out a movement for society, in order to bring justice to the realm, I must first see to my own morality and the regulation of my family so that I can avoid the grief of such concerns.[3]

[1] *Nikki to shokan*, p. 74.
[2] *Ibid.* p. 28.
[3] *Ibid.* p. 84. The 'life of poverty' Kōtoku refers to presents something of a problem. Earlier in the same diary entry (September 28, 1899) he described his income as being around forty yen a month. This may have constituted a 'life of poverty' in Kōtoku's eyes, but forty yen a month was a fairly substantial income in 1899. Katayama Sen received only twenty-five yen a month as director of Kingsley Hall. This Kublin tells us was 'a somewhat niggardly amount but really not ungenerous', at least in comparison with what others were receiving (*Asian Revolutionary*, p. 96). Six years earlier Kōtoku had started at seven yen a month, which appears to have been sufficient to support his mother and first wife. Instead of being 'poor', Kōtoku may well have become something of a spendthrift, particularly on 'entertainment' and 'alcohol'. This was probably as much a cause of his mother's complaints at the time as was her deprivation. Kōtoku was right when he complained that he had no idea of the value of money. As far as finances were concerned he could be extremely generous to his friends when he was well off; when things got tight he expected them to repay his generosity with loans. As a married man he simply continued the 'pawn shop' existence of his youth.

In a well-founded warning he added: 'If I do not pay close attention to this problem, the situation will become critical in a month or two.'[1]

Forced to admit that money was an important element of 'success' in the Meiji world, Kōtoku still felt compelled to rationalize his admission in terms of the Tokugawa warrior. Thus he wrote: 'Savings, although they were in some ways a disgrace to the warrior of old, constitute my honor and my defense. In order to provide for a rainy day or to maintain a solid appearance I must save money in the same way that the warriors of former days preserved their weapons and armor.'[2]

While savings were to constitute Kōtoku's new 'defense' and the solution to his financial and domestic difficulties, these, he soon discovered, could remain as elusive as the 'fame' for which he had deen searching for the past ten years. Without a political movement, without a name, and without money, Kōtoku came to regard himself as more and more of a failure. In addition, there was the problem of his health, which had never been good, and which now came in for its share of the blame for his lack of success: 'The unfortunate thing is my lack of health. It is because of this that I haven't written anything. It is because of this that I have no money. It is because of this that I am unable to organize sufficiently and am unable to attain power and glory.'[3]

A sense of failure, as had become apparent in his childhood, usually resulted in outbursts of anger and depression. The pattern was no different in 1899. Kōtoku's mounting difficulties were recorded by Sakai Toshihiko in his diary. Kōtoku frequently spoke to Sakai of his 'discontent' and 'restlessness'. Sakai was worried about Kōtoku's idealized view of himself. On one occasion Sakai observed: 'Kōtoku fancies himself a statesman...There is nothing wrong with such an opinion. But his concern with fame is not good. It is dangerous to overexaggerate one's abilities without understanding one's limitations.'[4]

The dark moods, the discontent, and the anger which we observed earlier as part of the adolescent Denjirō's personality were still very much a part of the personality of his thirty-year-old counterpart, Shūsui. In the closing months of 1899 the situation had indeed become 'critical' as he had predicted it might. Under no circumstances could he psychologically afford too many days like the following:

A gloomy day. It is nearing the end of the year and I haven't a sen in my pocket. Since ancient times it has been common for the poor to plow the fields of learning.

---

[1] *Nikki to shokan*, p. 84. [2] *Ibid.* [3] *Ibid.*
[4] Sakai Toshihiko, 'Sanjū sai ki', in *Sakai Toshihiko zenshū* (Tokyo, 1933), vol. I, p. 370.

Moreover, men of the same disposition have made light of their ability and much of their will power. They were satisfied with the barest minimum of rice and firewood. But women and children grieve over such a state. It is sad that my aging mother, who knows me so well, should have to complain about her present lack of freedom, when she once passed through life with so much confidence. Although it is sad, there is nothing I can do about it but cover my ears. If it were my wife I might argue, I might scold, I might boast, but since it is my mother there is nothing I can do but accept everything humbly.[1]

His financial situation had evidently not improved in the intervening months, for the entry continues:

Sitting down at my desk to write an article a day in advance in order to be able to attend the funeral of Furukawa's child which takes place tomorrow, the problem of family finances arose once more. I do not have the courage to firmly rebuff my mother on this issue and really do not know what to do about it. All I can do is grit my teeth and listen. In the process my mind was completely overwhelmed by trivialities. Although I tried to concentrate, it did no good. My ideas had been scattered in all directions. The more I tried to recapture them, the more my discontent gushed forth. Finally I threw down the brush without writing a single line. Yelling for sake I started drinking heavily. But the wine did not improve my mood. Instead, my dark anger swelled and swelled until it was uncontrollable. After telling my mother and wife exactly what I thought, I ran out of the house. Although I felt no pleasure I was extremely intoxicated and on the verge of passing out.[2]

Forced once more to face the everyday problems and pressures of the real world in which he lived, Kōtoku escaped into the realm of alcohol and anger. Needing a place of security he staggered to the offices of the *Yorozu Chōhō* where he felt people recognized his true talents:

Going to the newspaper office I entered the editorial room and started to complain and boast once more. When those present saw how drunk I was, they tried to console me, and Suzuki Shōgo put me in a rickshaw and sent me home. It was after four when I got back. My head was in a fog and I couldn't distinguish a thing. Twelve hours later I still wasn't sober. Making my wife accompany me, I set out once more. Staggering as far as the Kawashima [a drinking spot] in Hakkan Chō, I started drinking again. With nightfall it rained and I felt lonely. At twelve I walked home through the mud.[3]

Non-involvement may have been psychologically necessary for Kōtoku. Since childhood he had constructed for himself an ideal world in which he was to play a 'great' part, but the image of the 'hero' to which he aspired frequently contradicted that of the real Kōtoku which displayed itself in daily actions. When on occasion the curtain between the real and the ideal

[1] *Nikki to shokan*, p. 123. [2] *Ibid.* pp. 123-4. [3] *Ibid.* p. 124.

was rent asunder, the response could be traumatic. In the cold clear light of the following morning the contradiction between the ideals he advocated and the reality of his personal conduct seemed to clash all the more strongly. In the end he had not even made it to the funeral of his friend's child. For once Kōtoku had only himself to blame as he wrote: 'I myself always approve great capacity of mind. I believe in having an excess of broadmindedness and tolerance for all kinds of men. I am ashamed of myself. I must be truly a small man to allow my discontent to lead me to drink over a few family matters and then to become abusive under the influence of alcohol.'[1] Finally he concluded: 'Never have I been as drunk and out of my head as today. I must have angered my mother and become a burden to my wife. I am an unfilial son and a husband who lacks benevolence.'[2]

It seems strange that Kōtoku Shūsui under the favorable conditions of a growing reputation, influential journalistic position, and a widening circle of friends should have remained so volatile. But one must also remember that Kōtoku's goal, as he told Nakae, was the political world and not the life of journalism. In journalism the youthful Kōtoku had seen a means of unlocking political doors, but in the late eighteen-nineties his vision had become little more than a mirage that taunted him from a distance. Kōtoku had always been in a hurry. By 1899 it was hard for him to accept the fact that he was nearly thirty and still largely unknown.

For Kōtoku the ten-year span from 1889 to 1899 represents years of education and training. In many ways they were also years of anxiety and disappointment; for it was during these years that the young man, impatient and relentlessly driven by a need for recognition, confronted not only the complexities of the Meiji world, but the complexities of married life and professional responsibility. Unfortunately, Kōtoku's upbringing and early education failed to prepare him for these challenges. Having constructed for himself a world of ideals, a world in which his own identity was highly idealized, he found the confrontation with the real world, the world of imperfection, ambiguity, ugliness, and pain, more than he could bear. By 1899 the tensions between the real and the ideal could no longer be maintained. Overwhelmed by a sense of failure and pressured by the painful and traumatic experiences which he confronted in the closing months of that year, the ideal world of his youth collapsed.

For Kōtoku, failure aroused anger and depression but anger and depression were also followed by a new outburst of energy and by the attempt to

---

[1] *Ibid.*　　[2] *Ibid.*

master a new environment. In 1899 the new environment was the world of socialism. Thus, as the ideals of his youth were threatened by the changing environment and his private life deteriorated into strife and conflict, the need for a realm of purity and neatness asserted itself once more. Out of personal pain and suffering came a new and shining world of ideals – the world of socialism. From utopia in the past Kōtoku was to move to utopia in the future.

CHAPTER 3

From loyalism to socialism, 1899–1903

THE FOUR-YEAR SPAN from 1899 to 1903 was one of intense activity and intellectual growth for Kōtoku Shūsui. It was during these years that the Confucian humanist was to become the socialist-international-ist, that the *shishi* loyalist and patriot was to turn against nationalism and war, and that the young and unknown journalist was to gain a national reputation through his books and articles. Growing renown, aided by the successful restructuring of many of his former values, alleviated some of the tensions that had expressed themselves in the young journalist's private life. Domestic tranquility permitted a profusion of productivity. If our focus in dealing with Kōtoku's youth rested on the conflict between environment and personality, we must now turn to the realm of ideas.

Two forces did much to shape Kōtoku's attitude towards his society in the late 1890s. One was nationalism. The other was the emergence of Japanese imperialism.

Nationalism had played an important role in Kōtoku's life since childhood. As a young man he had rationalized much of his conduct in the name of the nation. In the process he discovered that filial piety and loyalty to friends and teachers could be transcended in the name of patriotic commitment, and that such commitment could even be used to justify the deviant behavior of a person like Nishino Buntarō, the assassin of Mori Arinori, the Minister of Education. For the young man, Denjirō, nationalism was a liberating force that cut through the fetters of tradition and particular loyalties; as such it was a force for change and progress which served as a carrier for many of the momentous changes that accompanied the Meiji Restoration.

And yet, it should also be pointed out that nationalism, as Kōtoku saw it, was not an unlimited force. For him the appeal of the nation was a trumpet call to arms only as long as that appeal could lead to the implementation of the universal principles of 'justice', 'righteousness', and 'benevolent government'. As was true of early French nationalists, Kōtoku envisioned nationalism as a means through which universal ends might be achieved. On the other hand, the universal ends towards which he aspired and towards which he willed the nation to move had undergone an important transition. Like Nakae, for whom, as Professor Ishida and others have pointed out, the cause of Popular Rights constituted Principle (*ri*) while the implemention of this great idea represented the 'way of the true gentleman',[1] Kōtoku had come to identify the universals of the Confucian tradition with the ideals of the French Revolution. 'Liberty', 'equality', and 'fraternity' had become synonymous with '*jin*' and '*gi*' (benevolence and righteousness).[2] Like many of his contemporaries who regarded the Restoration as popular and radical, the achievement of these goals through an all-out national effort seemed justified and proper. It was for this reason that many Japanese intellectuals, including well-known Christians like Uchimura Kanzō, entered the Sino-Japanese War with such high expectations. For them it was a war fought for civilization and enlightenment; as Kōtoku put it, a war for 'humanity and justice'. But when the war was finished what had become of 'humanity' and 'justice'? For those who had supported the war idealistically, who had seen in it an opportunity to have 'progress' conquer a 'decadent past',[3] the outcome of the struggle was mockingly ironic. Instead of the hoped-for reform that might save the continent from further encroachments by European imperialism, the war resulted in greater Chinese weakness and in an unprecedented 'scramble for concessions' by the European powers in China. Meanwhile, Japan herself entered the imperial fray with Taiwan as the cornerstone of her empire. Psychologically, the new-found arrogance of the imperial participant was suddenly underscored by an almost universal acceptance of the social-Darwinistic underpinings for the struggle-for-survival between nations. The popularity of the writings of Admiral Mahan and Herbert Spencer and the need to project an image of Japan as modern, vigorous, and united, even at the expense of despising China and 'leaving Asia', as Fukuzawa put it, was not just an overt reaction to the humiliation of the Triple Intervention and the forced retrocession of the Liaotung Peninsula; it was the conscious act of a government and people fully prepared to participate in the sphere of international politics according to the rules of the West.

[1] For a more extensive treatment of Nakae on this point see Ishida Takeshi, *Meiji seiji shisō shi kenkyū* (Tokyo, 1964), p. 299. Nakae's use of Confucian morality as the basis of a new world order is discussed by Hayashi Shigeru in *Kindai Nihon no shisōka tachi* (Tokyo, 1965), pp. 12f.

[2] Writing in the monthly *Chokugen* (not to be confused with the later weekly of the same name) on January 5, 1904, Kōtoku noted: 'Morality cannot be found in sutras, in ceremonies, or in superstition. Morality consists of *jin* and *gi* of liberty, equality, and fraternity. It can be found only in practicing *jin* and in realizing liberty, equality, and fraternity.'

[3] The words are those of Marius Jansen in *Changing Japanese Attitudes Towards Modernization* (Princeton, 1965), p. 78.

Kōtoku's disappointment with the outcome of the Sino-Japanese War was not just due to the realization that the universal goals he had postulated for the Restoration were being contradicted by an unbridled quest for national wealth and power based on the European model of imperialism; it was also a growing consciousness that the 'kindly' natural law thought of the Enlightenment, which had supported British and French liberalism, and which Nakae and he had seen as a means of preserving the former ethical order of Confucianism was being replaced by an 'amoral, struggle-for-survival natural law', which by its very nature seemed to be lacking in new positive social values.[1]

Kōtoku was not prepared to accept a theory, no matter how enlightened its goals, which based itself on a struggle-for-survival. At the same time, he was faced with the dilemma of how to transcend this stage of intellectual development. The question remained, where could he find a moral doctrine that could support his ideals while at the same time freeing him and his fellow Japanese from the overwhelming pressures of social-Darwinism?

By the late 1890s Kōtoku began to fear that the moral goals, the goals of 'civilization' and 'enlightenment', which he had postulated as the goals of a popular Japanese nationalism,[2] were being forfeited both at home and abroad. The great 'holy' war with China which had been fought for principles of humanity and justice had resulted instead in false pride and a new disdain for the humiliated enemy. The acquisition of territory whetted the appetite of those who sought to achieve wealth and power through foreign expansion,

[1] Albert Craig points out that the transition from the earlier natural law thought of the Enlightenment to that which tried to ally itself with the ideas of social-Darwinism was a phenomenon largely completed in the 1880s. This was certainly true in the case of Katō Hiroyuki and Fukuzawa Yukichi. But for Kōtoku an awareness of this transition did not develop until the close of the century. Albert M. Craig, 'Fuzukawa Yukichi: The Philosophical Foundations of Meiji Nationalism', in Robert E. Ward (ed.), *Political Development in Modern Japan* (Princeton, 1968), pp. 99ff.

[2] There seems to be little historical evidence to support Kōtoku's assertion that Meiji nationalism was 'popular' and 'radical'. Like many of the Meiji changes, nationalism originated with the warrior class. Far from the spontaneous product of a Japanese public, long isolated from political responsibility, nationalism had to be inculcated on the Japanese people from above under the guise of 'national emergency'. This was the type of crisis nationalism which Tokutomi Sohō referred to as the 'patriotism of national emergency'. Without native roots such nationalism could be highly superficial. Apparently aggressive and assertive on the surface, it often elicited the highest praise from Western observers, who were struck by the contrasting apathy of China and Korea. At the same time, there was always the danger that once the 'crisis' had been surmounted, national unity and commitment might dissipate as rapidly as they had formed. There are some signs that such a transformation followed the Sino-Japanese War. For the first time since the Restoration, the sense of 'crisis' weakened, and with its weakening the public's attention began to shift from national and international affairs to local issues and matters of 'self-interest'. It was this shift that Kōtoku interpreted as a loss of ideals and a deterioration of public morality. Moreover, it was this shift that he sought to rectify by providing the Japanese people with new ideals.

and shifted the focus away from vital domestic problems. The indemnity which Japan had won through the sacrifice of her people's lives and possessions had not been returned to them. Instead, the gains of war had gone almost exclusively into the hands of a minority class and added to the growing gap between poverty and wealth.

Coming out of the Confucian tradition, Kōtoku was convinced that one of the principal prerogatives of government was the preservation of national morality. The responsibility of those in leadership was to set a moral example for the people to follow. But to him the Japanese government of the late 1890s seemed completely incapable of such a role.

Some of Kōtoku's most bitter criticisms were leveled against the Japanese parliamentary system of the 1890s. In 1899 he published an article titled, 'An Essay Against Government' ('Hiseiji ron'), which was critical of government in general, and of the Japanese system in particular.[1] In it he wrote that the government that had arisen under the Meiji Constitution was nothing but a 'makeshift government', a 'patched-up affair', a government of 'degeneration and decay'.[2] Using the strongest Confucian invectives at his disposal he stated that Japan had developed a government in which 'cabinets and parliament', 'society and the people' are forced to 'wriggle about' like 'flies and maggots'.[3] 'Every law, every bill that is passed or rejected', he observed, 'is the product of bribery, pay-offs, and entertainments.'[4] Of the people's representatives he wrote, 'Today's members of parliament see nothing but their personal gain and seek nothing but their personal desires. They retain not a drop of concern for others.'[5]

Kōtoku considered party compromises and bureaucratic alliances, which lay at the heart of Japanese politics in the period from 1890 to 1911 as signs of disintegration and decline. He was appalled by the lack of principle in the political world. No one seemed to possess 'doctrines' and 'ideals'.[6] Even those who voted against the majority, he lamented, did so not on the basis of the 'dictates of their conscience', but for their own personal 'benefit'.[7] 'Today's Diet', he concluded with some bitterness, 'has no room for principles and feelings, all it has room for is money.'[8]

If the parties and members of parliament were vilified by Kōtoku's brush, the oligarchs also came in for their share of derision. Curiously, his dissatisfaction with the leaders of Meiji Japan did not include their firm grip

---

[1] 'Hiseiji ron' appeared in the *Yorozu Chōhō* on January 20, 1899. *Senshū*, vol. II, pp. 59–60.
[2] *Ibid.* p. 59.   [3] *Ibid.*
[4] 'Genkon no sieji shakai to shakai shugi', *Rikugo Zasshi*, no. 223 (August 15, 1899), p. 519.
[5] *Ibid.*   [6] *Ibid.*
[7] *Ibid.*   [8] *Ibid.*

on the reigns of power. Of this he approved.[1] What he objected to was their failure to direct the nation towards the goals he had postulated for the Restoration. It seemed contradictory to him that Itō Hirobumi should be calling for political reform in the late 1890s when Itō, Yamagata, and the other oligarchs were primarily responsible for the creation of the modern state which had led to the problems against which they now railed. 'After all', he wrote,

the cause of today's degeneration and decline can be attributed largely to the whole gang of elder statesmen like Itō. While free competition and the development of science gave birth to a rise of capital and a growing gap between the rich and the poor, and may unavoidably lead to the degeneration and corruption that accompany these, our own Restoration-Revolution (*isshin no kakumei*) was based on the spirit of liberty, equality, and fraternity. If these great ideas had been properly carried out, extended, and directed, then it might not have been difficult to bring about a healthy development and an elimination of the above evils before they could cause harm.[2]

Idealized as his interpretation of the Meiji Restoration may have been, Kōtoku remained fully convinced that the Meiji oligarchs had purposely 'forfeited the goals and spirit of the original revolution' and that this had resulted in a great setback to 'progress' and 'development'.[3]

The idea of an incomplete, or aborted, revolution was later taken up by Japanese Marxists who considered the Meiji Restoration an incomplete bourgeois revolution that culminated in absolutism. On the other hand, this interpretation was also adopted by twentieth-century Japanese nationalists like Nakano Seigō and Miyake Setsurei, who believed that the popular aims of the Meiji Restoration had not yet been achieved, and therefore called for another 'popular' Restoration. As Tetsuo Najita has pointed out in a recent article on Nakano, both groups appear remarkably similar in that they both attribute the failure of the Restoration to 'bureaucratic despotism' or 'the persistence of feudal patterns of exercising power'. At the same time, Najita points out the important difference that the Marxists based their criticism on 'social theory', while nationalists like Nakano relied on the 'historical significance' of the Restoration *shishi* (Najita's Satsuma *hayato*) like Saigō. Thus, Najita writes of Nakano stating that 'he did not see the fulfillment of the aims of the Meiji Restoration in terms of social determinism, but of the will of the extraordinary individual like Saigō'. Kōtoku's early position

[1] Kōtoku approved of transcendental cabinets, for example, on the grounds that given the corrupt nature of the political parties in the Diet the firm hands of the oligarchs would be required to provide political stability. See 'Yamagata naikaku o kangei su', *Shūsui bunshū*, pp. 82–4.
[2] 'Genkon no seiji shakai to shakai shugi', *Rikugo Zasshi*, no. 223 (August 15, 1899), p. 520.
[3] *Ibid.*

on the significance of Sakamoto Ryōma, Nakaoka Shintarō, and Yoshida Shōin, or more broadly speaking, his interpretation of the *shishi* as a whole, was very close to that of Nakano. It was only as his self-confidence and his belief in heroic individual action was shaken in 1898 and 1899 – which was accompanied by an almost simultaneous exposure to socialism – that one can detect a gradual shift from an emphasis on the individual to one on social theory. This shift, as I have tried to indicate in the previous chapter, was largely psychologically motivated. But it should also be pointed out that for Kōtoku this shift was neither permanent nor total. In later years one can frequently detect periods – usually emotional high points – when the 'will of the extraordinary individual' took precedence in his mind over 'social determinism'.[1]

'Self-seeking' citizens, 'avaricious' politicians, 'misguided' oligarchs may strike the reader today as mere caricatures of the men who contributed so significantly to the creation of modern Japan. But Kōtoku, it should be remembered, looked upon his society with the firm gaze of the Confucian moralist. He was convinced that everywhere in modern Japan the moral goals of society, the ends for which the individual was to sacrifice himself, had been lost.

Take a look at the state of our people today [he wrote in 1900], is there anyone who is willing to act in accordance with a high and lofty goal? Is there a single person of any age who is willing to act in accordance with a high and lofty purpose? . . . A people which possesses no loyalty and devotion towards goals and acts only on the basis of expediency is a people without discernment, a people without will-power, a people without stability, a people which deceives others as well as itself. In the past such a people has inevitably headed for decline and destruction.[2]

Despite his loss of faith in the government and people, Kōtoku became increasingly absorbed by the problem of reform. For him the question remained how to regenerate the public in order to mount it once more behind the continuing revolution which he believed symbolized early Meiji Japan.

Kōtoku's original hope had been that reform might be accomplished through a political movement. If only the Liberal Party, the Jiyūtō, with which he had identified so strongly as a young man could regroup and raise such a standard. But when Itō Hirobumi stepped down from his position in the oligarchy in 1900 to found a new political party (the Seiyūkai) which

---

[1] For Najita's discussion of Nakano see Tetsuo Najita, 'Nakano Seigō and the Spirit of the Meiji Restoration in Twentieth Century Japan', a paper delivered at the VI Seminar on Modern Japan, Puerto Rico, January 2–7, 1968. To appear in James Morley (ed.), *Dilemmas of Growth in Prewar Japan*, Princeton University Press.

[2] 'Mokuteki to shudan', *Yorozu Chōhō*, June 12, 1900. *Senshū*, vol. II, pp. 64–6.

included many of the former 'liberals', Kōtoku was struck once more by the lack of commitment and principle which governed the political world. At the request of Nakae, who also lamented the demise of the party with which his ideas and life had been so closely intertwined, Kōtoku composed a moving essay, 'A Requiem for the Liberal Party',[1] in which he eulogized the passing of Popular Rights ideals and revealed his own deep sense of loss.

With hopes for the Jiyūtō dashed, Kōtoku began to question the possibility of a political solution to the moral dilemma with which the Japanese nation was confronted. Certainly if a political solution were possible, he was now convinced that it would have to depend on a new ideology. 'Today when liberalism (*jiyū shugi*) and reformism (*kaishin shugi*) have become useless', he wrote, 'the political world which is to follow must await politicians and a party that adheres to new doctrines and new ideals which are suited to the conditions of the day.'[2] Moreover, in the 'present state of things', he insisted, men of 'action' and 'benevolence' must find their battlefields 'outside of government'.[3]

Kōtoku's growing interest in social issues and the question of reform brought him into contact with Japanese of similar concerns. As early as 1897 he had become a member of the Society for the Study of Social Problems (Shakai Mondai Kenkyūkai), a broadly-based organization that directed its attention to the problems emerging from Japan's early industrialization and rapid social change. It was through another member of this organization, Yasuoka Hideo's brother, Yukichi, who had studied social thought in England, that Kōtoku was first introduced to Albert Schaffle's *Quintessence of Socialism* and the works of other socialist writers.[4] While the Society for the Study of Social Problems left its imprint on Kōtoku, the same cannot be said for the opposite. Yamaji Aizan, who chronicled the history of the group, remembered him as just another member. 'No one would have guessed', he wrote, 'that ten years later he would become the most renowned socialist in Japan.'[5]

In 1898 Kōtoku wrote 'The Degeneration of Society: Its Causes and Cure'. The article brought him to the attention of Katayama Sen and Murai Tomoyoshi, who invited him to join another recently organized association, The Society for the Study of Socialism (Shakai Shugi Kenkyūkai). The stated aim of this association was to 'investigate the principles of socialism' in order

[1] 'Jiyūtō o matsuru bun', *Yorozu Chōhō*, August 30, 1900. *Senshū*, vol. II, pp. 80–2.
[2] 'Genkon no seiji shakai to shakai shugi', *Rikugo Zasshi*, no. 223 (August 15, 1899), p. 522.
[3] 'Hiseiji ron', *Senshū*, vol. II, p. 60.
[4] Itoya Toshio, *Kōtoku Shūsui kenkyū* (Tokyo, 1967), p. 122.
[5] Yamaji Aizan, *Genji no shakai mondai oyobi shakai shugi sha*, *Meiji bunka zenshū*, vol. XXI (Shakai hen), p. 377.

to determine whether they might be 'applicable to Japan'.[1] In essence the association represented an outgrowth of the social concern of a number of Japanese Christians who sought to extend the principles of their faith to society at large.[2]

The Society for the Study of Socialism held regular monthly meetings in the library of Unity Hall, the headquarters of the Japan Unitarian Association in Mita. Here a well-stocked supply of Western literature was available to its participants. The organizers made it clear from the start that the society was intended for 'study' and 'education'. Meetings were devoted to lectures and reports on Western social thinkers, and on the history of the socialist movement in Europe and America. Such figures as Saint-Simon, Louis Blanc, Proudhon, Lassalle, and Marx were discussed in rapid succession, though not always with the clearest perception. The members, as Ishikawa Sanshirō remarked, looked upon the group as a Japanese version of the British Fabian Society, although he was quick to add, 'with far less power and influence'.[3] While small in size – the total membership was less than twenty – The Society for the Study of Socialism included a high percentage of Japan's future socialist leaders. Among these were: Katayama Sen, Kōtoku's chief rival as leader of the socialist movement from 1900 to 1910; Abe Isoo, the Waseda University Professor who drafted the platform for Japan's first socialist party; and others like Murai Tomoyoshi, Kawakami Kiyoshi, and Saji Jitsunen.

As might have been expected of a group that combined ministers, labor agitators, university professors, and journalists, interests, as well as approaches to the problem of social reform, tended to be diverse. Katayama Sen, whose years as a student in America and whose early efforts at social work in Japan had introduced him to the plight of the urban worker, continued to emphasize the need to organize labor. In 1897 he had founded the Rōdō Kumiai Kiseikai, Japan's first association directed towards the promotion of trade unionism. Abe, too, was concerned with the conditions of labor and supported the Kiseikai. While Katayama and Abe looked to socialism as a means of undergirding Japan's nascent labor movement, other members of the group were attracted to it largely on scholarly grounds.

[1] For a discussion of the Shakai Shugi Kenkyūkai, see Akamatsu Katsumarō, *Nihon shakai undō shi*, pp. 90ff. Also Hyman Kublin, 'The Origins of the Japanese Socialist Tradition', *Journal of Politics*, XIV, no. 2 (May, 1952), pp. 261ff.

[2] The role of Christians in the early socialist movement in Japan is discussed by Cyril H. Powles in 'Abe Isoo and the Role of Christians in the Founding of the Japanese Socialist Movement: 1895–1905', *Papers on Japan* (Harvard University: East Asian Research Center, 1961), vol. I.

[3] Ishikawa Sanshirō and Kōtoku Shūsui, *Nihon shakai shugi shi*, in *Meiji bunka zenshu*, vol. XXI (Shakai hen), p. 363.

Kōtoku clarified his own position in a report before the society delivered in August 1899. In a paper titled 'Socialism and Today's Political Society', he noted that European and American socialism developed out of a concern for the plight of the worker that followed the Industrial Revolution. 'Although Japan appears to be headed for the same dangerous state,' he reported, 'our workers still retain a good deal of power and are not on the verge of losing their jobs and starving.' 'If one compares Japan with the countries of Europe and America on this point,' he continued, 'Japan might appear to have less of a need for socialism but, if one focuses instead on the political state of our country, one can see that our need for socialism far exceeds that of Europe and America.'[1] Kōtoku's concerns were predominantly ideological. The state of Japanese labor, something he knew relatively little about in 1899, did not elicit an overly sympathetic response on his part.

By the end of 1899 various forces were preparing Socialists for a more active political role. One of these was the general economic situation. The Sino-Japanese War had led to considerable economic expansion. Moreover, the boom-cycle which had begun with the war was further extended through the investment of the 360 million yen indemnity which Japan had received from China. When additional demands for capital appeared the Japanese government, no longer preoccupied with the threat of financial imperialism, regularly turned to foreign loans to support industrial growth at home. The government's investment strategy was designed to establish the industrial backbone for a powerful military machine. In the wake of the Triple Intervention military expenditures soared. The army's outlay, which had been under 15 million yen in 1893, more than tripled to 53 million yen in the period from 1896 to 1900. The navy, not to be outdone, moved from an expenditure of 13 million yen in 1895 to over 50 million yen in 1898. Combined military outlays in 1898 reached an unprecedented 51 per cent of the total national budget.[2] When one takes into consideration, as Professor Lockwood has pointed out, that general administrative costs and debt servicing ate up much of the remaining 49 per cent, there was little left over for the alleviation of social problems.[3]

While it is possible to argue that in the long run military expenditures of such proportions more than paid for themselves by stimulating a general industrial advance, it must also be admitted that in the short run they

[1] 'Genkon no seiji shakai to shakai shugi', *Rikugo Zasshi*, no. 223 (August 15, 1899), p. 522.

[2] William W. Lockwood, *The Economic Development of Japan* (Princeton, 1954), p. 292.

[3] *Ibid.*

contributed much to discontent and unrest, particularly in the urban sector which bore the brunt of the vicissitudes of industrialization.

By the late 1890s, rising wages, which had drawn increasing numbers of workers into modern industries during the war and in the immediate post-war years, had been largely offset by rising costs. The price of rice, perhaps the best commodity index for these years, more than doubled between 1893 and 1898.[1] At the same time taxes had become increasingly burdensome for the city dweller as the government shifted its financing from the land tax to indirect taxes on sake, camphor, tobacco, soya-sauce, drugs, sugar, and textiles. As long as wages kept pace with rising costs and taxes the situation remained tolerable. But by 1897 and 1898 – and here may well lie the reason for the initial success of Katayama and Takano Fusatarō in organizing urban labor during these years – wages in the cities were no longer able to keep up with inflationary prices. The difficulties Kōtoku experienced in making ends meet in 1898 were no doubt magnified considerably in the home of the average worker. And yet, while the cost–wage squeeze and the disappointment of rising expectations encouraged labor organization and strikes in 1898, the tilt from boom to bust in 1899 (a year that witnessed a significant growth in unemployment)[2] virtually brought to a halt trade union activity.[3] The passage of the Peace Police Law (Chian Keisatsu Hō) in February 1900, which outlawed labor agitation, strikes, and bargaining, was simply the *coup de grâce* for an already vitiated movement.

The decline in labor activism did not mean a decline in social discontent. It did, however, mean a shift in tactics on the part of labor leaders like Kata-yama from an emphasis on labor union activity to a new political focus. As Katayama's magazine, *Rōdō Sekai*, stated on March 1, 1900, with the Peace Police Law in effect 'labor agitation' would have to change to 'political agitation'. 'We can and must secure our inborn rights and heritage under the red flag of labor politics that is Socialism', Katayama wrote.[4] Two weeks later *Rōdō Sekai* stated flatly, 'The time is at hand for the formation of a political party consisting of workers.'[5]

Katayama's shift from labor agitation to politics was welcomed by Kōtoku,

[1] In January 1893 a *koku* of rice sold for 7·03 yen on the Tokyo Exchange. By August 1898 the price jumped to 16·80 yen per *koku*. See *Nihon kindai shi jiten* (Tokyo, 1958), p. 906.

[2] Statistics on employment vary. Kublin shows that male workers in factories dropped from 177,632 in 1898 to 158,937 in 1899; *Asian Revolutionary*, p. 108. Sumiya Mikio gives the figures 198,966 for 1898 and 184,559 in 1899; Iwanami Kōza (pub.) *Nihon rekishi, Gendai I*, p. 156.

[3] In 1899 strikes and other forms of labor protests dropped off sharply. In 1898 there had been forty-three strikes; in 1899 there were only fifteen. *Nihon kindai shi jiten*, p. 909.

[4] Hyman Kublin, *Asian Revolutionary*, p. 142n.

[5] Itoya Toshio, *Kōtoku Shūsui kenkyū*, p. 134.

who had never altered his fixed gaze on the political world. Unlike Katayama, Kōtoku did not look upon the establishment of a socialist party as a mere strategy move in the continuing battle for the Japanese worker. Although it is difficult to determine whether due to a lack of sympathy for the worker, or out of a deeper insight into the conditions of the labor movement – there were after all less than 200,000 male workers out of a population of 44 million in 1900 – Kōtoku was convinced that a socialist political movement would have to rest on a broader appeal. Kōtoku's vision was to unite the discontented, whether laborers, farmers, or intellectuals, into a powerful coalition against the central government.

In order to broaden his political base Kōtoku became active in a variety of organizations. In the autumn of 1899, after an unsuccessful attempt to unite the Hoshi Tōru wing of the Jiyūtō with the Kenseihontō in an anti-tax campaign, he accepted the position of secretary in Tani Kanjō's League for the Reduction of Taxes in Shikoku (Shikoku Genso Dōmeikai). Meanwhile he continued his trenchant journalistic attack on national priorities. In this he was aided by the festering Ashio Copper Mine problem, which not only became a *cause célèbre* for Japanese socialists, but aroused other Japanese to the need for social reform.

The Ashio Copper Mine was located in Tochigi prefecture. Under the direction of Furukawa Ichibe, who had bought the mine from the government in the 1880s, it had become one of the principal sources of copper in Meiji Japan. As the mine expanded, it annually dumped larger and larger quantities of pollutants into the Watarase River, thereby destroying the aquatic life of the river and the rice crop of a large segment of central Japan. Despite the extensive number of farmers and fishermen whose livelihoods were destroyed, and despite the fact that the issue was raised almost annually in the Diet by Tanaka Shōzō, the Christian representative from the Ashio district, virtually nothing was done to curb the activities of the mine from 1891 to 1900. In 1899, after flood waters had spread the pollution to an even wider area, farmers from Tochigi, Gumma, Saitama, and Chiba prefectures gathered to organize a direct protest to the Ministry of Agriculture. In February 1900 one thousand representatives of these outraged farmers started for Tokyo to present their grievances. They carried with them a petition calling for the closing of the mine and tax relief for those whose crops had been destroyed by the pollution. No sooner had they left Gumma prefecture than they were confronted by saber-wielding police and troops. Many of the leaders were arrested and the rest were dispersed.

It would be difficult to deny that the Ashio Copper Mine 'affair', which

65

continued to rage for a decade and was not solved until 1907 when it erupted in full-scale violence, represented a dark page in the social history of the Meiji period. It underscored the extent to which the commitment of the Meiji leaders to national wealth and power all too often required immense sacrifices. For those who had become immeshed in an international struggle for survival, copper had, in effect, become more important than the welfare of a few hundred thousand farmers.

To Kōtoku and others the sacrificing of 300,000 farmers for the well-being of one industrialist and the military symbolized the callousness with which the government treated the average citizen. The priorities which had come to be reflected in the military budgets, Kōtoku felt, were now finding further social expression. For police and troops to confront hard-working farmers and laborers with the expression 'dobyakushō' (stupid peasants) showed the extent to which equality had become a mockery. Kōtoku agreed with Tanaka Shōzō's complaint in the Diet that in Japan only the Furukawa Ichibes were treated as human beings.

By the beginning of 1901 Kōtoku was ready for a decisive political step. As a member of the Society for the Study of Socialism he had become increasingly attracted to socialism, but it was not until April 1901 that he announced his conversion to socialism in an article titled, 'I Am a Socialist'.[1] This was the same month in which his first major book, *Imperialism: The Specter of the Twentieth Century* (*Nijū seiki no kaibutsu teikoku shugi*), appeared. It was also at this time that Kinoshita Naoe records that Kōtoku came to see him at the offices of the *Mainichi Shimbun* and suggested that they start a socialist party.[2]

It would be unfair to attribute the creation of the Shakai Minshu-tō, Japan's first social democratic party, solely to Kōtoku's initiative. Many of the members of the Society for the Study of Socialism, and its successor, the Socialist Association (Shakai Shugi Kyōkai), had become convinced of the need for such a party. In 1900 there had been considerable debate on what kind of a stand the party should take, and by the spring of 1901 the stage was set for formal discussions on a platform. At the same time it would be well not to underestimate Kōtoku's influence in the formation of the party. Kinoshita, who along with Katayama served as secretary of the party and whose home became its headquarters, tells us that the invitation to the organizational meeting held in the offices of the Tokyo Iron Workers Union

---

[1] 'Ware wa shakai shugi sha nari', *Yorozu Chōhō*, April 9, 1901. Also in *Shūsui bunshū*, pp. 36–7.

[2] Kinoshita Naoe, *Kami ningen jiyū* (Tokyo, 1934), p. 19.

came from Kōtoku. When he arrived, he recalled, he found Abe Isoo, Katayama Sen, Nishikawa Kōjirō, Kawakami Kiyoshi, and Kōtoku present. Moreover, when it came time to put brush to paper, Kinoshita wrote, 'It was Kōtoku who was to have written the party's platform, but he deferred in favor of Abe Isoo, his senior.'[1] Kōtoku's ideas, if one can take *Imperialism*, about which more will be said shortly, as indicative of his thought at the time, were clearly apparent in the party's manifesto. The eight ultimate aims of the party were: universal brotherhood; disarmament and international peace; abolition of political and economic distinctions; public ownership of land and capital; public ownership of communications and transportation facilities; equitable distribution of wealth; equality of political rights; and free state-supported education for the people. These aims were closely in keeping with the ideals Kōtoku had expressed in the late 1890s. Many of these principals were taken from Richard T. Ely's *Socialism and Social Reform*,[2] a work which Kōtoku admired and later used to support his own study of socialism, *The Quintessence of Socialism* (*Shakai shugi shinzui*). Moreover, the quality of the manifesto, which made it, as Hyman Kublin has pointed out, 'more a well-founded indictment of the failures and betrayals of the liberals [than] a program of political action',[3] was also in keeping with Kōtoku's position that a socialist party would have to pick up the fallen standard of the Popular Rights Movement which had been deserted by Tokutomi Sohō and the Minyūsha group after the Triple Intervention and by the remnant of the old Jiyūtō in 1900.

The Shakai Minshu-tō was launched on May 20, 1901 with the publication of the party's manifesto in *Rōdō Sekai* and six of Tokyo's leading dailies, including the *Yorozu Chōhō* and the *Mainichi Shimbun*. Within a matter of hours the party was officially outlawed by command of Suematsu Kenchō, the Home Minister. All issues of the papers which had carried the declaration were ordered confiscated and the editors responsible were prosecuted for violations of the Press Laws. There can be little doubt that, with a life-span of less than a dozen hours, the Shakai Minshu-tō was among the shortest of Japan's frequently short-lived political organizations.

Kōtoku attributed the failure of the party to the Home Minister's hatred of socialism, a doctrine, Kōtoku was quick to add, that Suematsu, despite his Cambridge education and doctorate in literature, failed to under-

---

[1] Kinoshita Naoe, *Kami ningen jiyū*, p. 20.

[2] Kublin states that the party's manifesto was modeled on that of Marx and Engels; *Asian Revolutionary*, p. 145. Itoya Toshio shows, on the other hand, that it was largely influenced by Ely's work; *Kōtoku Shūsui kenkyū*, p. 141.

[3] Hyman Kublin, *Asian Revolutionary*, p. 147.

stand.[1] At the same time, Hyman Kublin has pointed out that the cause of the party's demise was less the government's fear or hatred of socialists (a group it regarded as cranks and eccentrics)[2] than its concern over certain features of the party's platform such as the proposed abolition of the House of Peers, the reduction in the size of the army, and the call for universal suffrage – policy positions that might allow socialists to link up with other liberal groups calling for reform.[3]

With the unsuccessful Shakai Minshu-tō revealing the extent to which political organization remained premature, Kōtoku, like other Japanese socialists, turned to the enlightenment of the public through lectures, articles, and books. The gradual transition to socialism which had begun for him as a member of the Society for the Study of Socialism and received its first public declaration in 1901 was carried to fruition in 1903 with the publication of *The Quintessence of Socialism*,[4] which remained the leading exposition of socialism in Japan prior to World War I.

For Kōtoku the move to socialism was accompanied by a new confrontation with the question of reform. It also involved a clash with the Christian values of the majority of Japan's pioneer socialists and reveals the extent to which Kōtoku stood for the maintenance of basic elements of the Confucian tradition.

As a young man Kōtoku had found it difficult to determine the causes of the discontent from which he suffered. Even as a student of Nakae Chōmin's he had been unable to decide whether it was the product of man's 'nature' or the 'environment'. Kōtoku's inability to answer this question affected his position on reform. If he had been able to decide that discontent was in fact the product of man's 'nature' then he might have been expected to side with those who proposed internal reform of man as the only basis for social reform. If, on the other hand, he had attributed it solely to 'environment' then one might have expected him to side fully with those who called for the reform of social and political institutions. The choice appears clear from

[1] 'Shakai-tō chin-atsu saku', *Yorozu Chōhō*, May 24, 1901. Also *Kōtoku Shūsui zenshū* (Tokyo, 1968), vol. III, p. 245.

[2] The government's attitude towards socialists was perhaps best expressed near the close of 1901 when the still unsolved Ashio problem led Tanaka Shōzō to attempt a direct petition to the Emperor as he returned from opening the Diet. Kōtoku had written the petition at Tanaka's request. In the aftermath of the incident, in which the sixty-one year old Tanaka nearly lost his life, both were arrested. However, they were soon released on grounds that they were 'insane', and that 'insane' persons were not subject to the law. Asukai Masamichi, 'Kōtoku Shūsui', in *Hangyakusha no shōzō*, p. 210.

[3] Hyman Kublin, *Asian Revolutionary*, p. 147.

[4] *Shakai shugi shinzui*. See *Senshū*, vol. II, pp. 98-151.

the Western perspective. Unfortunately, it was not nearly as distinct for the individual trained in the Confucian tradition.

The Confucian position on reform combined the two classical Western stands on the issue. Thus, Neo-Confucianism contained both an element of internal reform as well as an element of societal reform. The two were summed up in the phrase from the *Great Learning*, '*shūshin seika chikoku heitenka*', which implied that the individual must learn to 'control his actions' and 'manage his home' before he could 'rule a province' and 'bring peace to the realm'. In short, reform began with individual 'self-cultivation', and only the 'self-cultivated', or reformed individual was considered capable of reforming the institutions of society.

Kōtoku's early works reflect constant shifts between the poles of this tradition. On the one hand, he was aware that the moral political state depended on moral individuals. As a result, personal morality was of prime importance for the well-being of the state. At the same time, the maintenance of personal morality, as he was painfully aware, was becoming more and more difficult in an industrializing society. The average citizen was much too absorbed with daily concerns, with the struggle for survival, to give much thought to moral issues. Meanwhile, the state itself was becoming more dependent on a broadening base of the electorate.

Kōtoku realized that with government in the hands of the 'people',[1] and consequently susceptible to immoral forces, the old method of reform, namely, the reform of society through governmental power that rested in the hands of a morally qualified elite, no longer appeared workable. But what were the alternatives? One was, of course, to return to a position of internal reform. Man himself would have to be reformed before society could become whole. The entire public that was in any way connected with the political process would have to aspire to the kind of personal morality that had once been the concern of the warrior reformer. Kōtoku had rejected this idea in 1898 on the grounds that it was too late to save the individual by internal means. Only a transformation of the environment could now save the country from ruin. But by the spring of 1899 he had returned to his earlier position, writing, 'We must first instill in our society and its people morality, faith, ideals, sanctions, and confidence.'[2] A similar shift can be detecte

---

[1] Kōtoku's use of the term, the 'people' (*kokumin*), remains highly ambiguous. He stated, for example, that the 'people' had become politically equal through the Restoration. He also pictured the 'people' as the carriers of the Restoration. But the Restoration was almost exclusively the product of the warrior class, and in 1890 only 1.5 per cent of the population had the vote. His concept of the 'people' thus retains strong overtones of an elite class.

[2] 'Hiseiji ron', *Senshū*, vol. II, p. 60.

when after coming out openly for socialism in the spring he subsequently became active in the Risōdan, or Idealists Band, which was founded on the principle that the transformation of the individual would have to precede the reform of society.[1]

Through the eyes of the Western observer Kōtoku's oscillations between the poles of 'personal' and 'institutional' reform may seem erratic, but for Kōtoku the question appeared to be only one of emphasis since both polarities were fused in the Confucian position.[2] The influence of this fusion was to express itself not only in Kōtoku's approach to reform, but also in that of the Christians who had become his chief allies in the socialist movement.

Since the early years of the Meiji period Christianity had become one of the most powerful ideologies emphasizing 'internal' reform in Japanese society. For the ex-samurai elite that became increasingly concerned with the question of personal morality as the former feudal-based moral order collapsed, Christianity, particularly the highly ethical brand of Protestantism that was presented by American educators and missionaries, took over much of the personal morality sector that had once belonged to Confucianism.

In Confucianism personal morality constituted a means to be used for public ends. Thus, 'shūshin seika', the 'control of one's actions' and the 'management of the home' prepared the individual for 'chikoku heitenka', or the 'rule of the province' and the 'bringing of peace to the realm'. The first was a vital prerequisite for the second. As a result of this relationship it was not long before the Confucian 'samurai' who had turned to Christianity began to concern himself with the social implications of his new faith. Having successfully dealt with the problem of personal reform, he now felt compelled to focus his attention on the 'chikoku heitenka' side of the question. Unfortunately, the type of Christianity which confronted him was ill-suited for such endeavors. It was the more conservative branches of the Protestant Church that had taken up work in Japan, and these groups were often least concerned with the social implications of their faith.[3] With time, dissatis-

---

[1] The Risōdan was organized by Kuroiwa Ruikō, the editor of the *Yorozu Chōhō*, on September 2, 1901. Kōtoku, Sakai Toshihiko, Abe Isoo, Kinoshita Naoe, Saji Jitsunen, Katayama Sen, Uchimura Kanzō, and Kōtoku's close friend Koizumi Sakutarō, were among the better-known members of the group. For the reform program of the group see Kosaka Masaaki, *Japanese Thought in the Meiji Era*, p. 339.

[2] One is also reminded of Kawakami Hajime's well-known remark: 'I am a Marxist materialist who believes in religious truth.'

[3] While the early Meiji missionaries, many of whom came from the United States, were largely representatives of conservative denominations, it should be pointed out that by the turn of the century missionaries of more 'liberal' leanings were also active in Japan. These included the Unitarians and members of the German Liberal Movement. Christians, moreover, concerned themselves from the start with education, health, prison reform, outcasts, and other social work. But to the

faction on the part of Japanese believers mounted. And it was this dissatisfaction that led a number of Japanese Christians to turn to socialism as a means of implementing social reform. In the Christian-Socialism they developed one can detect an interesting restructuring of the former Confucian position on reform.

While Christianity allowed for a modern restructuring of the Confucian position on reform within the framework of Christian-Socialism, it also contained the seeds for the destruction of both Christian-Socialism and the Confucian position on reform. Kōtoku innately sensed this danger.

Like other Meiji 'samurai' Kōtoku was not without the personality needs that turned many of his contemporaries to Christianity. Having himself admitted the need for personal reform in 1899, a need which had become all the more apparent in his own life towards the end of that year, and being surrounded by those who had successfully dealt with similar problems through Christianity, there can be little doubt that Kōtoku must have been challenged by this new foreign faith. And yet, despite this challenge, his confrontation with Christianity was to remain strongly negative. While he cooperated with Uchimura Kanzō, Kinoshita Naoe, Katayama Sen, and some of the other Christians and Christian-Socialists, he always felt their values to be somehow foreign and dangerous. Nor were his fears unwarranted.

Confucianism in its combination of personal and societal reform stressed the fact that personal reform was never to be an end in itself. The premise was always that personal reform was a means to societal ends. Society could never be negated or transcended in the name of personal morality. Thus, while Confucianism was directed towards the concept of reform it left no ground for the idea of revolution. Many of those who turned to Christianity from Confucianism continued to relegate Christianity to the sphere of personal morality and assigned to it the traditional subservience to national and societal goals. But Christianity also possessed the potential for breaking down this traditional structure.[1] For some Japanese Christians total commitment could be shifted from the social system and placed instead in the area of personal morality. As such the individual's relationship to God transcended his relationship to the state. For the Confucian the mere conceptualization of such a position meant a new height in egoism and moral decline. By inverting means and ends, by placing the individual above the state, and by

man of Confucian background '*chikoku heitenka*' implied political action for social reform. Christianity's apolitical attitude was soon radically offset by the political implications of socialism.

[1] For a full discussion of the implications that Christianity had for traditional Japanese values see Robert Bellah, 'Values and Social Change in Modern Japan', *Asian Cultural Studies* (International Christian University, Tokyo), vol. III (1962), pp. 13–56.

legitimizing such a position by means of a powerful universal doctrine, the modern Christian was rejecting the basic tenets of the traditional state. This was a position of revolution. Moreover, it was a kind of revolution that Kōtoku opposed.

Kōtoku objected to any system that placed the individual above society and the state. He was convinced that Western individualism, both of the type advocated by Japanese Christians on the one hand and Fukuzawa Yukichi on the other, possessed disastrous implications for the Japanese people. On the moral front the emphasis on the individual meant the destruction of the relationship of means to ends upon which Confucian morality had been structured. If the individual were to be valued as an entity not subservient to the social body as a whole, but free and independent of that body, then egoism, self-interest, and self-aggrandizement, the enemies of morality, would become the rule of the day. Such a development could not help but have vast social and economic implications. A body of free individuals seeking only to fulfill their own selfish ends would plunge the nation into the struggle for existence and the survival of the fittest, elements of Western development that even European and American social and political thinkers seemed to be having second thoughts over. Kōtoku was not convinced that an acceptance of the competitive individualistic side of Western development insured the 'progress of civilization'.[1] What he searched for was a way to combine the cooperative values of his own tradition with the Western model of the industrial state.

Rejecting Fukuzawa Yukichi's assertion that the foundations of the modern state must rest on 'self-respecting', 'independent', individuals, Kōtoku wrote that the 'tragedy' of the age rested in the 'extremes' to which 'individualism has progressed'.[2] He pointed to 'flourishing egoism', 'free competition', and a 'lack of cooperation and equality' as the results of an effort to provide for the 'well-being of society' merely through the 'benefit and harm of the individual'.[3] Liberalism, with its stress on the individual, may have played an important role in breaking through the fetters of absolutism in the West, he conceded, but liberalism was also a double-edged weapon. The danger, as he saw it, rested in the fact that individualism in its 'extreme' forms led not to the achievement of the goals of liberalism, which he regarded as the continuing revolution towards 'liberty, equality, and fraternity', but to moral decline. 'Not to preach concepts of public honor and public morality

---

[1] He discussed this question in 'Ifu ku no mondai', *Senshū*, vol. II, p. 17.
[2] 'Shūshin yōryō o yomu', *Yorozu Chōhō*, March 6–7, 1900. Also *Senshū*, vol. II, p. 79.
[3] *Ibid.*

at a time like this', he concluded in 1900, 'is truly like trying to save a conflagration by pouring oil on it.'[1]

'Nations', he insisted, 'consist of combinations of individuals.'[2] Each citizen represents only 'a single molecule' of the whole. Where the good of the state is concerned, he emphasized, there must be a 'willingness to sacrifice the happiness and well-being of the individual for the happiness and well-being of society as a whole'.[3]

In summarizing his position on the relationship of the individual to the state, Kōtoku observed that 'people who do not fulfill to the utmost their duties to the nation do not possess the qualifications for citizenship; those who fail to fulfill to the utmost their duties to society are individuals who lack the qualifications for membership in that society'.[4] 'In the meantime', he wrote, 'there is no point in saying that such an unqualified individual possesses rights. For them to assert and brandish only their rights without fulfilling their obligations means licence not rights.'[5]

It is interesting that while Kōtoku questioned the possibility of achieving national wealth and power through a Western form of individualism, he still advocated highly individualistic behavior which he postulated must be based on the concept of 'duties' rather than 'rights'. Western individualism elevated the individual and made him subject to 'immoral' forces, but duty-based individualism was 'moral' in that the individual remained subservient to the social body as a whole. What added to the 'morality' of duty-based individualism was the fact that it was ultimately grounded on self-sacrifice. As Kōtoku wrote:

In a society with a perfect system of organization the interests of the individual and society will be in complete harmony...but in a society organized along today's imperfect lines the individual member who wants to fulfill to the utmost his obligations to that society must by all means determine to sacrifice himself for that society. Consequently the higher one's morality, the greater the corresponding sacrifice. The greater the sacrifice, the greater is the honor one gains.[6]

The individualism of self-sacrifice which Kōtoku advocated was not a new concept. This had been the individualism of the late Tokugawa *shishi* loyalist. And the same brand of individualism was to re-emerge in the thought of the rightist activists of the 1930s. Moreover, when one examines Kōtoku's stand on an issue like 'political assassination' it soon becomes apparent that he could serve as a link between the *shishi* tradition and the radical right of the

---

[1] *Ibid.*   [2] *Ibid.* p. 76.   [3] *Ibid.*
[4] 'Gimu no nen', *Yorozu Chōhō*, July 11, 1901. *Senshū*, vol. II, p. 67.   [5] *Ibid.*
[6] 'Hiranuma Senzō', *Yorozu Chōhō*, August 22, 1902. *Kōtoku Shūsui hyōron to zuisō*, pp. 183–4.

1930s as easily as he could be taken as a forerunner of the leftist movement in postwar Japan.

Commenting on the assassination of the well-known politician, Hoshi Tōru, in an article, 'On Assassination', in 1901, Kōtoku noted that 'when society loses its ability to judge and sanction, those who are immersed in its darkness and degeneration (men like Hoshi) no longer think of public morality or public good'. Under the circumstances, 'desperate men', he asserted, 'will inevitably arise... Yes, despairing of society's inability to judge and control the actions of groups and individuals, these men have taken it upon themselves to substitute for society in carrying out such judgements and sanctions... Those who truly despair of the societies of their day and through their act try to provide society with a means of escape,' he insisted, 'are certainly on the side of the majority of the people.' 'Yes, these assassinations', he concluded, constitute 'a force' which neither 'law, morality, nor social organization' could control. 'Perhaps', he added, ending on a traditional note, 'they should be called the will of heaven.'[1]

The values that reveal themselves in Kōtoku's writings on the question of reform and the relationship of the individual to the state were hardly those of a libertarian. He may not have been far from the truth when he later wrote a friend that his fundamentally 'Confucian' concerns had led him to socialism.[2] Certainly his early writings retain a strong nostalgia for the *gemeinschaft* values of a premodern, preindustrial age.

The theory of socialism constituted (along with the ideas of Christianity) one of the most potent universal doctrines to make inroads into the intellectual world of modern Japan. It was these universal doctrines that eventually posed the greatest threat to traditional Japanese values, and it was for this reason that they aroused such violent opposition from those who considered themselves the guardians of the tradition.

It is interesting to observe, however, that in their initial confrontation with the doctrines of Christianity and socialism most Japanese intellectuals were struck by what they considered a basic affinity between Western ideas and their own tradition, and not by the dimension of conflict. The Meiji warrior, whose moral system was undercut by the destruction of the feudal system, turned to Christianity precisely because it offered a means of preserving those values – loyalty, single-mindedness of purpose, sincerity, etc. – that lay at the core of the former warrior ethos. In the process of such intellectual borrowing, it should be pointed out, the new wine of Christianity

---

[1] 'Ansatsu ron', *Yorozu Chōhō*, June 27, 1901. *Senshū*, vol. II, pp. 31–3.
[2] See letter to Hayashi Sanjūrokurō, *Nikki to shokan*, p. 343.

rarely succeeded in bursting the traditional bottles into which it was poured. The same premises that lay at the heart of the former Confucian system were now transferred to Christianity. Just as personal morality had been subservient to societal ends, so Christianity was to remain subservient to national goals for the majority of the Meiji Christians. It was only with time, and with a deeper understanding of the implications of a faith which they had originally regarded as a fulfillment of the Confucianism of their youth, that a few perceptive and intellectually sensitive Christians were able to transcend nationalism and the imperial state in the name of ultimate loyalty to God.

Kōtoku's confrontation with socialism paralleled that of many of his contemporaries with Christianity. He saw in socialism a doctrine that closely resembled Confucianism or, more precisely, the Confucian values to which he remained firmly committed in the 1890s. As in the case of the Christians, it was the dimension of affinity on the value side, and functional utility in the area of 'psychological' and 'ideological' need that first attracted him to socialism. It is interesting to observe, however, that while Kōtoku almost instinctively felt Christianity to be a threat to Japanese values, he considered socialism to be the best way of preserving these.

As a study of Kōtoku's youth reveals, there were powerful pressures within his personality that demanded ideals and commitment. Without these Kōtoku was subject to periods of depression and doubt, which were exacerbated by feelings of moral impurity and failure. The idea may even be entertained that much of his concern with the morality of the nation and the people which preoccupied him during these years was an outworking of his own concern for his inner state. Later in *Kirisuto massatsu ron* (*Rubbing Out Christ*), which was published after his death in 1911, he noted that the Meiji Restoration had destroyed the foundations of the old morality without providing a new ethical system to take its place. In the interim, he added, men desperately searching for peace and faith had increasingly turned to Christianity.[1] The need for 'peace' and 'faith' that he attributed to the post-Restoration Japanese was no doubt an extension of his own needs. But the materialism to which he adhered, and which he regarded (perhaps somewhat mistakenly) as the core of his teacher Nakae Chōmin's thought, necessitated the rejection of the religious solution to which many of his companions turned. But rejection itself did not dispel the need. Driven by his search for ideals worthy of personal commitment and by a quest for a sense of wholeness, Kōtoku discovered in socialism a means of overcoming both the

[1] *Kirisuto massatsu ron* (Tokyo, 1911), p. 3.

personal and ideological dilemmas in which he found himself in the late 1890s.

To understand Kōtoku's sympathetic and open response to socialism, which contrasted so sharply with his reaction to Christianity, it is necessary to know something about the nature of the socialism with which he came into contact at this crucial point in his development.

In his association with the Society for the Study of Socialism and his initial introduction to Western social thinkers, Kōtoku appears to have been attracted more to the writings of Albert E. Schaffle, Richard T. Ely, and Thomas Kirkup than to those of such well-known socialists as Marx and Engels. One reason for this may have been the fact that popularizers like Schaffle, Ely, and Kirkup shared Kōtoku's predominantly 'ethical' and 'moral' concerns. Their attack, like his, was more a humanistic critique of the shortcomings of industrial society than an analysis of the economic forces that led to the rise of this stage of human development.

Thomas Kirkup, among whose admirers was another Asian revolutionary, Mao Tse-tung,[1] serves as a good example of the type of socialist thinker which appealed to Kōtoku. It remains unclear when Kōtoku first encountered Kirkup's *An Inquiry into Socialism*, but we do know that he quoted extensively from this work in an important article in 1902 and listed the work right behind Marx and Engels in the introduction to *The Quintessence of Socialism* in 1903.[2] Marx and Engels were invoked largely for their symbolic value,[3] while it was Kirkup's work, and Richard T. Ely's *Socialism and Social Reform* that contributed most to Kōtoku's interpretation of socialism. What appealed to Kōtoku about Kirkup's book deserves closer examination.

Socialism [Kirkup wrote] claims to be the economic and social side of a vaster movement, which in politics is democracy and in ethics means toleration, humanity, and unselfish service to society; a movement which set in long ago, but whose accumulating effects are only beginning to be really felt. While it professes first of all to be a movement for the deliverance of the poor, the aim of socialism is towards the renovation and progress of the entire human society.[4]

Kirkup's emphasis on the political and ethical ideals of socialism were guaranteed to arouse a sympathetic response from Kōtoku. Political democ-

---

[1] Mao Tse-tung considered Kirkup's *History of Socialism* one of the three books that led to his conversion to socialism. See Edgar Snow, *Red Star Over China*, p. 155.

[2] The article was 'Shakai Shugi to kokutai', *Rikugo Zasshi*, no. 263 (November 15, 1902). Also *Senshū*, vol. II, pp. 161–5.

[3] Sakai Toshihiko maintains that Kōtoku did not read Marx until 1905. See *Nihon shakai undō shiwa* in *Sakai Toshihiko zenshū*, vol. VI, p. 233.

[4] Thomas Kirkup, *An Inquiry into Socialism* (New York, 1888), p. 1. (Hereafter cited as Kirkup.)

racy had, after all, been something to which he had committed himself at an early age. Values like 'toleration', 'humanity', and 'unselfish service to society' closely paralleled those with which he identified and determined to implement in Japan.

Kirkup, moreover, shared Kōtoku's misgivings about the modernization process. The growth of an industrial system based on self-interest, Kirkup was convinced, would not necessarily lead to the improvement of the individual's lot:

But let us not forget [he wrote] that especially in its earlier stages the industrial revolution acted without social or ethical control, and being made the instrument of private gain resulted in the excessive enrichment of the few, and the impoverishment and degradation of the working classes. *Unless the material and technical appliances of civilization are subordinate to moral ends and to the promotion of true social well being, we have no guarantee that their influence will be beneficial.* Like the natural forces, steam and electricity, by which it is moved, the mechanism of the industrial revolution must be directed by intelligence acting on principles of justice and humanity, in order that it be a true instrument of progress.[1] [Italics added.]

For Kōtoku the concept that the 'mechanism of the industrial revolution must be directed by intelligence acting on the principles of justice and humanity' was a familiar one. Kōtoku could furthermore agree heartily with Kirkup's conclusion that 'under the new system, as under the old, the ethical factor is the dominant one'.[2]

In addition, Kirkup appeared to possess an insight into the role of the elite as morally upright individuals who were capable of understanding the universals of good government. 'Our present condition,' he wrote, 'strongly fortified though it be by prescription and conservatism of vested rights, is hopelessly at variance with the moral sense of the *elite* of men.'[3] It was this minority of morally upright men, Kirkup insisted, 'who have always been the pioneers of progress'.[4] At the same time, Kirkup's statement that 'there can be no real political advance without a corresponding moral improvement',[5] confirmed Kōtoku's own belief that the political state of the nation reflected the moral state of the people.

More important, Kirkup provided Kōtoku with an explanation for the failure of the Restoration to achieve the goals he had originally set for it. Kōtoku may well have thought that Kirkup was speaking to him personally when he stated:

By many it was thought that the boon of freedom was an effectual means of social

---

[1] *Ibid.* p. 41.   [2] *Ibid.*   [3] *Ibid.* p. 20.
[4] *Ibid.*   [5] *Ibid.* p. 24.

regeneration. The naive confidence of early reformers in the efficacy of liberty is indeed almost pathetic...Freedom was a social panacea. It could work miracles.

Freedom was undoubtedly one of the greatest gains of the new era, personal and political freedom, freedom of conscience, freedom of trade. All this was a new thing in the history of the world, and, as compared with the restraints of an earlier time, it was a splendid acquisition.[1]

But freedom had not led to the improvement of the average man's lot in Europe and America any more than it had in Japan. 'Unless wedded to moral law and resting on a secure economic basis', Kirkup wrote, 'freedom is not a special blessing.'[2] 'By itself freedom is no solution to the real and positive difficulties and necessities of social life.'[3]

Nor had freedom improved the moral state of the people. Kirkup too was aware of the corrupting influences of a system that stressed self-interest and a competitive quest for wealth and power as the ultimate meaning of existence. Kōtoku, like Kirkup, could personally vouch for the pressures of the system, pressures that had become increasingly telling in the late 1890s. Kirkup's position was not far from that which Kōtoku had expressed in 'The Degeneration of Society: Its Causes and Cure', when he wrote:

It is not too much to say that the prevailing system has perverted our moral judgements and debased our moral ideas. To get on is the accepted rule of life, which is followed with a persistence and energy truly astonishing, and with an indifference to the means of success that is most deplorable. Under the depraving influence of such a system the higher meaning of life is forgotten.[4]

Unbridled individualism, Kirkup moreover insisted, must sooner or later lead to 'social disaster'.[5] Survival depended essentially on the ability to repress the excessive individualism that had ruined other societies. On this point Kirkup wrote: 'Self interest will always have a large and permanent place in the evolution of humanity, but it must be subordinated to higher principles of moral and social order...Self interest can be trusted as a principle of human nature only when placed under higher ethical guidance.'[6]

As the foregoing passages suggest, Thomas Kirkup's 'moral' and 'ethical' concerns were highly similar to those which dominated Kōtoku's writings. There were additional areas of Kirkup's thought that appealed to Kōtoku and facilitated his smooth transition to socialism.

By the end of the 1890s Kōtoku had become increasingly aware of the inroads that Christianity was making on the *shūshin seika* side of the former Confucian reform dichotomy. Moreover, his fears were soon born out by

[1] Kirkup, p. 52.   [2] *Ibid.* p. 53.   [3] *Ibid.*
[4] *Ibid.* p. 78.   [5] *Ibid.* p. 85.   [6] *Ibid.* pp. 144–5.

Japanese Christians like Uchimura Kanzō and Kinoshita Naoe, who maintained that ultimate loyalty belonged to God and not to the state, Emperor, or social group. Kōtoku must have read with interest, therefore, Kirkup's statement that the division of reform into areas of internal and external reform, the one being the special goal of religion, and the other that of socialism, was a misunderstanding of the goals of this new doctrine. Socialism, Kirkup insisted, combined both the reform of the inner man and the reform of society. The two, he furthermore maintained, were inseparably linked and ought not to be disassociated from one another:

> To say that, while socialism insists on the external and economic influence for good, religion emphasizes the internal, is not altogether accurate. The two cannot be dissociated, and it is the mark of a superficial philosophy to separate them. Man must be treated as a whole. It should be the aim of all true reforms to improve him in soul, body, and estate.[1]

Here then was a means of overcoming the threat posed by Christianity that also promised to breathe new life into the traditional approach to reform. Personal reform and societal reform could be united once more within the framework of a single system. The schism which had emerged with the Restoration might at last be bridged by the new secular morality of socialism. Finally, the morality of socialism appeared to be based on its own *shūshin seika chikoku heitenka* formula which Kirkup expressed in the following words: 'Service rendered to the human society, beginning with the family and expanding through the wider social groups and the nation, till it embraces the whole human race: such is the moral law of socialism.'[2]

In reading this passage Kōtoku must have wondered if Kirkup had not himself read the *Great Learning*, and one can well imagine Kōtoku muttering to himself the standard Japanese expression of assent, *naruhodo*!

But while socialism revealed itself highly appealing because it paralleled certain of the fundamental premises of the Confucian system in which Kōtoku had been educated, it proved even more effective in that it stood in opposition to the very forces that had proved most threatening to the former system and to himself.

Kōtoku concluded that a major cause of decline in Meiji society resulted from the growing self-interest and egotism of the individual. This self-interest was spurred by an economic system that encouraged competition and was augmented by a philosophy that stressed the struggle for existence and the survival of the fittest. Kōtoku found the concepts of egotism,

---

[1] *Ibid.* p. 111.   [2] *Ibid.* p. 134.

competition, and a concern with money basically repugnant. And yet, buttressed as they were by strong historical arguments that bore the hallowed endorsement of modern 'science', and by an almost universal acceptance in the West, he found such concepts difficult to repulse. The fact that Kirkup and other socialists were able to inveigh the theory of evolution against the very elements that most seriously threatened the values of the old order, and refused to accept the existing conditions as anything more than a passing phase in a historical process, provided new support for his belief that human conduct ought not to be based on the Darwinian struggle, but on moral principle. Man was not one of the beasts and ought not to be judged by the standards of the animal world. 'As soon as man ends up making the following of nature the sole ideal of his existence', he wrote, 'he is no longer man, but a mere bird, beast, fish, or plant.'[1]

Thus Kirkup's socialism provided Kōtoku with the new ideology for which he had been searching. The ease with which he accepted Kirkup's ideas indicates the lack of tension that existed between his own intellectual tradition and Kirkup's thought. For Kōtoku the acceptance of socialism did not mean an immediate clash of values. Nor was it accompanied by a dramatic conversion experience. Socialism, instead, appeared to represent a refinement of the ideas of selfless devotion to society, strengthened by the weight of modern science and a program for political and economic reform. Basically a transformation of his Confucian values, Kōtoku's socialism reflected the extent to which his new ideology was molded by the values of the past.

Kōtoku is frequently criticized by current historians and political scientists for his insufficient understanding of certain of the cardinal tenets of the materialistic socialism to which he ascribed. His study, *The Quintessence of Socialism*, has often been attacked for its failure to deal adequately with the proletariat as a revolutionary force, with the contradictions of class-based societies, and the position of socialism *vis-à-vis* the Imperial Institution. These criticisms are valid if one assumes that Kōtoku intended to establish Marxism in Japan. But this is a somewhat dubious assumption given the fact that he had not yet read Marx. Perhaps it is more important to focus on the fact that it was precisely in these areas of so-called 'insufficient understanding' that socialist values promised to clash most sharply with elements of the Confucian tradition. The problem expressed itself on the question of revolution.

Kōtoku was not untutored in the field of Western revolutionary history.

[1] *Teikoku shugi*, p. 39.

Nor was he unaware of the role assigned to the proletariat in the revolution anticipated by Marxists. At the same time, he remained basically an elitist. His picture of the revolutionary was not that of the worker defending the barricades, but that of the Tokugawa loyalist sacrificing himself for the good of society and the nation. The morally upright assassin whose violent act was designed to restore society to its naturally good order by eliminating those who had corrupted that order had his roots in the Mencian, and not the Western, revolutionary tradition.[1] Mencius also provided the optimism for the coming revolution. It was an inevitable part of the historical process that the passage of time itself insured the restoration of the natural order. 'Revolutions', Kōtoku wrote in 1903, 'are the product of heaven and not man. They can be directed but not manufactured. When they come there is nothing man can do about them, nor can he do anything about them once they have passed . . .'[2]

Lassalle, Kōtoku noted in *The Quintessence of Socialism*, described revolution as the 'midwife of a new age'.[3] Kōtoku compared it to the process of birth itself. The revolutionary he pictured as the 'obstetrician' whose duty it was to keep a constant watch over the health of the mother and to prescribe those measures that might render the birth an easy one. In the hands of a good 'obstetrician', revolutions, like natural births, proceeded tranquilly and without violence.

Kōtoku conceived of revolution as part of the natural order. Just as there had once existed a universal ideal (*ri*) of 'good government' which it was the duty of the statesman to investigate and understand in order to insure the tranquil functioning of the state, so there existed a universal ideal (*ri*) of revolutionary change which it was the duty of the revolutionary to investigate and understand in order to insure the peaceful transition of society from one stage to the next.[4]

As a socialist Kōtoku saw the revolutionary's role as neither creative nor destructive. Revolutions were not man-made, he insisted again and again. The responsibility of the revolutionary centered in the realm of knowledge, not action, and his function was to educate himself and the public and not to prepare and organize for violence. Since Revolutions lay beyond man's control, the revolutionary's only means of influencing their outcome, or

[1] For a discussion of this point see Teradani Takeshi, 'Kōtoku Shūsui ron', *Kokugo to koku bungaku*, vol. 37, no. 5 (May, 1960), pp. 68ff.

[2] *Shakai Shugi shinzui, Senshū*, vol. II, p. 144.   [3] *Ibid*. p. 143.

[4] *Ibid*. p. 144. 'It is the concern of the revolutionary', Kōtoku wrote, 'to check on the state of the organization of society and to lead the great forces of evolution in order to bring about peaceful revolutions.'

'leading' them, was to deal with the human response. It was man's willingness to bow to the inevitable, or to resist it with dogged determination, that decided whether a revolution would develop along peaceful or violent lines.

While Kōtoku's revolutionary thought reflects the extent to which the Confucian concept of the 'natural order' could accommodate the theories of evolutionary change, the relationship of the individual to that order remained fundamentally unaltered. The power of the natural order, which remained sacrosanct, still dwarfed and limited the individual. Given these limitations, the revolutionary's only recourse lay in providing his fellow men with clearer insights into the inevitable workings of the system. He could not change the system itself.

It remains a curious paradox in Kōtoku's thought that such a passive response to the idea of revolution and the role of the revolutionary should have coexisted with his forceful rejection of late Meiji nationalism.

Kōtoku's dissatisfaction with Japan's new imperialistic course, his distrust of aggressive nationalism, as well as his search for values and a program of reform became the core of his first major book, *Imperialism: The Specter of the Twentieth Century*, which appeared in 1901.

Like Hobson's well-known study published in 1902, Kōtoku's investigation of imperialism first appeared as a series of newspaper and magazine articles.[1] As Hobson's concerns were stimulated by British involvement in the Boer War, so Kōtoku's study was influenced by Japanese participation in the efforts to quell the Boxer Rebellion. Kōtoku viewed Japanese involvement in the expedition to relieve the legations at Peking with apprehension. In his estimation, the chief beneficiaries of such an involvement were the military and other groups committed to national expansion. The chief victims were

---

[1] Although it is possible that Kōtoku may have encountered some of Hobson's articles in the *Contemporary Review*, a journal with which he was no doubt familiar from his translating days, there is no reference to Hobson's articles in Kōtoku's writings. There are, however, some parallels worth pointing out. Certainly an important part of Hobson's analysis centered on his economic theory of finance capital's search for better investment opportunities abroad, a theory that could hardly be applied to capital-impoverished Japan, and for this reason might have been expected to appeal little to the Japanese critic of imperialism. But economic arguments represented only one side of Hobson's critique. Hobson was also concerned with the relationship of an increasingly aggressive nationalism to foreign expansion, and with the implications of such a nationalism for domestic liberal reform. Here Hobson and Kōtoku share a common concern. Occasionally there is even some similarity of rhetoric. Thus, Hobson's concluding statement that 'imperialism is a depraved choice of national life, imposed by self-seeking interests which appeal to the lusts of quantitative acquisitiveness and of forceful domination surviving in a nation from early centuries of animal struggle for existence. Its adoption as a policy implies a deliberate renunciation of that cultivation of the higher inner qualities which for a nation as for an individual constitute the ascendency of reason over brute impulse', comes remarkably close to Kōtoku's language in the introduction and conclusion of *Imperialism: The Specter of the Twentieth Century*.

inevitably the common people, who, shouldered with increased taxes, would find themselves further deprived of much needed social reform and tax relief. At the same time, Kōtoku was concerned with the ethical implications of the conflict. Unlike Hobson and Lenin, whose *Imperialism: The Highest Stage of Capitalism* was to appear fifteen years later, Kōtoku was less concerned with the economic imperatives of capitalism than with its moral implications. His critique, by contrast with that of Hobson, was basically humanistic, the work of a Confucian moralist and not of a political economist.

Kōtoku began his study by counterposing what he considered the responsibility of the modern state with what he was convinced had become the all too obvious pattern of late nineteenth-century imperialism. 'The goal of national policy', he wrote, 'is to secure lasting progress for society and happiness and well being for all mankind.'[1] 'I believe, moreover,' he added, 'that the progress of society must await the establishment of true scientific knowledge, and that the happiness and well being of mankind can be achieved only by a return to the fountainhead of a pure civilized morality.'[2] Kōtoku did not believe that imperialism could meet either of these requirements. 'What leads to the rise and popularity of imperialism', he wrote, 'is not scientific knowledge, but superstition. It is not civilized morality, but fanaticism. It is not liberty, righteousness, fraternity, and equality, but tyranny, wickedness, perversity, and strife.'[3]

Kōtoku's combination of a one-armed hold on the past with a one-armed grasp for the future, which is readily detectable in the preface of *Imperialism*, outlines the curious middle position in which he found himself in the late 1890s. On the one hand, he was tied to the traditional ethic; on the other, he had come to admit that modernization through 'scientific knowledge' was inevitable. Like many another Meiji thinker, Kōtoku found himself in the difficult position of needing somehow to reconcile the Confucian ethic with the modernization process. This was no easy matter.

And yet, while Kōtoku accepted 'science' – a term he never fully defined but vaguely associated with 'modern' and 'western' – he was quick to distinguish between 'true' science, or 'true' scientific knowledge, and what he termed 'so-called' scientific knowledge. 'True' science constituted those ideas from the West which blended with the tradition without jeopardizing the fundamental premises upon which the tradition rested. 'So-called' scientific knowledge was anything that threatened the tradition. Thus, Kōtoku regarded liberty, equality, and fraternity as 'truly scientific' because they

---

[1] *Teikoku shugi* (Tokyo, 1959), p. 15.
[2] *Ibid.* p. 16.   [3] *Ibid.*

represented Western expressions of the Confucian universals of good government. By the same logic, patriotism, militarism, and their combined result, imperialism, were 'unscientific' because they threatened these universals.

Japanese imperialism, Kōtoku maintained, was the product of militarism (the outgrowth of an unbridled commitment to wealth and power) and jingoistic patriotism. The latter, he insisted, was based on hatred, scorn, and vain pride – subhuman qualities of the individual immersed only in self interest.[1] Such a policy, which took the immorality of the individual and sanctioned it in the name of the nation, stood in direct opposition to humanism, justice, and righteousness, the goals of true progress and enlightenment.[2]

Nationalism, on which Kōtoku concentrated his attack in the first half of his book, had once liberated the individual from the ties of a feudal society, he admitted, but nationalism in its new aggressive form could well return the individual to a new form of slavery. This he believed was true in Japan as well as abroad.

Instead of searching for peace and focusing on the multitude of unsolved social and economic problems that plagued the public at home, the government, he felt, was trying to shift the attention of the Japanese nation abroad by constantly dangling before it the carrot of 'empire' and prodding it with the stick of 'national emergency'. 'By shifting the hatred at work among individuals and directing it towards a foreign enemy', he wrote, 'the government hopes to serve its own ends.'[3] Under the circumstances the individual became a mere pawn. 'Anyone who opposes this', he wrote apprehensively, 'is suppressed by being called "unpatriotic" and labelled a "traitor".'[4]

Kōtoku was aware of the potential for reaction inherent in a combination of jingoistic nationalism with a policy of national expansion. He was quick to see the serious implications of such a union for those who supported liberal reform. Using England as an example, he wrote: 'In modern times England has been called an extremely liberal nation. It has, moreover, been called a humanistic nation, and a peaceful nation. But even in England those calling for liberty, advocating reform, or pleading for universal suffrage are accused of treason and suppressed as traitors during periods of ardent nationalism.'[5]

Kōtoku was convinced that if this were true of England, a nation with a long liberal tradition, it would be far more true of Japan which had no liberal tradition. The rejection of nationalism was therefore of crucial importance for the implementation of reform in Japan.

[1] *Teikoku shugi*, p. 34. [2] *Ibid.* [3] *Ibid.* p. 24.
[4] *Ibid.* [5] *Ibid.* p. 25.

In opposing nationalism Kōtoku was forced to go beyond the premise that the given was 'natural', which determined his position on revolution. Now he called instead for the conquest of the 'natural' by the 'man-made'.[1] Here was the start of a break with the past.

Kōtoku's rejection of nationalism was accompanied by his affirmation of socialism. It was no accident that *Imperialism* and 'I Am a Socialist' were published almost simultaneously in 1901. Just as he had once turned to nationalism in order to transcend the particularistic concepts of loyalty and filial piety that were part of his village environment in Tosa, he now turned to internationalism and to the new universal moral order of socialism to reject a nationalism which he no longer regarded an aid to Japan's healthy development.

But such a rejection was not an easy step for a person who considered himself a patriot and an heir of the warrior tradition. Kōtoku's difficulty lay in the fact that while he found himself intellectually convinced of the need to reject nationalism, he found it difficult to reject some of the specific elements of the Japanese tradition with which that nationalism identified itself. Thus, although he saw quite clearly the need for man to consider institutions, and even ideas, 'man-made' in an effort to oppose them and bring about reform, this intellectual awareness was not accompanied by an emotional break with the past. Kōtoku's life continued to be lived on two planes: the intellectual and the emotional. On the one he was slowly developing into a revolutionary; on the other, he continued to adhere to the values of the old order.

The complexity of his split loyalties can be seen in his response as a socialist to the national polity (*kokutai*) and the Imperial House.

From childhood Kōtoku had modeled himself on the late Tokugawa loyalist. Like other of Meiji Japan's 'liberals' he had combined the advocacy of greater popular rights with loyalty and devotion to the Throne. The tone of many of his early pieces reflects this commitment. But with the increasing deification of the Emperor he found himself in a difficult position. While he remained loyal to the Emperor and nation, he became sharply critical of the government. At the same time the government began to use the symbol

[1] On this point Kōtoku wrote: 'Do not say that these [love of war, vain pride, hatred, and other elements of nationalism] constitute the nature of man's history, that they have always existed, and that they cannot be eliminated ... The reason for man's progress lies in his effort to rectify the evils of nature. It is those people who have made the greatest progress in controlling the natural passions who have made the greatest moral progress. Moreover, it is those people who have made the greatest effort to offset the natural with the man-made that have achieved the greatest material progress. Those who desire the happiness and well being of civilization must refuse blind submission to nature.' *Ibid.* p. 39.

of the Emperor and nation to suppress those who dissented with its position on domestic and foreign affairs.

Under these circumstances, some of Kōtoku's fellow socialists – particularly those of Christian background – called for the rejection of the symbols of authority upon which the government was based. One of the leading advocates of such a stand was Kinoshita Naoe, who called for an open rejection of the Imperial myth. Ultimate loyalty, Kinoshita maintained, belonged to God and not to the state or the Emperor. Kōtoku was highly annoyed by Kinoshita's adamant stand on this issue. 'The aim of socialism', he told him in no uncertain terms, 'is to reform the economic organization [of society]. It has nothing to do with the national polity (*kokutai*), or with the system of government (*seitai*). Because of men like you socialism is misunderstood by the public. This is highly unfortunate.'[1]

Kōtoku's position on the Japanese Emperor contrasted sharply with Kinoshita's. In 'Socialism and the National Polity' ('Shakai Shugi to kokutai'), which he wrote in 1902, he presented his own approach to the question of Imperial authority. 'Extreme individualists like Louis XIV, who recklessly declared himself to be the state, have always been the enemies of socialists' Kōtoku wrote.[2] On the other hand, Japanese Emperors like Nintoku, who considered 'the well being of the people the treasure of the court', he maintained, 'were in complete agreement and accord with the principles of socialism'.[3] In *Imperialism* Kōtoku wrote that the Japanese Emperor differed from the German Kaiser in that he favored 'peace over war', 'freedom over oppression', and 'the happiness and well being of the entire world over the barbaric vanity of a single nation'.[4] Kōtoku made every effort to identify the Imperial Institution with the universal and moral, rather than the particular and Japanese. 'Humanism', 'justice', and 'peace' had always been the chief concerns of the Japanese Emperors, he felt, and such a tradition was clearly not in keeping with the goals of nationalism which stressed 'hatred', 'contempt', and 'vain pride'.[5]

The trouble with Japan, as he was well aware, was that there were too few 'lonely morning stars' among her people who were willing to back the true Imperial tradition and oppose the kind of nationalism that was built on hatred and the desire to subjugate others. 'A heart of loyalty is good,' he wrote, 'so is doing things for the Emperor, but to say that one knows nothing of

[1] Kanzaki Kiyoshi, *Taigyaku jiken* (Tokyo, 1964), p. 57. The quotation is from Kinoshita Naoe, *Kami ningen jiyū*.
[2] *Senshū*, vol. II, p. 165.   [3] *Ibid.*
[4] *Teikoku shugi*, p. 34.   [5] *Ibid.*

justice and humanity, this is barbaric nationalism, this is loyalty based on superstition, this is no different from theft and prostitution carried out in the name of filial piety.'[1]

Finally, Kōtoku was convinced that socialism would overcome the evils of nationalism and militarism without jeopardizing the position of the Emperor. Nor did he feel socialism to be incompatible with the goals of wealth and power. Consequently, he saw no conflict between socialism and the national polity. To support this position he quoted Kirkup, who had written:

> Though socialism most naturally allies itself with the advancing democracy, there is no absolute reason why the actual control of the movement should be democratic. In Germany it is quite possible to imagine with Rodbertus that it might proceed from the Emperor... It is possible that the imperial court and its servants, tired of compromise with the monied middle class, might throw themselves unreservedly on the workers both of town and country, and establish a socialist empire. Such an empire, served by capable officials like the present and supported by a people's army inspired with the enthusiasm of a better social order, might find its strength and stability immeasurably increased.[2]

On the question of wealth and power Kōtoku was willing to go a step further. 'There can be no doubt', he wrote, again quoting Kirkup,

> that in the struggle among nations which at least in the immediate future is likely to become more intense than formerly, the people that first brings its social organization into harmony with the new conditions will have an immense advantage. The country that can first raise its working population to an intelligent and enthusiastic solidarity of feeling and interest, a compact nation of free instructed men, would in the scientific warfare of today have an exceptionally strong position against a government of capitalists dragging after them an unwilling, demoralized, and ignorant host of proletarians.[3]

Kōtoku therefore saw no reason why a socialist could not make his peace with the Japanese state. The goals of socialism, he was convinced, were identical with those to which benevolent Japanese Emperors had always addressed themselves. Socialism did not clash with what he considered the fundamental elements of the Japanese tradition. At least so he thought in 1903. His confrontation with the authority of the state which resulted from his pacifist opposition to the Russo-Japanese War soon dispelled any illusions he might have had over the possibility of compromising with the existing order.

---

[1] *Ibid.* p. 15.

[2] 'Shakai Shugi to kokutai', *Senshū*, vol. II, pp. 163–4. The original source is Thomas Kirkup, *An Inquiry into Socialism*, pp. 102–3.

[3] *Ibid.* p. 164. Original in Kirkup, p. 103.

CHAPTER 4

Pacifist opposition to the Russo-Japanese War, 1903–5

AT THE TIME OF THE SINO-JAPANESE WAR Kōtoku Shūsui had been little more than a fledgling journalist with few personal convictions on the subject of war. Highly ambitious, constantly restless and impatient, Kōtoku had enthusiastically followed the progress of the war first from Tokyo and then from Hiroshima. There is no evidence that he opposed what was taking place on the continent.

By 1900 Kōtoku's attitude towards war had begun to change. Sensing a need to take a stand against the mounting tide of nationalism, which he was convinced was being directed towards the acquisition of empire rather than internal reform, he adopted a firm pacifist stand.

The Sino-Japanese War had created new problems for Japan. No one could deny that the quick and easy victory over China had added greatly to Japan's prestige abroad. At last Japan had gained a measure of equality with the West, and this realization greatly buoyed up the nation's self-confidence. Success in war, furthermore, confirmed the wisdom of the Meiji leaders' emphasis on guns over butter, and significantly underscored the importance of the army and navy. But victory was not without further humiliation. A week after the signing of the Treaty of Shimonoseki the Triple Intervention forced the Japanese to divest themselves of the territorial concessions they had won from China. Overnight the joyous lantern-waving celebrations, which had marked the nation's response to victory, turned into public indignation. The situation became even less tolerable a few years later when Russia, France, and Germany, the countries which had forced Japan to give up the Liaotung Peninsula, acquired new concessions from China.

The hard lesson in international politics which the Japanese learned through the Triple Intervention was not soon forgotten. In order to insure that such indignities would not recur, the Japanese government embarked on an ambitious program of military expansion. The extent to which this military buildup weighed on the Japanese public has already been mentioned. Given the shock of the Triple Intervention, few Japanese complained however. While Kōtoku decried the growing influence of the military and what he regarded as the waste of vital national resources for defense purposes, the majority of his countrymen supported the priorities of national strength.

Under these conditions, nationalism, which was already bellicose at the time of Japan's victory over China, grew increasingly jingoistic by the turn of the century. To Kōtoku the public appeared 'paralysed' in its grip. And to the extent that many Japanese allowed their mood of bitterness to lead them to accept the ideas of nationalistic extremists, his charge was not totally unfounded.

While concentrating on the domestic problems of her military and economic buildup, matters of foreign policy continued to trouble the Japanese government. With Chinese influence eliminated from Korea, Japan was confronted more directly by growing Russian power in Korea and Manchuria. Efforts to assure Japan's 'strategic' interests in Korea through diplomatic agreements with the Tsar's government were made in 1896 and 1898. These recognized Japan's predominant interests in Korea, but did not halt the Russian push to the east which had begun with the commencement of construction on the Trans-Siberian Railroad in 1891. Russian actions, moreover, were less assuring than her diplomacy. If her role in the Triple Intervention aroused Japanese fears, her subsequent attempts to gain a foothold in Manchuria by arranging extensive loans for the Chinese (to repay the indemnity owed Japan), signing a secret treaty with the Ch'ing government in 1896, and leasing the strategic tip of the Liaotung Peninsula, which included Port Arthur and Dairen, in 1898, did little to alleviate Japanese fears.

Japanese-Russian tensions reached a new peak in 1900 when the Russian government, using the pretext of the Boxer Rebellion, garrisoned Manchuria with Russian troops. Vigorous protests by Japan, England, and the United States did little to dislodge the Russian forces, and it was not until the Japanese and British signed the Anglo-Japanese Alliance in 1902 that Russia agreed to troop withdrawals, to be completed in three stages over a period of eighteen months.

The first stage of Russia's pull-back was carried out on schedule in October 1902. But the second stage, set for April 1903, failed to materialize. Instead, all signs indicated that the Russians planned a new advance.

Despite growing public outbursts and a clamor for war by the press in Tokyo, Prime Minister Katsura continued to make efforts to reach a diplomatic solution with the Russian government. In June 1903 the Japanese proposed a plan that would have called for mutual recognition of the territorial integrity of China and Korea. At the same time the Japanese agreed to recognize Russian railway rights in Manchuria if the Tsar's government would reciprocate by recognizing Japanese political and economic rights in Korea. The Russian reply, delivered in October 1903, made it clear that while it agreed on territorial guarantees for Korea it opposed such guarantees for China. Moreover, it insisted that the Japanese declare Korea outside of their 'sphere of interest' and refrain from fortifying the Korean coast. As soon as the Russian terms were made public in Japan the press insisted that they were unacceptable to the Japanese people.

The Katsura Cabinet found itself in a difficult position. To accept the Russian proposal would be politically suicidal and might well lead to violence at home. On the other hand, to engage Russia in war, as the public demanded, might prove an even greater tragedy. And yet, as a follower of Yamagata, who had been convinced for some time that Japan would have to fight another war within the decade after the conflict with China, Katsura was hardly a coward who feared decisive action. In January 1904 he delivered a counter-ultimatum to the Russians. When no reply was forthcoming, he and his cabinet, conscious of the rush of Russian reinforcements to the Far East over the Trans-Siberian Railroad, decided that further negotiations would simply jeopardize Japanese chances for victory. Japanese–Russian discussions were consequently terminated on February 6, 1904. Two days later in a daring night raid Japanese torpedo boats inflicted heavy losses on the Russian fleet at Port Arthur. On February 10, 1904, the Japanese officially declared war on Russia.

For Kōtoku who had come to reject war the course of events leading to the outbreak of hostilities between Japan and Russia represented a new lowpoint in the moral life of the Japanese people.

Kōtoku's first anti-war articles appeared in 1900. This was the year in which he composed most of the short pieces that were included in the book, *Imperialism: The Specter of the Twentieth Century*. This was also the year of the Boxer Rebellion which once again saw Japanese troops deployed on the continent. Despite Western approbation of Japanese military conduct, to men like Sakai Toshihiko and Taoka Reiun, two of Kōtoku's friends who accompanied the Japanese army to Tientsin as war correspondents, the Japanese effort to impress Western powers through a careful observance of military etiquette seemed to contrast sharply with the attitude of the Japanese military towards hapless Chinese who all too frequently became the victims of derision and brutality. The reports Taoka and Sakai sent back confirmed Kōtoku's conviction that war was basically brutal and barbaric. He stated his position clearly in the *Yorozu Chōhō* in an article on 'Pacifism' in which he wrote that while the abolition of war and the reduction of arms was not feasible in the 'near future', the ideal of a peaceful world without arms was one towards which all civilized nations must gradually advance. The need for war and arms symbolized an ailing and imperfect society, not a healthy and advancing one.[1] 'Never call this honor', he wrote in another essay in which he insisted that the Japanese warrior tradition had always identified with 'honor' and not with mere love of fighting and killing.[2] At the same time, Kōtoku realized that the Japanese public was becoming increasingly belligerent in its attitude towards China and Russia, and that the influence of the military was growing in almost every sphere of public life. For many Japanese, he lamented, the idea had arisen that 'the nation belongs to the military'.[3]

Nor had the intellectuals remained free from such influences. Kōtoku was particularly outspoken in his denunciation of writers and scholars who mouthed 'barbaric' and 'unenlightened' ideas in support of war and patriotism. This, he insisted, was not the function of the man of letters, whose dual role was to provide 'moral sustenance' and 'pleasure', and not to arouse suspicion and hatred among his readers.[4]

Kōtoku's attraction to pacifism aroused a new militancy in his prose. Certainly his personality had always been far from pacific. As a journalist he continued to see himself as a *shishi* whose role was to attack the established authorities of his society. Pacifism provided a new way of pressuring the government.

With the growing influence of the military, and the political parties' need for compromise with bureaucratic factions within the government, Kōtoku felt that only a strong stand on the question of increased military budgets could create an effective party protest against a central government dominated by men from Satsuma and Chōshū. The failure of the parties to take such a stand convinced him of the bankruptcy of Japanese democracy and of the need for a new ideological basis of protest.[5]

Kōtoku's pacifism, unlike that of Japanese Christians like Uchimura Kanzō, was not the product of a fundamental value transformation. Thus, while he criticized war and militarism as Spencer did, seeing it as the product of a 'militant' age, an age that society should leave behind on its path to an 'industrial' order, he found it difficult to underscore his pacifism with the

---

[1] 'Hisensō shugi', *Kōtoku Shūsui shisō ronshū*, p. 34.
[2] 'Konsen kokumin ya', *Senshū*, vol. II, p. 51.
[3] 'Heishi no kōgū', *ibid*. p. 54.
[4] 'Hisensō bungaku', *ibid*. p. 57.
[5] 'Nihon no minshu shugi', *ibid*. p. 42.

type of moral conviction available to a person like Uchimura. Uchimura was able to take the position that the Christian–Samurai transcended society and owed loyalty directly to God. In the process the fighting ethos of the warrior could be transformed into a commitment to peace. For Kōtoku the task was far more difficult. It was all very well to identify the warrior tradition with 'honor' and not with a love of 'fighting' and 'killing', but to go a step further to show that this 'honor' was 'pacific' was almost a contradiction in terms. Without Uchimura's type of commitment to universal values as ends in themselves, Kōtoku's pacifism remained a means to specific political ends. As a result, it was not free from what Kinoshita Naoe later called a 'lust for revolution' and a 'lust for power'.[1] Kōtoku had not discarded his original goals.

Like socialism, pacifism became an area of considerable interest and debate in Japanese intellectual circles at the turn of the century. At the center of this debate stood the *Yorozu Chōhō*, the paper for which Kōtoku had begun to write in the spring of 1898. The *Yorozu* was an unusual paper. Under the vigorous leadership of its editor, Kuroiwa Ruikō, a complex man whose humanism was second only to his shrewd business sense, the paper had become a champion of controversial causes. In doing so it attracted to its staff some of the outstanding critics of the age. Uchimura Kanzō, Taoka Reiun, Sakai Toshihiko, and Kōtoku represented a wide spectrum of those dissatisfied with the course of modern Japan's development. Most remarkable about the paper was its circulation figure which jumped to an unprecedented 120,000 in 1902 making it the most widely-read newspaper in Japan.

Pacifism was one of the central issues that united the staff of the *Yorozu*. Uchimura, Taoka, Sakai, and Kōtoku may have differed in their tactical approach to the question of social reform, but they were united in their opposition to war. Moreover, as long as the actual question of war and peace hung in the balance their anti-war stand was given full support by Kuroiwa. By the autumn of 1903 the outbreak of hostilities had clearly become imminent, however, and when the paper's editorial stand began to affect sales, Kuroiwa decided that changes were necessary. On October 8, the terminal date for Russian troop withdrawals, the *Yorozu* made a dramatic about-face and began to support those calling for war. The same evening, after re-confirming their opposition to war with Russia, Kōtoku, Uchimura, and Sakai resigned from the paper.

With the *Yorozu* silenced, an urgent need was felt for a new paper through

---

[1] From Kinoshita Naoe, *Kami ningen jiyū*, quoted in Kosaka Masaaki, *Japanese Thought in the Meiji Era*, p. 357.

which Japanese socialists might continue to speak out against the war and agitate for their ideals. This was particularly true after the enforcement of the Peace Police Law made organized trade union activity virtually impossible, and after the short-lived Social Democratic Party revealed the limitations of political action. In the wake of these measures Japanese socialists had been forced to concentrate their efforts on enlightening the public. Newspapers were central to this educational strategy and the voice of the *Yorozu* had played an important role in presenting socialist views on current problems.

A few days after submitting their resignations to the *Yorozu* in an open letter in which they stated that the forced 'silence' demanded of them by the paper's new policy was not in keeping with the 'basic responsibility of the *shishi* to society',[1] Kōtoku and Sakai laid plans for a new paper. With the financial backing of Kojima Tatsutarō, a former student of Chōmin's who had supported the left wing of the Jiyūtō, and Katō Tokijirō, a physician sympathetic to socialism, the way was cleared for the establishment of a new socialist organ.

In the meantime, a power struggle emerged between Kōtoku and his followers and Katayama Sen, who had traditionally headed the movement. In part this was the result of a shift away from a focus on labor which Katayama insisted must lie at the core of the Japanese socialist movement, but which had become increasingly difficult after the Peace Police Law of 1900. Kōtoku's appeal was less to workers than to young intellectuals. By nature and upbringing he was fundamentally an elitist, and while he admired the efforts of others – particularly those of the Russian narodniks – to take their cause to the common man, he found it difficult to do so himself. Katayama feared that Kōtoku's highly theoretical and intellectual approach would alienate the Japanese worker. Kōtoku, for his part, wanted the control of the movement in the hands of 'materialists', not 'Christians'.

The struggle came to a head at the same meeting of the Socialist Association at which Katō promised Kōtoku and Sakai financial support for the proposed paper. At this meeting Katayama was forced out of his position as secretary of the organization and replaced by Nishikawa Kōjirō.[2] With the establishment of the Heiminsha, the mother organization for the new paper, the *Heimin Shimbun* (*The Commoner's News*), in November 1903, the mainstream of the Japanese socialist movement gradually shifted from Katayama to Kōtoku and Sakai. This shift was further dramatized by

[1] Sakai Toshihiko, *Sakai Toshihiko zenshū*, vol. VI, p. 213.
[2] Nishio Yōtarō, *Kōtoku Shūsui*, pp. 90-1.

Katayama's sudden departure for the United States in December. The Socialist Association which had previously met in Katayama's home now moved to the offices of the Heiminsha in Yūrakuchō.[1]

The first issue of the *Heimin Shimbun* appeared on November 15, 1903. In it Kōtoku and Sakai noted that 'liberty, equality, and fraternity are the essential reasons for man's existence in this world'.[2] In order to achieve these, the paper pledged itself to the principles of 'Commonerism' (*heiminshugi*), 'Socialism' (*shakaishugi*), and 'Pacifism' (*heiwashugi*).[3] The paper made it clear from the start that it intended to 'arouse the public opinion of the masses within the limits of the law'.[4] At the same time it categorically rejected the use of violence to achieve its aims.

In the closing months of 1903 and the early months of 1904 the *Heimin Shimbun* rapidly built up its reputation as the leading radical paper in Tokyo. As its circulation increased, its staff was augmented by Ishikawa Sanshirō and Nishikawa Kōjirō. Regular contributors to the weekly included Kinoshita Naoe, Abe Isoo, Katayama Sen (from abroad), Itō Ginsuke, Taoka Reiun, Murai Tomoyoshi, Koizumi Sanshin, Uchimura Kanzō and Saitō Ryoku-u. Meanwhile, students and young intellectuals, attracted by the paper's clear-cut stand on the war issue, flocked to the meetings of the Heiminsha.

Ideologically the Heiminsha incorporated a curious mixture of ideas. Ishikawa Sanshirō later described the 'spirit' of the organization as basically 'romantic' and 'humanistic'.[5] No doubt there was some truth to Ishikawa's claims, for despite Kōtoku's ardent defense of materialism, the majority of his colleagues and youthful followers persisted in their basically Christian orientation. The eclectic nature of the association was perhaps best symbolized in the offices of the *Heimin Shimbun* where portraits of Marx and Engels hung alongside those of William Morris, Zola, Bebel, and Tolstoi. Had there been room for more, there would no doubt have been others. And yet, the diversity of ideological positions contributed much to the intellectual ferment of the association. It was the excitement of debate that added greatly to the popularity of the Heiminsha among the young people of the day. As Kinoshita Naoe noted:

What the youth of that period was searching for was not really systematized thought, or an organized body of ideas; on the contrary, they thirsted for confusion, they craved great confusion, and behind this great confusion there was the thirst for

---

[1] *Kōtoku Shūsui*, p. 92.   [2] *Shūkan Heimin Shimbun*, vol. I, p. 3.
[3] *Ibid.*   [4] *Ibid.*
[5] Ishikawa Sanshirō, *Jijoden* (Tokyo, 1956), p. 71.

some great creation. Kōtoku's *Heimin Shimbun* was a small crater for the whirling gaseous passions of these young people.[1]

Many of the youthful members of the Heiminsha, which included Ōsugi Sakae, Arahata Kanson, and Shirayanagi Shūko, recognized the revolutionary potential of Christianity.[2] As Ōsugi wrote: 'For the intellectual world of that day Christianity was the most progressive force. At least it incorporated the largest proportion of those who opposed the ruling ideas of loyalty and patriotism.'[3] Kōtoku and Sakai, for their part, were attempting to shift the vision of the young from Christianity to a materialistic form of socialism. Under the circumstances, it was only natural that Kōtoku, Sakai, and Nishikawa's 'materialism' should sooner or later clash with the 'Christian' principles of Kinoshita and Ishikawa. Kōtoku's own anti-Christian stand must have been intensified by the fact that so many young Japanese intellectuals looked to Christianity, rather than to socialism, as the real revolutionary force in their society.[4] He was frequently biting in his criticism of those who professed Christian convictions. Ishikawa, who was not immune to Kōtoku's attacks, compared him to a 'razor' whose style was to 'cut' and 'stab' in contrast to Sakai whom he regarded as more 'round' and 'mellow'.[5]

Despite the gradually growing rift between the Christian and materialist socialists in the Heiminsha, both groups remained united by their opposition to the war. In the months before the outbreak of hostilities (February 10, 1904) the *Heimin Shimbun* fought ceaselessly against the insurmountable tide of pro-war sentiment that gripped the public. Kōtoku's arguments against war were basically those formulated in his two books, *Imperialism* and *The Quintessence of Socialism*. While his original pacifist position had corresponded to that of Chōmin's 'Gentleman', his increasing contact with the writings of Marx and Engels convinced him of the economic motives behind international conflicts. And yet, he never totally discarded his earlier moral arguments. Instead, he emphasized his growing conviction that morality was itself the product of economic conditions. Wars were caused by greedy

[1] Kosaka Masaaki, *Japanese Thought in the Meiji Era*, p. 354.
[2] All three became important figures. Ōsugi Sakae (1885-1923) played a central role in the Japanese socialist and anarchist movement until he was cruelly murdered in the violence that followed the Tokyo Earthquake of 1923. Arahata Kanson (1887-) served as one of the founders of the Japanese Communist Party. Shirayanagi Shūko (1884-1950) became the close associate and biographer of the Prime Minister and Elder Statesman, Saionji Kimmochi.
[3] Ōsugi Sakae, *Jijoden*, p. 185.
[4] One can detect here a reason for Kōtoku's final book, *Kirisuto massatsu ron* (*Rubbing Out Christ*) which appeared in 1911.
[5] Ishikawa Sanshirō, *Jijoden*, p. 71.

capitalists in league with corrupt and power-hungry politicians. They were never fought in the interest of the worker or common man.[1]

Writing on the eve of the war (February 7, 1904), Kōtoku noted in an editorial titled, 'Those Who Decide on Peace and War' ('Wa-sen o kessuru mono'), that the whole conflict between Japan and Russia (in fact, the whole 'Far Eastern Problem') was the product of the monied interests of both countries, whose object was to expand markets and acquire colonies. The decision for war, he furthermore stated, was neither that of the Emperor nor that of the people. To the contrary, it was those in financial power who decided the fate of the nation. 'Ah! Is this the Japan of the people,' he wrote; 'is this the Japan of the Constitution? Is this not the Japan of a few money lenders?'[2]

In the first issue of the *Heimin Shimbun* to appear after the outbreak of war, Kōtoku wrote, 'We commoners will never recognize war... so long as we have mouths, so long as we have brushes and paper, we will continue to cry out against war...'[3] The opening of hostilities merely served to increase the virulency of the paper's attack on the war policy of the government. In the months that followed Kōtoku's prose, which a contemporary described as having a quality not unlike a 'cat fight', poured forth in a series of biting articles and editorials.[4] Among these were 'The Results of War' ('Sensō no kekka'), 'The Delusions of Soldiers' ('Heishi no byūsō'), and 'The Heavy Burden of Patriotism' ('Aikoku no omoni'). None of these ingratiated the *Heimin Shimbun* in the eyes of the government. But at the same time, there was little the government could do as long as the paper continued to operate 'within the limits of the law'.[5]

On March 28, 1904, in response to the government's request for additional war funds from the Diet, Kōtoku published an editorial titled 'Ah, Woe! The Rising Taxes' ('Aa Zōzei!') in which he wrote in a vein that was by no means new, questioning the need for 'nations', 'governments', and 'taxes'. At the same time, obviously conscious of the 'limits of the law', he tried to soften his arguments by couching them in theoretical terms. 'As far as the

---

[1] In keeping with his earlier theme, Kōtoku had written in the third issue of the *Heimin Shimbun* (November 29, 1903) under the heading, 'A Strange Logic': 'It certainly seems strange that individuals are required not to fight, while nations are encouraged to do so, and that individuals ought not to rob, while nations should. The peculiar logic of those calling for war would have it that the greatest evil [for the individual], when perpetrated by the nation, becomes the greatest good.' *Shūkan Heimin Shimbun*, vol. I, p. 50.

[2] *Ibid.* pp. 280–1. [3] 'War Has Come' ('Senso rai'), p. 302.

[4] The description is that of Itō Ginsuke in the first issue of the *Heimin Shimbun*, p. 24.

[5] Hyman Kublin emphasizes this point in 'The Japanese Socialists and the Russo–Japanese War', *Journal of Modern History*, vol. XXII, no. 4, p. 329.

present is concerned', he wrote, 'we do not, like Tolstoi, maintain that individuals desert from the army or refuse to pay their taxes. We only recognize the harm of military service and feel the agony of taxes.'[1]

If Kōtoku's ambiguity was designed to save the *Heimin Shimbun* from the wrath of the Home Ministry, it failed. As soon as the paper reached the news stands the government initiated legal proceedings against it for an infringement of the Press Laws.[2] Sale and circulation of the issue were prohibited immediately and the government moved to close the paper permanently. By the decision of the Tokyo District Court handed down in April the *Heimin Shimbun* was ordered to discontinue publication, and Sakai, the official editor, was sentenced to three months' imprisonment.

Seeking a reversal of the lower court's decision the paper appealed to the Tokyo Higher Court, where, after an 'impressive speech' by Kinoshita Naoe on Sakai's behalf, the sentence was repealed – the ban on the paper was lifted and Sakai's prison term was reduced to two months.[3] Kōtoku regretted the fact that the paper had not set up a dummy editor. He lamented that Sakai's loss, even for two months, would hamper the activities of the paper at this critical juncture. On the other hand, the decision of the higher court clearly represented a victory for the *Heimin Shimbun*. It furthermore revealed the extent to which even the 'autocratic' Meiji leaders were forced to operate 'within the limits of the law'.

With Sakai in prison, Kōtoku was now in full charge of the paper. Having successfully challenged the government and won, Kōtoku felt confident to push the anti-war fight with renewed vigor. The government, having lost the legal battle, turned to new forms of harassment. A high proportion of the paper's weekly circulation, which in April 1904 averaged 4,500 copies, was sold over the counter in small news stands.[4] The police soon began to use their authority to search and badger news stands and dealers who continued to handle the paper. Direct subscribers were visited by policemen and 'advised' to take another paper. Government pressures may have had some effect on sales, for by June the paper's circulation was down to 3,700.

Late in May Kōtoku was informed by the government that it intended to

---

[1] *Shūkan Heimin Shimbun*, vol. II, p. 77.

[2] The paper was prosecuted under Article Thirty-three of the Press Laws which stated that persons responsible for the publication of materials 'detrimental to public order and morality' were liable to fines and imprisonment. The article makes no mention of the government's right to prohibit further publication.

[3] *Shūkan Heimin Shimbun*, vol. II (English Section), p. 11.

[4] Shirayanagi Shūko, *Saionji Kimmochi den*, p. 486. Shirayanagi, who provides us with the information on police tactics, mentions that of the paper's weekly circulation over 3,000 copies were sold through small dealers.

keep a strict watch over the paper's anti-war activities as well as any statements it made about the Imperial House.[1] To government intimidation the *Heimin Shimbun* replied that while it was quite easy to 'foresee how stringent the governmental inquisition will be', it hoped the government would soon learn 'as severe a lesson as the German or Austrian governments have learned'.[2]

In the summer of 1904 Kōtoku and the *Heimin Shimbun* extended their anti-war appeals to international socialists. The English column of the paper now began to carry long editorials, and these were sometimes reprinted in Western magazines. As early as the eighteenth issue of the paper (March 13, 1904) Kōtoku had addressed an editorial to socialists in Russia.[3] In order to make this appeal available to Western readers it was translated and appeared in English in the following issue. In it Kōtoku wrote:

Dear Comrades! Your government and our government have plunged into fighting at last in order to satisfy their imperialistic desires, but to socialists there is no barrier of race, territory, or nationality. We are comrades, brothers and sisters and have no reason to fight each other. Your enemy is not the Japanese people, but our militarism and so-called patriotism. Nor is our enemy the Russian people but your militarism and so-called patriotism. Yes, patriotism and militarism are our common enemies; nay, all the socialists in the world also look upon them are [*sic*] common enemies. We socialists must fight against them. Here is the best and most important opportunity for us now. We believe you will not let this opportunity pass. We too will try our best.[4]

'We cannot foresee which of the two governments shall win the fighting', the editorial continued, 'but whichever gets the victory, the results of the war will be all the same – general misery, the burden of heavy taxes, the degradation of morality and the supremacy of militarism.'[5] The American magazine, *Arena*, published this editorial for its readers under the title 'The Socialists of Japan to the Socialists of Russia'.[6] Consequently, Kōtoku's article received considerable publicity abroad and was hailed by international socialists as a symbol of the solidarity of the anti-war movement. The Russian socialists soon responded with an article of similar tone in their magazine, *Iskra*.[7]

[1] The June 5 editorial comments on the government's warning. *Shūkan Heimin Shimbun*, vol. II, p. 304.
[2] *Ibid.* (English Section) p. 17.
[3] 'Letter to Russian Socialists' ('Yo Rōkoku Shakaitō sho'), p. 28.
[4] 'To the Socialists in Russia' appeared in English on March 20, 1904. *Ibid.* (English Section) p. 5.
[5] *Ibid.*
[6] See Kublin, 'The Japanese Socialists and the Russo–Japanese War', p. 330. The article was in *Arena*, vol. XXXII, p. 322.
[7] Shirayanagi Shūko, *Saionji Kimmochi den*, p. 494.

Quite naturally none of this acclaim pleased the Japanese government. The Katsura ministry, cautious about the coverage of the war abroad, had gone out of its way to assure itself of a favorable press in Europe and America. Occasionally, as in the case of Jack London, it had barred from Japan Western newsmen of 'radical' leanings who might jeopardize a favorable Western response.[1] Under these circumstances, the alliance of Japanese and Russian socialists, as well as the foreign airing of domestic discontent, could not help but increase the apprehension with which the government leaders viewed the activities of the *Heimin Shimbun* and its staff. The editors of the paper were not unaware of the fact that this was an issue with the government, and that they would have to tread softly if they were not to become vulnerable to official reprisals.[2] Kōtoku was quick to grasp the situation. As Kinoshita has pointed out, this was a period in which Kōtoku was still willing to work within limitations.[3] Thus, while Kōtoku admired the activist revolutionaries of Russia he was fully aware that any identification with anti-imperial violence would be interpreted as treason by the authorities and would doom the socialist movement. The Russian reply to the *Heimin Shimbun*'s appeal had urged 'force against force, violence against violence!' but Kōtoku took great pains to distinguish Japanese socialists from their more extreme Russian counterparts, writing:

We are neither Nihilists nor Terrorists, but Social Democrats, and are always fighting for peace. We object absolutely to using military force in our fighting. We have to fight by peaceful means; by reason and speech. It may be very difficult for you to fight with speech and produce a revolution by peaceful means in Russia where there is no constitution, and consequently you may be tempted to overthrow the government by force. But those who are fighting for humanity must remember that the end does not justify the means.[4]

It must be remembered that Kōtoku, as well as the other members of the staff of the *Heimin Shimbun*, were still committed parliamentarians. Their goal, in the realm of strategy, was to produce a revolution by 'peaceful means'. In a country which had reached the enlightened stage of constitutional rule,

[1] Despite Japanese restrictions London made his way to Korea and Manchuria and sent back some of the first photographs of the war. Another young journalist with left-wing sympathies who appears to have slipped past Japanese authorities was Leopold Fleischmann who had close ties with American socialists and while in Tokyo as a war correspondent became friendly with members of the Heiminsha. Later he appears to have made efforts to solicit funds for the Heiminsha in the United States.
[2] It is worth noting that in explaining the reasons for the government's stiff attitude towards the paper in the closing months of 1904 the editors attributed it to the paper's growing international influence. *Shūkan Heimin Shimbun*, vol. IV, p. 146.
[3] Kinoshita Naoe, 'Hakaba', in *Gendai Nihon bungaku zenshū*, vol. 53, p. 257.
[4] *Shūkan Heimin Shimbun*, vol. II (English Section), p. 5.

violence represented a throwback to an earlier, more primitive age. True, Japanese constitutionalism was still imperfect, and Japanese socialists would have to fight for universal suffrage, yet, when compared to Russia and the position of Russian socialists, Kōtoku and the other members of the Heiminsha could not help but feel a sense of pride in the achievements of their country since the Restoration.[1] At the same time, they regretted that the government did not understand the true nature of their pacifism. 'If one thinks that there are not more than two hundred professed socialists in Japan,' Kōtoku wrote, 'it seems strange that the government is rather nervous about our propagandism.' In Kōtoku's eyes Japanese socialists had done nothing to provoke the authorities:

If socialists were reckless enough to resort to violence it would be quite proper for the government to use the police force for the sake of social peace, but not an accusation of this kind can be brought against them. Are we not denouncing war all the time because we believe that no violent action is justifiable at any time?... Perhaps none can better tell the government that we are harmless people than its own detectives, yet, the government is too nervous to let us alone.[2]

Despite the increased government pressures that followed the paper's legal battle with the authorities, the *Heimin Shimbun* continued to agitate against the war at home and appealed to Western socialists to join it in its anti-war campaign.[3]

On June 19, 1904, the *Heimin Shimbun* published a resolution passed by the Socialist Association which was to be presented to the Second International at its sixth congress in Amsterdam in August. The resolution, which was delivered to Amsterdam by Katayama Sen, noted:

Whereas, the Russo-Japanese War is carried on by the Capitalist government of both nations and in consequence brings a great deal of suffering upon the working classes in Japan and Russia, therefore be it resolved, that the Japanese Socialist Association ask the members of the International Socialist Congress that will be

[1] The government, Kōtoku thought, seemed unaware of Japan's advances. In an article titled, 'Our Government Fears Socialism Too Much', he wrote: 'Our government does not like to be placed in the same standing with the Russian government, but is it not dragging itself down to the level of the semicivilized countries by putting rigid restraints on freedom of speech and the press? Our proverb says, "Despise yourself, and others will despise you." If our government repeats what Bismarck did, and what the present Emperor of Germany is doing, it will become the laughing-stock of the civilized world.' *Shūkan Heimin Shimbun*, vol. II (English Section), p. 17.

[2] *Ibid.*

[3] That Western socialists had begun to respond to the appeal is witnessed by the resolution of the Socialist Party of America which appeared in the *Heimin Shimbun* on June 19, 1904, and read: 'this convention of the Socialist Party of America sends greetings of fraternity and solidarity to the working people of Russia and Japan, and condemns the Russo-Japanese War as a crime against progress and civilization'. *Ibid.* p. 354.

held in Amsterdam the coming August to pass a resolution to the effect that they will do their best to urge their respective governments to take proper steps to put an end to the Russo-Japanese War as soon as possible.[1]

Again the editors of the paper felt it necessary to make it quite plain that 'by passing this resolution, we do not mean to ask our comrades in Europe and America to use some direct means to urge their respective governments to interfere with the war, but we believe our comrades can use their pens and tongues so as to make their influence felt indirectly'.[2]

Nor were tongues and pens lacking in the West. A week after the publication of the above resolution, Leo Tolstoi issued his own denunciation of the war in the London *Times*.[3] Tolstoi's 'Bethink Yourselves!' created a sensation not only in Europe and America but also in Japan. When a translation of the article appeared in the *Heimin Shimbun* in August the demand was so great that the editors had to run off reprints.

Although 'Bethink Yourselves!' was well received by the Japanese socialist community, it also served to aggravate the struggle between the Christian and non-Christian wings of the movement.

In the years preceding the war the mainstream of Japanese socialism had been founded on the Christian humanism of men like Katayama Sen, Abe Isoo, Kinoshita Naoe, Nishikawa Kōjirō and Kawakami Kiyoshi. When the Shakai Minshu-tō, the short-lived social democratic party, was organized in 1901, Kōtoku had been the only non-Christian member of the group. While his position on reform as a member of the Risōdan, the 'Idealists Band' which Kuroiwa Ruikō organized in 1898,[4] was similar to the Christian emphasis on the need to change the inner man, he had little use for the puritanical side of the Christians with whom he associated. 'I hate anyone who tells me not to "smoke", "drink", or "run into debt",' he noted on one occasion.[5] Meanwhile he determined to work with Sakai and other non-Christian socialists to shift the focus of the movement away from Christian humanism towards what he considered a firmer 'scientific' and 'materialistic' base. As his own knowledge of 'materialistic' socialism expanded, his writings on this subject became more outspoken.

In March 1903, while still a journalist on the staff of the *Yorozu Chōhō*, Kōtoku published an article titled 'Socialism and Religion' ('Shakai Shugi to

[1] *Ibid.* p. 18.   [2] *Ibid.*
[3] 'Bethink Yourselves!' appeared in *The Times* (London) on June 27, 1904. The Japanese translation was published in the *Heimin Shimbun* on August 7, 1904.
[4] The 'Idealist Band' took the position that the reform of society would have to begin with the reform of the individual.
[5] *Uchimura Kanzō shinkō chosaku zenshū*, vol. XIV, p. 315.

Shūkyō') in the magazine, *Chūō Kōron*. In the same month, Uchimura Kanzō published a piece titled 'Christianity and Socialism' ('Kirisuto Kyō to Shakai Shugi') in his own journal, *Seisho no Kenkyū*. The articles are of interest in that they show a hardening of positions on the part of both Uchimura and Kōtoku.

In his article Uchimura maintained that Christianity and socialism, while sharing a common concern for the poor and lowly, were fundamentally different. The Christian 'kingdom', Uchimura insisted, was not 'of this world'.[1] Moreover,

from the point of view of Christianity [he wrote], the injustices of society are consequences of man's having rejected God and do not come from the imperfections of the social system. The way to remedy these injustices is for man to return to God and not by his being given new social organization. For this reason Christianity does not place much significance on such things as system or organization.[2]

Kōtoku, for his part, argued that the 'injustices of society' had in fact led man to create God. They had also led men to create the concepts of 'heaven', and 'hell', and the 'after-life'. Primitive religions, whether in Japan or the West, he maintained, had made no distinctions between the religious, the social, and the political. For them, all of these realms were united into one whole. In these faiths there was, moreover, no concern with an after-life, with a distinction between 'flesh' and 'spirit', or with a separation of religion and government. By contrast, all modern religions like Christianity based themselves on dualisms, and in the process had lost their concern over man's existence in this world. What the modern world required was once again a faith that was monistic and not dualistic. Government, religion, and society must be reunited. The emphasis of such a faith must be on man in this world, and not on the after-life. It is clear that Kōtoku visualized the religion of the future that would overcome the flaws in the contemporary religious world as socialism. For him this was the 'one true faith' that would eventually replace all other religions.[3]

While Uchimura was concerned that Christianity was being confused with socialism by the Japanese public, Kōtoku, to the contrary, was concerned by the fact that most Japanese identified socialism with Christianity. On this point Kōtoku had written:

In Japan socialism is frequently seen as a special product of Christianity, or as one of its accessories. Moreover, it is generally believed that a person who is a socialist

---

[1] Kosaka, *Japanese Thought in the Meiji Era*, p. 350.
[2] *Uchimura Kanzō shinkō chosaku zenshū*, vol. XXI, p. 316.
[3] 'Shakai Shugi to shūkyō' in *Senshū*, vol. II, pp. 181ff.

is also a Christian...So-called 'modern socialism', which stands for the theory of 'scientific socialism', actually originated with Hegel's philosophy, was nourished by Darwin's theory of evolution, and first became influential when it reached Marx's theory of materialistic economics. It was neither the special product nor the accessory of any religion.[1]

Kōtoku's attempt to distinguish socialism from Christianity was not limited to polemical writings of this nature. On this subject he was often blunt and brutally cutting. With time his anti-Christian sentiments proceeded to take the form of morbid exchanges with the Christian members of the movement. Kinoshita Naoe, who was often the victim of these, later wrote about one such incident. On this occasion Kōtoku, Kinoshita, and Katayama were returning from a socialist rally in Yokohama.[2] On the train Kōtoku suddenly turned to Kinoshita and said: 'Kinoshita, why don't you give up God! If you'd only do this, I'd gladly untie your shoelaces for you!' Kōtoku's voice was as 'sharp and penetrating as an owl's', and Kinoshita not knowing how to reply remained silent. Meanwhile Katayama broke in with a half-smile on his lips saying: 'Kōtoku, be careful that you yourself are not vanquished by God.' Without listening to what Katayama said, Kōtoku continued to stare at Kinoshita and muttered: 'I'll make you give up God yet! I really will!'

This incident took place in the summer of 1903. While he may have failed to make anyone 'give up God' by the close of that year, Kōtoku had, with the establishment of the Heiminsha and the *Heimin Shimbun*, won over the momentum of the movement from Christians like Katayama, Abe, and Kinoshita. The appearance of Tolstoi's 'Bethink Yourselves!' in the summer of 1904 provided him with another opportunity to distinguish his position from that of the Christians.

In answer to the question of war Tolstoi had written:

However strange this may appear, the most effective and certain deliverance of men from all the calamities which they inflict upon themselves and from the most dreadful of all – war – is attainable, not by external general measures, but merely by that simple appeal to the consciousness of each separate man which, one thousand nine hundred years ago, was proposed by Jesus – that every man bethink himself, and ask himself, who he is, why he lives, and what he should and should not do.[3]

---

[1] *Ibid* p. 181.

[2] Kublin states that the anecdote was originally set forth in Kinoshita Naoe, 'Katayama Sen to boku', *Chūō Kōron* (December, 1933), and that the incident took place on the way to Yokosuka. See *Asian Revolutionary*, p. 152. The earliest source is Kinoshita's *Yajingo* (1911) in which he states that the exchange took place on the way back from Yokohama, *Yajingo*, pp. 105ff.

[3] Leo Tolstoi, *The Times* (London), June 27, 1904.

A week after the publication of Tolstoi's essay in the *Heimin Shimbun*, Kōtoku submitted to the paper a critical evaluation of Tolstoi's position. In answer to Tolstoi's ideas on war Kōtoku wrote:

When we socialists air our arguments against the war the proposed solution and goals we uphold are not vague and obscure. On these points we possess clear logic and a concrete plan. According to our view the present international conflict is not just the outcome of the fact that men have forsaken the teachings of Jesus, as Tolstoi maintains, but is in fact the result of the extremes of economic competition that exist between the powers. Moreover, the reason for this extreme competition can be found in the fact that modern social organization is based on the capitalistic system. If one wants to eliminate war and its harm, one must destroy today's capitalistic system and substitute for it a socialistic system...Tolstoi ascribes the cause of war to the debasement of man and consequently desires to save him by means of repentance. We socialists attribute the cause of war to economic competition and consequently seek to prevent war by abolishing economic competition.[1]

While Kōtoku debated with Tolstoi, and with Japanese socialists of Christian background, the war continued to hold the attention of most Japanese. Despite a series of impressive early victories, by the end of 1904 the war had bogged down into a number of slow and costly campaigns. After more than six months of investment, Port Arthur still flew the Russian flag. Meanwhile disconcerting news reached Japan that the Russians planned to sail their Baltic Fleet to Far Eastern waters. Under these pressures, anxiety suddenly replaced self-confidence. Both the government and public grew less tolerant of the anti-war agitation of the *Heimin Shimbun*.

The November sixth issue of the paper intended to deal primarily with education. When it appeared it contained among other 'educational' articles one titled, 'Advice to the Teachers of Primary Schools' ('Shōgakkō kyōshi ni tsugu'). The article had been written by Ishikawa Sanshirō and called upon elementary school teachers, who were suffering from low pay and a struggle with inflation, to turn to socialism to alleviate their 'lamentable conditions'.[2] Other articles in the same issue, particularly 'The Confusion of So-called Patriots' ('Iwayuru aikokusha no rōbai') and 'The Attitude of the Educator Towards the War' ('Sensō ni tai-suru kyōiku-sha no taido') continued the paper's attack on patriotism and reiterated its position on the whole question of war.

The above articles contained little that was new. Kōtoku and his staff had made similar points – sometimes in more scathing language – throughout the summer. A small advertisement announced that the paper intended to

---

[1] *Shūkan Heimin Shimbun*, vol. III, p. 170.
[2] *Ibid.* vol. IV, pp. 76ff.

publish *The Communist Manifesto* in its next issue to commemorate its first anniversary. A garden party for all socialists was also planned to mark the occasion. While there was nothing startling about the paper's content, the government was growing less tolerant. Since any socialist effort to meddle in the education of Japan's young people could be construed as detrimental to peace and order in time of war, the sale and circulation of the issue was prohibited by the police and legal proceedings were once more initiated against the paper to close it permanently.

The government's new hard line was no doubt influenced by the growing public reaction against Kōtoku and his associates. Many of the leading papers had begun to criticize the *Heimin Shimbun* for its anti-war stand. The editors of the paper commented on this shift in public attitude late in November when they wrote:

We do not know what has made the government so nervous again, but we cannot doubt that there must be some special reason for this change. It is not the government alone this time that persecutes us, but many papers and magazines are criticizing us as if with one voice. One of the magazines goes so far as to say that it would have socialists beheaded if it only had the power of executing them.[1]

Disappointed by the progress of the war and apprehensive about the future, the Japanese public seems to have turned to witch-hunting at home. Kōtoku's advice to socialists was that they would have to prepare themselves for 'persecutions' fast gathering around them, but that they ought not to complain since 'the cause of socialism will make a greater advance under persecution'.[2]

Anxiety was not, however, the only reason for the government's stiff stand. In the closing months of 1904 Japanese socialists increasingly violated the fine line between violence and non-violence which Kōtoku had made every effort to defend earlier in the year. This had been a touchy issue throughout the history of the paper. The editors of the paper had again and again gone out of their way to show that the position they maintained was 'pacifist' in every sense of the word. But Kōtoku was also faced with a problem that was to recur at later stages of his radical career. While his public declarations reaffirmed the need for compromise and suggested a moderate policy, the private image that he left with his young followers was often quite different. As one of them observed, no matter how much he 'bathed himself', how much he 'cut his hair', or how much he 'changed his dress', Kōtoku would always remain a 'revolutionary *shishi*'. 'With Shūsui', he wrote, 'one

---

[1] *Ibid.* (English Section), pp. 7-8.
[2] *Ibid.* p. 8.

wants to plot either how to kill people, or how to raise them from the dead.'[1] Thus, while the paper continued to adhere to a policy of non-violence, the behavior of the youthful followers of the Heiminsha were not always conducive to peace and tranquility.

Early in November a socialist rally was held at the Y.M.C.A. Hall in Kanda. Sakai Toshihiko was to be one of the principal speakers at this rally, and the *Heimin Shimbun* reported the event as follows:

On the evening of the 2nd, a large meeting of socialists was held at the Y.M.C.A. Hall, in which seven leading socialists were to speak. The audience numbered more than one thousand and even the galleries were filled. It was an inspiring scene when the audience welcomed each of the speakers with clappings of hand. But the first three speakers were stopped by the chief of the policemen present without any adequate reason, and, to our great disappointment, he ordered the dissolution of the meeting. The audience, having become indignant, did not withdraw even a bit, and demanded that the policeman should explain why he had dissolved the meeting. When he began to speak, his voice was drowned by loud shrieking and noisy stamping on the floor. By this time more policemen came in and there were now more than fifty. Seeing that the audience would not disperse, one of the policemen dragged comrade Sakai, one of the speakers, down from the platform. The audience became enraged at this violent action, and struck the policeman down on the floor and trampled on him. Two more policemen met the same fate. Some cried: 'Despotism like the Russian government.' Another said: 'Down with despotism!' We socialists could not do anything to silence them, and therefore we were for a while mere spectators. Two hours passed before the angry audience returned home and order was restored.[2]

While Kōtoku and Sakai may have considered themselves mere spectators in this riot, and disclaimed all credit for the violent behavior of the audience which was packed with their young followers, the government held them responsible and was not about to apply kid gloves to a group that 'trampled' officers of the law.

On the sixteenth of November, no doubt in consequence of the above meeting, Nishikawa Kōjirō was informed by the police that the Home Minister had ordered the dissolution of the Socialist Association on the grounds that it was 'detrimental to public peace and order'.[3] Three days earlier the *Heimin Shimbun* had published its anniversary issue featuring *The Communist Manifesto*.[4] Sale and circulation of the issue were immediately pro-

[1] The description is that of Itō Ginsuke. See *Shūkan Heimin Shimbun*, vol. I, pp. 24-5.
[2] *Ibid.* vol. IV (English Section), p. 7.
[3] *Ibid.* p. 137.
[4] *The Communist Manifesto* appeared in the *Heimin Shimbun* on November 13, 1904. This was the first translation of Marx' and Engels' work into Japanese. The translators were Kōtoku and Sakai.

hibited by the police. Kōtoku and Nishikawa, who were already being prosecuted on charges of violating the Press Laws due to the November sixth issue, were indicted on the additional counts of 'disturbing public peace and order'. Charges were also brought against Sakai. On the nineteenth Kōtoku and Nishikawa were found guilty of violating the Press Laws and were sentenced to five months of imprisonment and a fine of fifty yen each. On top of this the paper was ordered to close. Hoping for a repetition of their earlier confrontation with the government the editors of the paper decided to appeal the decision. Meanwhile they were busy defending themselves against the second charge arising out of their publication of *The Communist Manifesto*. On December 18 the Tokyo District Court found Kōtoku, Nishikawa, and Sakai guilty as charged and fined each of them an additional eighty yen. While a temporary stay – allowing for an appeal – permitted the paper to continue publishing through December, things did not look promising. Welcoming in the New Year, the editors noted rather gloomily:

We see no reason to congratulate the new year...The old year of an international war, capitalist system, oligarchy, and bribery has over [*sic*], but a new year of international war, capitalist system, oligarchy, and bribery has come. The newness of the new year is just the same as the oldness of the old year. We can't see any reason to congratulate the dawning of the new year.[1]

With the passing of January the situation did not improve. Fighting to keep the paper alive, Kōtoku and the others had involved themselves in a series of legal maneuvers to gain time. But by the end of the month they were aware that they had exhausted all legal possibilities without success. Rather than have the government close down their paper, Kōtoku and Sakai decided to disband it. On January 29, 1905, the sixty-fourth, and final, issue of the *Heimin Shimbun* appeared on the news stands. Following the example of Marx' *Neu Rheinische Zeitung* the issue was printed in a bold red type. Kōtoku summed up the feelings of the entire staff when he wrote: 'struggling to hold back our tears we sadly announce the discontinuation of the paper'.[2]

The dissolution of the *Heimin Shimbun* virtually brought to a close the socialist anti-war movement. With two of its most important leaders about to enter prison, and without the unifying force of the paper, the various dissident groups within the movement began to move in separate directions. Materialists and Christians now began to cluster around their own small journals, often more concerned with internal debates than with a sense of

[1] *Shūkan Heimin Shimbun*, vol. IV (English Section), p. 15.
[2] *Ibid*. p. 368.

mission directed against the government. Split and fragmented they presented no further challenge to the authorities.

By the end of February time had run out for Nishikawa and Kōtoku. On the twenty-eighth both entered Sugamo Prison to serve seven- and five-month terms respectively.

With Kōtoku's imprisonment the socialist anti-war movement lost its principal voice. Meanwhile the war had taken a turn for the better. In January Japanese troops captured Port Arthur, and in March they followed this victory with the defeat of the Russians at Mukden. In May, Admiral Tōgō destroyed Russia's last hopes for success by annihilating Admiral Rodjest-vensky's fleet in the Battle of Tsushima. In the wake of these victories many Japanese breathed more freely, knowing that their country had weathered the most serious threats of the war. Under the circumstances, the small minority who opposed the war once more faded from the public limelight. Five months later Kōtoku was to emerge from prison just in time to witness the final drama of the war when thousands of Japanese dissatisfied with the Treaty of Portsmouth rioted in the streets of Tokyo.

CHAPTER 5

The transition to anarchism, 1905–6

ON FEBRUARY 28, 1905, a few hours before Kōtoku and Nishikawa were to enter Sugamo Prison, the remnant of the socialist anti-war movement gathered in Hibiya Park for a commemorative photograph (see plate 2). The picture, published in the following issue of *Chokugen* (*Plain Talk*), the magazine which had replaced the *Heimin Shimbun*, shows Nishikawa and Kōtoku surrounded by a host of friends. Kōtoku and Nishikawa were meticulously garbed in the traditional *haori* and *hakama*. Both wore western hats. Kōtoku's solid and defiant stance reveals no sense of contradiction between his large black bowler and the crest-embroidered *haori* which his mother had sent from Tosa nearly a decade earlier. Like other members of his generation Kōtoku had been quick to combine elements of his own tradition with those imported from the West. Bowler and *haori* could coexist as easily in the world of dress as could socialism and native values in the world of ideas and ideals. At least so he thought in the spring of 1905. Five months of confinement followed by six months of self-imposed exile in the United States did much to alter his views. The man who returned from San Francisco in the summer of 1906 was no longer the same Kōtoku whose friends had urged him to take care of himself on that cold morning in February.

On the day that Kōtoku was to enter prison Kinoshita Naoe visited him at the Heiminsha. When Kinoshita arrived Kōtoku was in the process of bundling up a 'mountain' of books. He was about to add a copy of the Bible when Kinoshita, surprised, asked what he hoped to do with it. 'What? Oh, that...,' Kōtoku answered, hesitating nervously, 'in my cell I plan to search for a flaw in Christ.' Making this reply he burst into a strange peal of laughter.[1]

For Kōtoku Shūsui the five months spent in Sugamo Prison constituted a period of intensive reading and introspection. For over a year he had been faced with constant duties. Agitating against the war, lecturing on socialism, and performing the more mundane functions of keeping the *Heimin Shimbun*

[1] Kinoshita Naoe, *Yajingo*, pp. 107–8.

and the Heiminsha alive, left little time for intellectual pursuits. Prison, despite its cold austerity, provided Kōtoku with the leisure necessary for study and contemplation. Once before, as a student of Chōmin's, he had disassociated himself from the political arena for a period of quiet introspective reflection. So now he once more disassociated himself from the events of the previous year in order to read and think.

A few months after he entered prison Kōtoku wrote to Sakai that time was passing like a 'firecracker'.[1] With each passing day the 'mountain' of unread books diminished. Engels' *Feuerbach* and Kropotkin's *Fields, Factories, and Workshops* received special mention in letters to Sakai, but the book that impressed him most was a little-known work by Michael A. Lane titled *The Level of Social Motion* about which he wrote to Sakai: 'Of the works I have read since entering prison, the most interesting is *The Level of Social Motion* by the Boston professor Lane. Reasoning along the lines of social evolution he comes to conclusions that are totally at one with our own ideals.'[2] The affinity between Lane's 'conclusions' and Kōtoku's 'ideals' is worth looking into in greater detail.

The Level of Social Motion is a curious book. As Lane announced in the preface, his object in writing the book had been to 'discover a law of social motion' which would 'harmonize the bewildering facts of human history'.[3] Convinced that he had discovered such a law, he concluded:

Human society is rapidly moving towards a state of equality very similar in all essentials to that which is advocated by socialist philosophers as the ideal of a genuinely Christian life. The forces drawing the human race to this remarkable end are the very forces by which human history has been thus far wrought out. They are the same forces described by Darwin in his law of natural selection.[4]

The essence of Lane's 'law of social motion' was that Western society was steadily evolving towards a state of economic equality, and that the equal distribution of wealth would overcome the problem of population growth by creating a 'mean, or normal number which, when once reached, can never be disturbed'.[5] To support this thesis Lane produced a variety of scientific and pseudo-scientific arguments. Many of these must have been of questionable validity even in their day. For example, he wrote on the problem of equal rights for women: 'The brain of civilized woman is increasing in weight. Her intellect is rapidly developing a new and extraordinary capacity,

[1] *Nikki to shokan*, p. 191.
[2] *Ibid.* pp. 191–2.
[3] Michael A. Lane, *The Level of Social Motion* (New York, 1902), p. v.
[4] *Ibid.* p. vi.   [5] *Ibid.*

1 Kōtoku as a child surrounded by the women of his family (his mother Tajiko sits to his right)

2 Kōtoku (in center with bowler) on his way to prison in 1905

4 Kōtoku and Kanno Sugako in 1910

3 Kōtoku and his wife Chiyoko in 1905

and the ultimate end of this progress in woman will be a social state in which men and women will be intellectually equal, or nearly so.'[1]

Curiously enough, Kōtoku considered Lane's rather dubious arguments of greater 'scientific' value than those of Bebel whom he had read earlier.[2] Kōtoku's lack of scientific training no doubt left him vulnerable to Lane's quasi-scientific approach. His response to Lane furthermore indicates the extent to which he lacked a solid foundation in Marxism. The fact that Lane attempted to accommodate both the ideas of Marx and Spencer, and at the same time sought to go beyond them, further served to attract Kōtoku, who was himself constantly seeking to reach the frontiers of Western social thought.

Finally Kōtoku was attracted to Lane for the same reason that he had been drawn to Kirkup. Lane, too, was ultimately concerned with morality. His book begins with a chapter on 'The Flow of Moral Energy' and ends with one on 'Moral Equilibrium'. The end product of social evolution was to be a harmonious world of moral men. Not unlike Chōmin's Gentleman, Lane conceived of morality as a great universal that united all men. On this point he wrote:

And surely he would be a bold man who would underestimate the importance of moral force in social development. There is yet to be found a human group which is not altogether swayed by this powerful implement of progress ... We desire at the beginning of our discussion to emphasize this all-important fact: that the most conspicuous relation observable in the drift of modern social reform is inextricably combined with that sense of right and wrong found to be universal with mankind.[3]

Lane's theory on the relationship of morality to wealth furthermore paralleled that which Kōtoku had developed in 'The Degeneration of Society: Its Causes and Cure'. 'At the present time', Lane wrote, 'the moral and intellectual characters of civilized men vary in high degree because the quantity of wealth possessed by individuals varies in like degree. If the average man is less moral and intellectual than some exceptional men, it is because the average man is comparatively poor.'[4]

Confronted with the need to find a secular alternative to the moral and ethical position of his Christian associates, Kōtoku had further reason to be attracted to Lane, who stressed the secular and 'scientific' foundations of morality and ethical conduct. As Lane noted: 'The morality of religion is not defined by religious opinion, but by economic and political opinion. And so we are brought to the conclusion that while religious codes have no influence

---

[1] *Ibid.*
[2] *Nikki to shokan*, p. 192.
[3] Lane, *The Level of Social Motion*, pp. 16–17.
[4] *Ibid.* p. 518.

upon moral codes affecting wealth and life, these latter codes have every influence upon religious theory and conduct.'[1]

Kōtoku had already taken a stand against what he considered the 'dualism' that lay at the heart of Christianity. This 'dualism', which stressed the division of flesh and spirit, the individual and the social body, this life and the next, he was convinced, was not a part of the East Asian tradition which emphasized the unification of the moral, economic, and political spheres.[2] Lane took a similar stand when he wrote: 'Hence it is seen that economic systems, governments, and moral codes are, at their root, one and the same thing.'[3]

For Kōtoku, who had gone to prison searching for a 'flaw in Christ', Lane provided new anti-Christian arguments. In this Lane was not alone. A large part of the 'mountain' of books Kōtoku had carted to prison consisted of anti-religious treatises. Many of these had been sent to him by Albert Johnson, the American anarchist with whom he had begun to correspond towards the close of 1904.[4] Among the works over which he pored in his cell were John William Draper's *History of the Conflict Between Religion and Science*, Ernst Heinrich Haeckel's *The Riddle of the Universe*, Ernest Renan's *Life of Jesus*,[5] and Parish B. Ladd's *Commentaries on Hebrew and Christian Mythology*.[6]

In addition to investigating the anti-religious tradition of the West, he also reread Kropotkin's *Fields, Factories, and Workshops*. Soon after reading this work for the first time, he had written to Albert Johnson asking for Kropotkin's address, intending to translate the book into Japanese.[7]

Under the influence of Kropotkin and the anti-religious literature in which he absorbed himself, Kōtoku's ideas began to make a gradual transition. It is difficult to ascertain whether this transition had not actually begun in the previous year,[8] but it seems to have become more pronounced at this time.

[1] Lane, *The Level of Social Motion*, p. 559.

[2] Kōtoku elaborated this point in 'Yūshin yūkon setsu to dōtoku' published in the *Yorozu Chōhō* on November 8, 1901; *Shūsui bunshū*, pp. 179ff.

[3] Lane, *The Level of Social Motion*, p. 536.

[4] Kōtoku had written to Albert Johnson on December 30, 1904: 'I am an atheist or agnostic, and always fighting against the dogma of Christian and all other religions.' *Nikki to shokan*, p. 431.

[5] That Kōtoku was highly impressed by Renan's study of the life of Jesus is reflected in his letter to Sakai in which he wrote: 'This is how a biography should be written! In comparison, my own *Lasalle* seems crude and primitive.' *Ibid.* p. 192.

[6] Kōtoku subsequently became quite interested in Ladd and his work. In San Francisco he had Albert Johnson introduce him to Ladd. On May 15, 1906, he spent over two hours talking to him in Alameda. *Ibid.* p. 144.

[7] *Ibid.* p. 431.

[8] According to Nishio, Kōtoku had begun to question the state and had already started to preach the 'gospel of non-recognition' of its authority in the summer of 1904. Nishio, *Kōtoku Shūsui*, p. 120.

In May Kōtoku had maintained in a letter to Sakai: 'If anyone were to question me at this moment regarding my views on life and the universe, I would still answer that I am a materialist and a scientific socialist. My readings and meditations during the next sixty days will, I suppose, only strengthen and affirm my beliefs.'[1]

In August, a few days after leaving prison, Kōtoku wrote to Albert Johnson:

Five months of imprisonment not a little injured my health, but it gave me many lessons of the social questions. I have seen and studied [a] great many of [the] so-called 'criminals' and became convinced that the governmental institutions – court, law, prison – are only responsible for them – poverty and crime . . . Indeed, I had gone [to prison] as a Marxian Socialist and returned a radical Anarchist.[2]

Kōtoku's assertion that he had gone to prison a 'Marxian Socialist' and that he had emerged as a 'radical Anarchist' must be seen as something of an oversimplification written for the sake of foreign consumption. Kōtoku knew that Johnson was an anarchist, and that such an assertion would appeal to him. No doubt he considered himself a 'Marxist' when he entered prison, but then, he had also just completed a biography of Lassalle, whom he praised highly and compared to Yoshida Shōin.[3] Perhaps nothing reveals more clearly the limitations of his 'Marxian Socialism' than his attraction to the pseudo-scientific arguments of an author like Lane.

If any generalizations can be made about Kōtoku's career as a socialist until his imprisonment in 1905, it may be said that his involvement with the ideas of socialism was itself a part of his quest for the frontiers of Western social and political thought. In the short period of five years Kōtoku had moved rapidly through much of the socialist tradition from Henry George to Kropotkin. Like other Japanese thinkers of his generation, he found little time to assimilate and digest the ideas of individual Western thinkers. Ideas, in fact, rarely appear to have become ends in themselves. For Kōtoku ideas were always means to some specific political goal, and as such could be taken up and discarded with surprising rapidity. Shortly after being introduced to socialism Kōtoku toyed, for example, with the possibilities of the 'initiative' and 'referendum', concepts which he soon abandoned for the formula of 'parliamentarianism'. This formula, as we shall see, was in turn to give way to 'syndicalism', 'direct action', and a belief in the 'General Strike'. The pace with which he moved from position to position reveals something of the

[1] *Nikki to shokan*, p. 192.
[2] Letter to Albert Johnson dated August 10, 1905. *Ibid.* p. 433.
[3] See introduction to Rasāru, in *Senshū*, vol. I, pp. 203ff.

intensity with which he searched for the frontiers of Western revolutionary thought. And yet, the closer he came the fewer became the signposts. Lane or Kropotkin? Whose ideas represented the tide of the world revolutionary movement? Kōtoku was uncertain.

A further dilemma of this rapid movement from position to position was the fact that ideas rarely acquired the emotional support necessary to sustain them and to cause them to flow in new and original channels. At the same time there was always the danger that, because thought and feelings were compartmentalized, periods of crisis would result in a victory of the emotional realm over the realm of ideas. Since the tradition flowed more strongly in the emotional realm, crisis experiences easily resulted in a reversion to traditional attitudes and solutions.

Through socialism Kōtoku had hoped to change his environment. As he had pointed out in *Imperialism*, man must not accept the existent state of society as 'natural', but must be willing to struggle against it in order to institute change. Within the framework of the *Heimin Shimbun* and its program he had tried to put this idea into practice. He had personally attempted to resist the power of the state by carrying the anti-war standard against the pro-war government leaders. In doing this he had sought to mount the people once more behind his own vision of the continuing revolution towards 'liberty', 'equality', and 'fraternity'. In all these efforts he had failed. Prison provided ample opportunity to reflect on his shortcomings. As on previous occasions the consciousness of failure aroused a strong need to strike out in rejection.

Writing about his prison experience Kōtoku noted in a mood that recalls his 'Fuhei no Rireki':

Late at night in Sugamo Prison, listening to the rain under the faint glow of the weak electric light, the events of the past thirty years dimly passed before my vision. When I saw how small, how mean, how impure and ugly I had been; how I had run after self interest and searched for fame, jealous of others and resentful of the world; how I had been impatient and ambitious, relied on cleverness, become proud of heart and self-willed in action, I was both mortified and ashamed. No matter how often I shook my hand, I could not drive away the ugly figures of my past which rose before me.[1]

Confronted with his own imperfection, Kōtoku once more wrestled with the question of responsibility. Was the fault his? Was his imperfection the product of his nature? Were Kinoshita and the other Christians possibly right? Was the inner reform of man still a possibility? These were the

[1] 'Kashiwagi yori', *Chokugen*, September 10, 1905, p. 5.

questions which haunted him. In response he appears to have undergone something of a brief conversion experience. About this struggle with the inner man he wrote:

At the time I secretly thought that I should make an about-face, repent of my wrongs, and address myself whole-heartedly to the following of the 'way'. Hereafter I would be totally different from what I had been before. For a while I felt as if my unclean heart had been cleansed, and my muddled mind had become lucid. I felt liberated in both body and spirit.[1]

Under the influence of his new sense of purity Kōtoku entertained the possibility of a utopian existence after his release from prison. Writing to Sakai towards the end of June he listed some of the things he wanted to do. After stating a desire to reconstitute a 'great daily paper' with headquarters in the heart of Tokyo, and toying with the possibility of a trip to the United States and Europe in order to 'examine the activities of other comrades in the field of battle',[2] Kōtoku went on to write:

My third desire is to withdraw from all wordly concerns and taking with me books on science, philosophy, and religion to escape into the mountains and there devote myself to the composition of a new treatise on materialism. Finally, I should like to buy some land in Hokkaido or Korea, where in the company of several hundred farmers, I might lead an ideal life, quietly nourishing simplicity.[3]

But Kōtoku's new sense of purity was little more than a temporary moral mirage. The reform of the inner man was a possibility only as long as he remained isolated from the world outside. What he had not counted on, he confessed, was that:

this frame of mind was only the product of extreme leisure and tranquility; nothing more than the product of a separate world without responsibility, of sitting alone facing a stone wall reading books. One step outside of the prison gates and I was once again carnal, wrathful, and arrogant. I was the same man of small character, the same person of low taste.[4]

From his new height of moral and mental purity Kōtoku plunged once more into the morass of mental anxiety and gloom. 'I am a small man', he wrote, castigating himself in the old Confucian terminology.[5] At the same time he insisted that the fault belonged to the 'system' and not to the individual. Unwilling to accept personal responsibility he struck out once more against the social order. In his cell he had read Kropotkin. No doubt he had mentally begun to question the need for authority before his release.

---

[1] *Ibid.*   [2] *Nikki to shokan*, p. 194.   [3] *Ibid.*
[4] 'Kashiwagi ori', *Chokugen*, September 10, 1905, p. 5.   [5] *Ibid.*

But in none of his letters from prison is there the slightest indication of a conversion to anarchism. It was only faced with personal disillusionment and despair, which did not overwhelm him until his departure from prison, that Kōtoku began to strike out against his environment in the name of this new foreign creed.

Meditating in his cell under the influence of Draper, Haeckel, and Ladd, Kōtoku had become convinced that Christianity (and religion in general) was based on 'myth'. While regaining his health at the home of Katō Tokijirō, his socialist friend and personal physician, in Odawara, where he had gone after his release from Sugamo, Kōtoku began to extend some of their principles to the Japanese Imperial Institution itself. Thus, Kōtoku, who had gone to prison seeking a flaw in Christ emerged having found a flaw not only in Christ but in the heart of the Japanese national polity as well.

In prison Kōtoku had toyed with the idea of going abroad. With his release and growing depression, friends, who were concerned over his mental and physical condition, urged him to take such a trip. Moreover, the change of environment was strongly recommended by Dr Katō, who was about to send his son to study in the United States and welcomed the chance to have a friend accompany him on the journey to America. Money remained an obstacle, but Dr Katō offered a generous contribution, and his family and friends promised the rest.[1] In August 1905 Kōtoku wrote to Albert Johnson in San Francisco, 'if my health allows and money... could be raised, I will start in the coming winter or next spring'.[2] A month later he wrote, 'I am intending to start for America in the next November.'[3]

Meanwhile his antagonism to Japanese society had grown. Even the Emperor now came in for scathing criticism. Japan had deteriorated to the level of a police state and the Imperial House acquiesced in this decline. Kōtoku's attitude towards the Emperor was expressed in a letter to Albert Johnson in which he stated that one of the reasons for his proposed visit to the United States was 'to criticize freely the position of "His Majesty"... from [a] foreign land where the pernicious hand of "His Majesty" cannot reach'.[4] A few years earlier he had reprimanded Kinoshita Naoe for a similar stand.

But Kōtoku's rejection went beyond a mere rejection of the Japanese Emperor. Under the influence of Kropotkin he began to question authority of any kind. On November 13, 1905, the day before his scheduled departure

---

[1] The sums donated by Dr Katō, Kōtoku's family and friends are itemized in *Nikki to shokan*, p. 130.

[2] *Ibid.* p. 434. [3] *Ibid.* p. 436. [4] *Ibid.* p. 434.

for the United States, Kinoshita once more visited him in Tokyo. Sitting on a stump on the outskirts of the city they discussed their mutual positions. Kōtoku constantly referred to Kropotkin's ideas,[1] and Kinoshita was struck by how much Kōtoku had changed. 'Oh! What a gap one little phrase could create between two individuals,' he recalled, 'the rejection of authority, this was the phrase that had come between us. Kōtoku discussed the theory of Anarchism, while I spoke of the love of God.'[2]

It is possible to regard Kōtoku's rejection of the Japanese Emperor, the state, and authority in general as the outworking of an inner crisis that elicited responses deeply rooted in his personality. Defeat had always led to rejection. At the same time, it had also resulted in clouds of self-doubt. Kōtoku summed up his feelings in a diary entry in which he wrote:

At the farewell meeting on the eighth given by my friends Kinoshita said that seeing me off was like seeing off a wounded hero. Though I am no hero, I am indeed a fugitive from a defeated army searching for a place to conceal myself from the world. When can I rise again? The road ahead is so uncertain.[3]

Perhaps there is an interesting parallel here between the young boy Denjirō, who had locked himself up in his room and subsequently tried to escape to China, and the mature Shūsui, who sought to conceal himself from the world by running away to San Francisco.

Finally, one cannot overlook the fact that the seeds for an anarchic rejection of authority had in some ways begun to germinate in Kōtoku before his encounter with Kropotkin. Certainly 'Hiseiji ron' ('An Essay Against Government') shows that he had begun to question the role of government as early as 1899. 'What is this thing called government? What is this thing called the state?' These were questions that appeared with increasing frequency in his articles in the summer of 1904. And yet, while he questioned both the state and the government on theoretical grounds prior to his imprisonment, his criticism never reached the level of open rejection. More important, his criticism never extended itself to the core of the national polity, the Imperial Institution. Frustrated in his attempt to conquer the political world, defeated, and imprisoned, Kōtoku struck back by excommunicating the Emperor.

On November 14, 1905, the Meiji Emperor journeyed to the Imperial Shrines at Ise to report to his ancestors the Japanese victory in the Russo-Japanese War. At two o'clock on the afternoon of the same day Kōtoku

---

[1] Kinoshita noted that Kōtoku constantly referred to Kropotkin as 'Sensei' (teacher) at this time. Kami ningen jiyū, p. 28.
[2] Ibid.　　[3] Nikki to shokan, pp. 129-30.

Shūsui quietly slipped out of Yokohama aboard the *Iyo Maru* bound for Seattle and San Francisco.[1]

It should be pointed out that Kōtoku left behind a highly fragmented socialist movement. The farewell meeting held for him on November 8 was to prove one of the last cooperative ventures for the group that had opposed the war through the *Heimin Shimbun* and its successor, the *Chokugen*. The Heiminsha had itself been dissolved on October 9, after basic disagreements between its Christian and non-Christian members over a variety of issues which included the question of 'free love'.[2] On November 10, two days after Kōtoku's farewell, Kinoshita Naoe, Abe Isoo, and Ishikawa Sanshirō formally inaugurated the Shin Kigen Sha (New Era Association), whose monthly organ, *Shin Kigen* (*New Era*) became the mouthpiece for the Christian wing of the movement.[3] The materialists, on the other hand, gathered around the bimonthly journal, *Hikari* (*Light*), which was founded by Nishikawa Kōjirō and Yamaguchi Kōken on November 20.[4] Both groups spent considerable time and energy attacking one another and debating points of theory. In effect, the movement had become highly intellectualized (as Katayama Sen had originally feared it might) and in the process had lost sight of the worker and common man. Kōtoku's influence in this process cannot be totally disregarded, but perhaps the fault must be shared equally by the others who like him failed to establish any real rapport with the masses in whose name they claimed to be speaking.

Still in the throes of the depression which gripped him after his release from prison, Kōtoku showed little of the enthusiasm and excitement that overwhelmed so many of his contemporaries on their first trips to the West. Instead, his travel diary is full of somber tones that reflect a mood of despondency. 'Ah! Why was it that I left Japan?' he asked a few days out of port. 'It was for the very reason that I could not stay. After government pressure forced the collapse of the *Heimin Shimbun*, sickness and poverty prevented me from accomplishing anything.'[5] On another occasion he noted:

Many of those who have gone to the West have done so to earn fame and personal gain. For them such a journey was the way to wealth and honor and the stairway to success. For such individuals it was a so-called 'fabulous trip' full of joy and glory. But this was not the case with me. I did not leave because I wanted to. I wanted to stay, but could not.[6]

---

[1] *Nikki to shokan*, pp. 129–30.
[2] Akamatsu Katsumarō, *Nihon shakai undō shi*, pp. 131ff.
[3] Hosokawa, *et al.*, *Nihon Shakai Shugi bunken kaisetsu*, pp. 60ff.
[4] *Ibid*. pp. 58ff.   [5] *Nikki to shokan*, pp. 129–30.
[6] Kōtoku Shūsui, 'Kyōran yōmatsu', *Senshū*, vol. III, p. 261.

For Kōtoku, leaving Japan contained an element of the inevitable. No one seems to have actually pressured him to leave, but he somehow felt compelled to go. Growing friction with Chiyoko's family may have contributed to his decision.[1] And yet, it is interesting that in his farewell address before his friends on November 8, he spent most of his time discussing the question of freedom and determinism. 'I cannot believe in freedom of the will,' he stated, 'all I believe in is fate.'[2] For a man who was advocating the rejection of all authority, this seems a curious contradiction. Libertarians, while they may have occasionally seen revolution as an inevitable force, have, after all, rarely been fatalists on the level of personal action. What then lay behind Kōtoku's concern with the problem?

The answer remains puzzling. Perhaps its source rested in the continuing conflict of values to which he was subject. Kōtoku's proposed trip to the United States forced him to confront once more the particularistic loyalties and duties in which he had been raised and educated. Filial piety, duty to his family, loyalty to friends – these were elements of the tradition with which Kōtoku identified. And yet, it was precisely in areas of his private life where these values applied that the greatest conflict between the past and his new revolutionary ideology took place. To leave behind a sick wife, an aging mother, and comrades who depended on his help, could not be regarded as anything but selfish by the standards of the past. On his way to the United States Kōtoku was to berate himself with the same phrase he had used in 1899: 'I am an unfilial son and a husband who does not know benevolence.'[3] At the same time, he realized that his future as a revolutionary necessitated a trip to the West. The conflict over loyalties which Kōtoku experienced reveals the extent to which his revolutionary ideology failed to cut through the values of the past. Instead of clearly stating that his new revolutionary faith required these sacrifices, no matter how difficult they might be, he equivocated. The argument of fate provided him with an avenue of escape. Once again he was forced to rationalize his failure to act decisively in terms of the inevitable.

Aboard ship Kōtoku suffered from an additional affliction – seasickness.

---

[1] A curious, if somewhat tenuous, reason for Kōtoku's trip is given by his nephew, Yukie. Writing in 1933 Yukie maintained that the trip was the result of a family dispute which involved Chiyoko's elder sister, Matsumoto Sugako, who was married to the younger brother of a Diet member. Sugako's husband considered Kōtoku's anti-war stand detrimental to his brother's career and tried to persuade Chiyoko to divorce him. According to Yukie, his uncle was 'greatly troubled' by this situation and attempted to alleviate it by leaving the country. Kōtoku Yukie, 'Oji Shūsui no omoide', *Chūō Kōron*, April, 1933, p. 163.

[2] Kinoshita Naoe, 'Hakaba', in *Gendai Nihon bungaku zenshū*, vol. LIII, p. 257.

[3] *Senshū*, vol. III, p. 265.

After nearly a week's confinement to his cabin, he was happy to record, 'I feel a little better today and made it to the dining room three times.'[1] With three solid meals his spirits improved sufficiently for him to observe: 'Life aboard ship is a life free from competition for food. Society aboard ship is socialist society. Men are at harmony with one another.'[2]

At least so it seemed to Kōtoku in his second-class accommodations. Third-class, in which his nephew, Yukie, traveled, appears to have elicited a different response from his uncle. Not only was Yukie's food so unpalatable that Kōtoku had to save him bread from his own table, but on the lower decks disease was also rampant. Once in Seattle he was only too glad to get his nephew out from among disease, prostitution, and other forms of vice. Once more Kōtoku's egalitarianism showed itself somewhat limited. He had few sympathetic words for the impoverished Japanese in steerage who were hoping for a better life in the United States.

Having recovered from his seasickness, Kōtoku spent his leisure hours reading Kropotkin's autobiographical *Memoirs of a Revolutionist* and a critical analysis of the struggle between Marx and Bakunin.[3] In many ways he came to identify his trip to the United States with Kropotkin's flight to Switzerland.[4]

On November 28 the *Iyo Maru* reached Victoria harbor in British Columbia. After spending the night in Victoria, the ship continued on to Seattle. Kōtoku, still melancholy, stuffed a letter into an empty wine bottle and dropped it out of his porthole into the dark ocean below, wondering if its message would ever reach land, or whether it might not be doomed to float forever or to disappear immediately into the belly of some fish. Then, as if meditating on his act, he reflected: 'Ah! We are really very much alike, that bottle and I; neither of us knows the fate that lies before him.'[5]

That afternoon, after reaching Seattle and setting foot on American soil for the first time, his mood seems to have improved. One of the reasons for this was the warm welcome given him by the local Japanese community. Two days of sightseeing, visits, and discussions with young men interested in the study of socialism, were capped by an address before the Japanese Association on the first of December. Speaking to an audience of over five hundred, Kōtoku finally broke the self-imposed silence which had lasted since his imprisonment in February.

[1] *Nikki to shokan*, p. 131.
[2] *Ibid.*
[3] Kōtoku's diary simply states that he read Kropotkin's 'autobiography'. *Ibid.* pp. 131–2.
[4] Diary entry for November 22. *Ibid.*
[5] 'Warera no unmei', in *Senshū*, vol. III, p. 265.

As he later observed, entering the hall in which he was to speak he could not refrain from smiling bitterly. 'Contemporary Japan' – which was also the subject of his speech – was represented all too clearly in the decor with which he was surrounded. In front, by the speaker's platform, could be seen two large portraits of the Emperor and Empress. On the sides there were photographs of the 'heroes' of the war with Russia, including those of Admiral Tōgō and General Nōgi. Occupying the rear wall was an impressive piece of calligraphy done by Itō Hirobumi. Amidst such an array of 'Japanese authority', Kōtoku thought it somewhat 'strange' that a person who had been imprisoned for a violation of the Constitution, and frequently branded a 'traitor' by the press, should be allowed to speak out against war and in favor of socialism. Despite the setting, the audience soon revealed itself responsive to his appeal, and Kōtoku, pleased to note the absence of 'police inspectors, patrolmen, and plain-clothesmen', continued 'freely [and] honestly' for an hour and a half.[1]

Greatly heartened by his reception in Seattle, and by the concern shown by the young people of the area in social and political questions, Kōtoku began to look forward to his arrival in San Francisco. Leaving his fifteen-year-old nephew in the care of a local Japanese family,[2] he continued overland by train, and on December fifth arrived in Oakland to the warm welcome of Oka Shigeki, a friend of Sakai's and a former journalist for the *Yorozu Chōhō* who had organized a branch of the Heiminsha in San Francisco.[3] Within a matter of hours he was shaking hands with Albert Johnson, Mrs Fritz, and a delegation of representatives from the Heiminsha which had come to the

[1] 'Shiyatoru shi yori' in *Senshū*, vol. III, pp. 266-7.
[2] Yukie constituted something of a burden for Kōtoku. Kōtoku does not appear to have been fond of children in general, and while Yukie, the son of Kōtoku's deceased brother Kameji, was hardly a child, Kōtoku often treated him as if he were. Kōtoku did not hesitate to leave Yukie with virtual strangers in Seattle, while he traveled on to San Francisco in the company of Katō Tokiya, the son of his patron, Dr Katō Tokijirō. Later in San Francisco Kōtoku roomed with Tokiya, who was not much older than his nephew, while Yukie, for whom Seattle had become unbearable, was put out to work in Oakland. Yukie subsequently studied art and became a painter in the Los Angeles area. In the mid 1930s he committed suicide.
[3] Oka Shigeki was a cousin of Kuroiwa Ruikō, the editor of the *Yorozu Chōhō*. Like Kōtoku he came to Tokyo from rural Tosa and served as a writer on the staff of the *Yorozu*. As a journalist he appears to have become particularly friendly with Sakai Toshihiko who introduced him to socialism. At the same time he got along badly with Matsui Matsuba, one of the paper's popular novelists, and after several fights between the two men Kuroiwa fired his cousin. Oka next moved to Alaska where he became a salmon fisherman. With the money he saved in Alaska he finally moved to San Francisco and set up a branch of the Heiminsha. According to Karl Yoneda, a long-time friend of Oka's to whom I am indebted for this information, Oka's warm and friendly disposition, as well as the fact that he was one of the few married members of the group, attracted to the Heiminsha many of the alienated young Japanese students and workers of the San Francisco area. Some of these young men Kōtoku subsequently molded into the Social Revolutionary Party of Oakland.

Ferry Building to welcome him. By nightfall he was exploring the city which was to serve as his home for the next six momentous months.

No sooner had he arrived in San Francisco than his mood changed. Evidence of such a change was already detectable in his meeting with Oka about which he wrote: 'Seeing the warmth with which he welcomed me, I grasped his hand firmly and for some time found myself unable to say anything. Oh! the feelings of that moment!'[1] It was also reflected in his response to the San Francisco Heiminsha to which he was almost immediately introduced by Oka. Writing to his fellow socialists in Tokyo he stated:

Friends and comrades at home, just imagine my joy when arriving here crestfallen and forlorn, the remnant of a defeated army, and a man on the brink of despair . . . I saw on the entrance of a splendid building a black plaque inscribed with gold letters in Japanese and English reading, 'Heiminsha, San Francisco Branch'. Yes, the Heiminsha is not dead, it still lives. Here, where the poisonous hand [of the Emperor] cannot reach, this branch will grow strong in the future.[2]

Having weathered his own despair, Kōtoku plunged once more into a whirlwind of activity. A quick glance at his diary for his first week in San Francisco reveals some of the scope of his interests.

Kōtoku had arrived in San Francisco on December 5, 1905. On the evening of the sixth he met with other Japanese socialists at the Heiminsha to plan strategy for a local movement. On the seventh he was invited to the home of Albert Johnson, where he came to know the *émigré* Russian anarchist into whose home he was soon to move, Mrs Fritz, and the American atheist journalist, Kidder. On the eighth he visited Golden Gate Park with a friend (and tried to nurse a cold which had been bothering him for several days). On the ninth he met someone named Eitel from the 'Socialist Party', and later in the evening attended a banquet held in his honor by the Japanese press of the San Francisco area. On the tenth he followed up an invitation to attend a socialist discussion group at the 'Imperial Hotel' – he notes fifty attended – and this was followed by a visit from George Williams, a local organizer for the Socialist Party. On the eleventh his cold appears to have deteriorated into laryngitis, and he complained that due to an unending stream of visitors he found himself unable to nurse his ailment.[3]

In the spare moments between visitors, consultations, and meetings of all kinds, Kōtoku began to plan his own stay in the United States. Months

---

[1] *Senshū*, vol. III, p. 268.
[2] 'Sanfuranshisuko yori' in *Senshū*, vol. III, p. 269.
[3] *Nikki to shokan*, pp. 134-5.

before he had written to Albert Johnson that among the things he would like to accomplish in America were an extension of his contacts with foreign revolutionaries and their movements, as well as his knowledge of foreign languages.[1] In a later letter he had added: 'I'm now intending to organize the Japanese laborers in America. There is no other means to get freedom of speech and press than to quit the soil of the state of siege and go to a more civilized country.'[2] Under the influence of Kropotkin's *Memoirs of a Revolutionist* his vision seems to have expanded a dimension further. The first flush of his American encounter was still very much with him as he wrote home on December 8, expressing his hopes for the future:

At present I would like to recuperate quietly; then, when I know more about local conditions I should like to exert myself fully to establish here a base for the work of the Heiminsha. I believe that here, where there is freedom of speech, assembly, and the press, and where money can be made with ease, it may be possible to establish, through a concerted effort, a sanctuary for our persecuted comrades at home, as well as a base of supply and operation for the Japanese socialist movement, much as the Russian revolutionaries made Switzerland a base for their movement. This may be a wild dream on my part, but I shall make every effort to see it realized.[3]

In the months that followed Kōtoku poured himself with full vigor into the tasks he had set for himself. It is clear from his diary that his attempts to come into closer contacts with Western revolutionaries was greatly aided by two individuals: Albert Johnson and Mrs Fritz. Unfortunately, our knowledge of both remains limited.

Albert Johnson, with whom Kōtoku was to carry on a warm correspondence until 1910, had been introduced to him by Leopold Fleischmann, a journalist of radical leanings whom Kōtoku had come to know in Tokyo at the time of the Russo-Japanese War.[4] Johnson was a fireman on one of the ferries that plied between Oakland and San Francisco, and ideologically seems to have been more an atheist than an anarchist, although Hyppolyte Havel, writing in *Mother Earth*, referred to him as the 'veteran Anarchist of California'.[5] While Johnson had never met Kōtoku in person before his arrival in San

---

[1] Letter to Albert Johnson dated August 10, 1905. Originally published in *Mother Earth*, vol. IV, no. 6 (August 1911), p. 184. Reprinted in *Nikki to shokan*, p. 434.

[2] Letter to Albert Johnson dated October 11, 1905. *Nikki to shokan*, p. 437.

[3] *Senshū*, vol. III, p. 270.

[4] According to a news brief in *Hikari*, no. 7 (February 20, 1906), p. 1 (in *Meiji Shakai Shugi shiryo shū*, vol. II, p. 51) Fleischmann is said to have been a member of the Independent Labor Party of America, who had made an appeal to American socialists to support their Japanese friends with financial aid during their period of 'persecution' in the previous year.

[5] Hyppolyte Havel, 'Kōtoku's Correspondence with Albert Johnson', *Mother Earth*, vol. IV, no. 6 (August, 1911), p. 180.

Francisco, their friendship soon blossomed, and throughout his stay he was a constant visitor in the Johnson home. It was Johnson who introduced him to Mrs Fritz, Kidder, Sanford, Maievsky, Ladd, and other atheists and anarchists. It was also Johnson who saw to it that he received a card to the public library where he might pursue his interests in the significance of religious symbols.[1]

Kōtoku first met Mrs Fritz on the day of his arrival in San Francisco. She and her seventeen-year-old daughter, Anna, had joined Albert Johnson at the Ferry Building to welcome him. A week later he accepted her offer to board in her home which was close to the Johnsons, as well as to the Heiminsha and the Y.M.C.A. (where he usually went to have his meals). Mrs Fritz, herself an *émigré* Russian revolutionary and anarchist acquainted with Kropotkin,[2] was exactly the type of person Kōtoku had hoped to meet. He was delighted with his new quarters, particularly his room which contained two large portraits – one of Kropotkin, the other of Bakunin – and numerous books by Gorki, Zola, Kropotkin, and others.[3] As Kōtoku wrote home, Mrs Fritz and her daughter were 'extremely kind';[4] they were, moreover, concerned that their lodger learn as much as possible during his stay. While Anna undertook to tutor him in conversation, her mother presented him with Jean Grave's *Moribund Society and Anarchy*, then one of the most popular works on the subject of anarchism in the English language.[5] A few days later she began to debate with him anarchist theory; introducing him at the same time to other members of the anarchist and *émigré* community such as the Swedish revolutionary, Widen, and the American anarchist, Pyburn. Within a matter of weeks Kōtoku had come to know many of the revolutionaries active in the Bay Area.

Meanwhile Kōtoku was also interested in furthering his contact with American socialists. Soon after his arrival he joined the San Francisco

---

[1] Under Johnson's influence Kōtoku built on, and expanded, his anti-Christian research which he had begun in prison the year before. Much of the research for *Kirisuto massatsu ron* (*Rubbing out Christ*) was carried out in the San Francisco Public Library. In his attempts to organize the local Japanese who gathered at the Heiminsha he was to encounter again and again what he termed the 'religious problem'. In one report to his Tokyo colleagues he commented: 'I had imagined before coming that there might be quite a number of Christians among our Japanese comrades in America, but I had expected nothing like this!' *Nikki to shokan*, p. 227. On the other hand, he considered the Japanese Christians living in San Francisco more liberal than their Tokyo counterparts and hoped that the schism between Christians and materialists which had rent the movement in Japan might somehow be avoided in the United States.

[2] See letter from P. Kropotkin to Kōtoku dated September 25, 1906. Reprinted in Kanzaki Kiyoshi (ed.), *Taigyaku jiken kiroku*, vol. II, p. 209. Mrs Fritz seems to have been the contact between the two men.

[3] 'Sanfuranshisuko yori' in *Senshū*, vol. III, p. 272.

[4] *Ibid.*   [5] *Nikki to shokan*, p. 136.

Socialist Party in order to 'study their campaign methods',[1] and became a regular participant in its discussion groups. On the fifteenth of December he was visited by three members of the Industrial Workers of the World (I.W.W.), who asked him to speak at a meeting of their organization.[2] This was to be his first introduction to American 'syndicalism', whose formula of 'direct action' he was to take back to Japan.

By the end of December Kōtoku had due cause to be satisfied with himself. In the month that had passed he had made a wide circle of friends and acquaintances, and had gained some insight into American radicalism. Earlier in the month he had written to his friends in Japan: 'As yet, I know nothing of middle or upper class American society, nor do I want to. These have been made public all too clearly by others who have gone abroad. All I would like to do is come into contact with the tide of the social and revolutionary movements of the lower classes.'[3] This is exactly what he thought he had accomplished in the weeks after his arrival, and while his health still had not recovered to the extent he had hoped – little wonder given his schedule – he was much improved in spirit. As others observed, it now became a common sight to see Kōtoku, dressed in a black morning coat and bowler hat, and carrying a wooden sword that substituted as a cane – a style of dress strangely out of keeping with his mission to the 'lower classes' – briskly striding to and from the Heiminsha, and other appointments, with a new air of self-confidence.[4]

While a good deal of time and effort had gone into making contacts with American socialists and foreign revolutionaries, Kōtoku had not neglected his other goal of organizing the local Japanese through the Heiminsha. Following the model of the Tokyo Heiminsha, he established a regular Sunday evening 'discussion group', which was soon well attended by serious-minded young men. About these he wrote: 'I expect that someday the members of this group will become the driving force behind the rise of

---

[1] 'Sanfuranshisuko yori (II)', *Senshū*, vol. III, p. 271.

[2] *Nikki to shokan*, p. 218.

[3] 'Sanfuranshisuko yori (II)', *Senshū*, vol. III, p. 272.

[4] Perhaps the best personal description of Kōtoku in San Francisco can be found in Iwasa Sakutarō's 'Zai bei undō shiwa' ('Tales of the Movement in America'). Iwasa was one of the members of the San Francisco Heiminsha who later went on to head the Oakland Shakai Kakumei tō (Social Revolutionary Party). Iwasa mentions that Kōtoku's look and manner reminded him strongly of the Meiji Emperor, and that his dress, which might have passed as that of a well-groomed gentleman in Tokyo, seemed curiously grotesque in San Francisco. One day, according to Iwasa, the boys of the neighborhood decided to make fun of Shūsui by calling everyone's attention to his clothes. Kōtoku became angry and chased them away waving his wooden sword. 'From then on', Iwasa concludes, 'he came to dislike America'. See Iwasa Sakutarō, 'Zai bei undō shiwa', in Shakai Bunko (ed.), *Zai Bei Shakai Shugi sha – Museifu Shugi sha enkaku* (Tokyo, 1964), pp. 527ff.

socialism in Japan and the Far East.'[1] At the same time his activities began to branch out to include Japanese outside of the immediate San Francisco area. By the middle of April he was able to write:

On the first Sunday of this month I addressed a woman's meeting in San Francisco. The next Saturday there was a study group in Oakland. This evening I have promised to make a speech in Alameda. Next Sunday, at the request of American comrades, I am lecturing at two places in the Sacramento area. Although all this keeps me extremely busy, I am heartened by the fact that the number of our Japanese comrades has been increasing rapidly. I believe that it will not be many years before our comrades here will serve as a large partisan force for our struggle at home.[2]

If Kōtoku was beginning to affect his San Francisco environment through his organizational activities, that same environment was also beginning to affect his thought.

Upon his arrival in December Kōtoku had continued to propagate the basic parliamentarian line which he had adopted in the *Heimin Shimbun*. While he told a Japanese friend that he did not hesitate to tell inquiring Japanese that he was an 'anarcho-communist' (Westerners being told that he was a 'socialist'), there are no signs in his early speeches that he actually advocated a new position.[3] Addressing an audience of four hundred at the Golden Gate Hall on December 16, he 'talked for an hour and a half about the degradation of the Japanese people at the end of the war and about the state of the poor; reporting the urgent need for the implementation of universal suffrage and socialism'.[4]

Mrs Fritz, no doubt in the audience during this speech, began to debate the whole issue of parliamentarianism with him the following day.[5] Jean Grave added further fuel to her arguments that a reliance on parliamentary

---

[1] 'Sanfuranshisuko yori (V)', *Senshū*, vol. III, p. 281.

[2] *Nikki to shokan*, p. 234.

[3] Iwasa, to whom this statement was made, questioned Kōtoku's understanding of anarchism. Shūsui's desire to seize power through an organized party seemed to Iwasa to be out of keeping with the anarchist ideal. 'Anarchists', he wrote, 'maintain that political parties are useless, and consequently do not concern themselves with seizing power through them. They do not plan to carry out a revolution in the wake of such a power seizure. Instead, they intend to transform all systems, whether political, economic, religious, or educational, through personal sovereignty and independence which is based on the freedom of the individual. Under no circumstances do they dream of seizing political power. It may be that his birthplace and upbringing made Kōtoku, quite unconsciously, into one who dreamed of being a revolutionary hero. Then too, he was only a young man of thirty at the time.' Iwasa Sakutarō, in Shakai Bunko (ed.), *Zai bei Shakai Shugi sha–Museifu Shugi sha enkaku*, pp. 527–8.

[4] 'Sanfuranshisuko yori (III)', *Senshū*, vol. III, p. 273.

[5] She began by stating firmly that it was pointless to work for universal suffrage. Diary entry for December 17, 1905. *Nikki to shokan*, p. 136.

tactics was useless. To anarchists he wrote, 'The ballot...is a perfected instrument of authority;' it must be repudiated 'equally with authority itself.'[1] Moreover, Kōtoku could easily agree with Grave when he wrote, 'It is impossible for the Anarchists to be pacific, even if they so wished... there comes a moment when, pacific though the sufferers be, force is answered by force, and exploitation by revolt.'[2] Kōtoku and his fellow socialists had been close to such a point in the autumn of 1904, and he was to have good reason to recall Grave's words a few years later. It should also be pointed out that while Grave advocated the use of violence largely in the direct confrontation of labor and capital, Mrs Fritz tried to convince Kōtoku of the need to 'assassinate government leaders'.[3]

Perhaps of even greater influence than the arguments of Mrs Fritz and Jean Grave was Kōtoku's personal involvement in the social and revolutionary ferment of the San Francisco area. His search for the tide of revolutionary activity, a tide which one suspects he visualized as a great inevitable force into which he might plunge himself in order to be carried to fame and glory,[4] had brought him into contact with a broad spectrum of those concerned with the social and labor issues of the day. As an outsider he could move freely in and out of a variety of groups, observing, recording, and occasionally commenting on the great debate between conservatives and radicals which raged during his stay. He recorded the debate quite clearly when he wrote:

Recently a controversy has developed between two factions in the American Socialist Party regarding the movement's policy. One group particularly stresses public ownership (state or municipal) of monopolistic enterprises and desires to use the polls as its weapons. The other group desires to raise the ideals of pure socialism as its banner.

The first group maintains that we must advance step by step in order to improve the actual well-being of the working classes, and that it is not sufficient to concentrate merely on ideals to the neglect of the real problems that confront us. They furthermore state that the reason why our German comrades have steadily gained ground, and why our English comrades reaped victory in the last elections, is due to the fact that they shaped their platforms out of issues that were directly related to the worker's well-being.

The second group maintains that today's so-called public ownership does not eliminate the wage system, and simply substitutes government or municipal

---

[1] Jean Grave, *Moribund Society and Anarchy* (San Francisco, 1899), p. 119.

[2] *Ibid.* p. 117.

[3] Diary entry for December 23, 1905. *Nikki to shokan*, p. 137.

[4] 'This is a revolutionary age', Kōtoku told the young Japanese of San Francisco, 'and we are the children of that age ... if we aspire to revolution today, it will be easy to make a name for ourselves and win fame'. Quoted by Iwasa Sakutarō, in Shakai Bunko (ed.), *Zai bei Shakai Shugi sha–Museifu Shugi sha enkaku*, p. 527.

capitalism for private capitalism. Socialism, they insist, stresses complete elimination of the wage system. To agree to state or municipal ownership under the present system is to make concessions to social reformers and state socialists.[1]

Kōtoku, who had grown familiar with the more radical elements of this debate through his contacts with Anthony and other members of the Industrial Workers of the World, stated his own sympathies in no uncertain terms: 'As for me, were I to choose between the two, I would side with the idealists, the revolutionaries, and the progressives. I do not like lukewarm socialism, "sugar-water" socialism, state socialism.'[2]

While Anthony and the other members of the radical wing of the I.W.W. were soon to discover that the main current of the American revolutionary tide was to continue in the reformist camp of the socialist movement,[3] Kōtoku, who was forced to leave San Francisco before their disillusionment, returned to Japan fully convinced that the tide of the world-wide revolutionary movement was cresting in an anarchistic direction, and that, given this trend, the new formula for revolutionaries everywhere should be 'direct action' and the 'General Strike' rather than 'parliamentarianism' and 'universal suffrage'.

Several elements of Kōtoku's San Francisco experience joined to mold his stepped-up radicalism. One may presume that his contacts with Mrs Fritz, Albert Johnson, and other anarchists did a great deal to bring into sharper focus ideas which had already begun to germinate under the influence of his readings in Kropotkin. There was much, for example, in the writings of Jean Grave that could appeal to a man who had originally modeled himself on the *bakumatsu shishi*. Grave's position on action – that 'action is the flowering of thought'[4] – was readily understandable to one who had studied the late Tokugawa emphasis on the relationship of knowledge to action. Moreover, Grave's 'propaganda by deed' – acts of violence carried out not for selfish motives but for the good of the whole laboring world[5] – were not far from the type of violence Kōtoku had applauded in his earlier study of assassination. Yet, while 'direct action' was perhaps more in keeping with the warrior values in which he had steeped himself as a young man, one cannot disregard the fact that parliamentarianism, too, had played a significant role in the creation of his youthful ideals. The rejection of this idea must have had its roots in something deeper.

---

[1] 'Sanfuranshisuko yori (VII)', *Senshū*, vol. III, pp. 287-8.   [2] *Ibid.*

[3] At the Second Convention of the I.W.W. (held in August 1906) the west coast radicals were defeated in their attempt to seize control of the organization. See Paul Frederick Brissenden, *The I.W.W.: A Study of American Syndicalism*, pp. 136ff.

[4] Grave, *Moribund Society and Anarchy*, p. 124.   [5] *Ibid.* p. 125.

For Kōtoku America had always symbolized a haven of democracy, freedom, and liberty. In the first flush of his arrival, breaking out of his personal despondency, it seemed to him that America was everything he had hoped for. Here was a country in which socialism had every chance to flower and grow.

Within a few months his evaluation of American democracy was to change drastically. Increased radicalism of the I.W.W. type had not gone unchallenged in the Bay Area; strikes and sabotage had led to police reprisals. Witnessing these, Kōtoku wrote in a more sober vein:

America is the country of democratic government and freedom. But even now her freedoms of speech, assembly, and the press are daily and monthly chipped away and stolen. All those who make the least attempt to violently oppose the present bourgeois government, religion, customs, or habits are subjected to severe persecutions. Here too, a few days ago, at a great rally held by the workers of San Francisco, many were clubbed down by the police and thrown into prison.[1]

By April he agreed with an American worker who told him that 'America is a land of liberty for the rich and the religious. The way the workers are oppressed and persecuted differs not the least from their treatment in Russia or Japan.'[2] 'Anglo-Saxon hypocrites', he wrote on the twenty-first of the same month in response to Gorki's treatment in New York, 'there is no country in the world that pretends to be as liberal, but is in fact as illiberal, as America.'[3]

With the hopes of a 'parliamentarian' solution to the worker's plight growing dim even in the American democratic setting (a setting which he considered in many ways more favorable for the growth of socialism than that of his homeland), the arguments of Mrs Fritz, Jean Grave, and his friends in the I.W.W. became more and more forceful. The tide of revolution seemed to be clearly moving in the direction of violence and 'direct action'.[4]

It was at this juncture that the cataclysmic events which engulfed San Francisco on April 18, 1906 were to confirm and cast a final seal on the metamorphosis of his thought which had begun in prison the year before.

On April 18, 1906, Kōtoku noted in his diary:

[1] *Nikki to shokan*, p. 233. [2] *Ibid.*

[3] 'Goruki to Beijin gizen', *Hikari*, no. 13 (May 20, 1906), p. 6. In *Meiji Shakai Shugi shiryō shū*, vol. II, p. 104. Gorki had come to New York with his mistress. The press made much of this and he was forced out of several hotels.

[4] Needless to say, events transpiring in Russia also confirmed this view. 'Isn't the Russian Revolution something to rejoice over?' he wrote in January after speaking at a sympathy rally held for the victims of the Bloody Sunday Massacre. Expecting the Russian Revolution to spread, he observed, 'Every corner of Europe will be entering an age of worker's revolutions.' *Nikki to shokan*, pp. 220–1.

Earthquake after 5 A.M. Fires started in numerous downtown areas. Hayes, too, is on fire. It has spread to the neighborhood of the Heiminsha. The members of the Heiminsha have taken refuge in a vacant lot nearby. Mrs Fritz and daughter are seeking refuge in another vacant area. Katō and I have bedded down in Mrs Fritz' house for the night. Can't sleep because we are constantly awakened by others.[1]

On April 19, he continued: 'Fires still haven't stopped. They're spreading out to all areas north and south of the downtown area...many have lost their homes and do not know where to flee...The terrible sight is beyond description.'[2] On April 20 he simply recorded: 'The fires still haven't ceased.'[3]

On the twenty-first, in the comparative safety of Oakland (where he had fled with Takeuchi Testugorō) Kōtoku wrote home to Koizumi Sanshin, Sakai Toshihiko and his wife, Chiyoko. Assuring them that he was well and unscathed, and describing to them how he had watched the 'grand sight' and 'magnificent spectacle' of San Francisco's destruction with binoculars from his room, he insisted that what he had witnessed was 'one of the rare events of history' not unlike Nero's burning of Rome.[4] At one point his letter grew almost rhapsodic: 'Aah! Fire! Wonderful, isn't it! Everywhere it turns there is no god, no wealth, no authority. The countless magnificent churches, the high and lofty city hall, the vast [amounts of] wealth and treasure – all have gone up in a rain of fire and ashes.'[5] The next instant he was more sober: 'Needless to say, hunger and cold followed. Unemployment also followed. A hundred thousand of the poor have been forced to taste bitter suffering. But all this is not the fault of the fire, this is the fault of today's social order alone.'[6]

Despite the destruction, despite the pain and suffering that it unleashed on the citizens of the San Francisco area, Kōtoku saw in the earthquake and its aftermath a momentary glimpse of the process of regeneration through which man would be freed from the fetters of the social order and once more given a chance to live by his true cooperative and communal instincts. Disregarding all evidence to the contrary – theft, looting, pilfering, and the hoarding of vital supplies, which necessitated the calling out of troops and the declaration of martial law – he was convinced that what he had seen was the transient flash of the new order that would someday replace capitalism everywhere.[7] Addressing his comrades in Tokyo he stated:

[1] *Nikki to shokan*, pp. 142–3.   [2] *Ibid.*   [3] *Ibid.*
[4] *Ibid.* pp. 234–5.   [5] *Ibid.* p. 235.   [6] *Ibid.*
[7] It is worth noting that the vision of a new order emerging spontaneously out of the ashes of the old was as much a part of the East Asian tradition in which Shūsui had been brought up, as it was a part of the anarchism of men like Kropotkin and Bakunin.

This terrible disaster in San Francisco afforded me a most valuable experience, which is none other than this: since the eighteenth of April the entire city of San Francisco has existed under a state of Anarchist Communism [*museifuteki kyōsan sei*].

Commerce is at a complete standstill; the mails, trains and ferries [of the vicinity] are completely free of charge. Food is distributed daily by a relief committee. All able-bodied men work as a matter of duty, transporting foodstuffs, caring for the sick and wounded, clearing up the fire's debris, and building shelters. Since there is nothing to buy, even if one wanted to, money has become totally useless. Property and private ownership has been completely eradicated. Interesting, isn't it? But this ideal paradise will continue for only a few more weeks before things will revert once more to the original capitalist system of private property. How regrettable.[1]

Within a few weeks Kōtoku was only too aware that San Francisco had returned to its former 'capitalist system'. Prices skyrocketed, and Kōtoku, whose small savings had gone up in smoke in one of the banks on Market Street, found himself in financial difficulties.[2]

Most of his Japanese friends were no better off. The majority left the city for Sacramento, Oakland, and other points. Kōtoku himself decided to go to Oakland, but even there prices were exorbitantly high and housing almost unattainable. After a long and fruitless search for a room, he was finally given shelter in the attic of a local Japanese church, where he bunked in dormitory fashion with a number of young men whom he was quick to engage in 'daily revolutionary discussions'.[3]

Early in May Kōtoku received an urgent request from his friends in Tokyo asking him to return to Japan.[4] In the spring of 1906 prospects for the Japanese socialist movement had suddenly improved. A period of recession had ushered in renewed labor unrest. Early in January the more liberal Prince Saionji, who had been in France with Nakae Chōmin and had drunk deeply from the wells of French liberalism, replaced the doctrinaire and sometimes heavy-handed General Katsura, as Prime Minister. By mid-February Sakai Toshihiko and Fukao Shō petitioned the new government to establish a socialist party. To their surprise their petition was granted, and on February 24 an organizational meeting for the Japanese Socialist Party (Nihon Shakai-tō) was held at the office of Katō Tokijirō.[5] A need was immediately felt for a newspaper which might speak in the name of the party, and Kōtoku represented the logical choice to head such a paper.

---

[1] *Nikki to shokan*, p. 236. [2] *Ibid.* [3] *Ibid.* p. 237.

[4] This was reported in *Hikari*, no. 14 (June 5, 1906), p. 1. In *Meiji Shakai Shugi shiryō shū*, vol. II, p. 107.

[5] For the details behind the establishment of the Nihon Shakai-tō see Akamatsu, *Nihon Shakai undō shi*, pp. 135ff. Also Kublin, *Asian Revolutionary*, pp. 190ff.

Coming at a time when financial difficulties seemed to necessitate an early return to Japan, Sakai's offer was welcomed by Kōtoku. On May 24 he wrote: 'I have decided to return to Japan on the fifth of June via the *Hong Kong Maru* and should arrive in Yokohama around the twenty-third. I intend to go to Tosa for a month or two to rest and recuperate, and then plan to start to work with vigor.'[1]

In the six months since his arrival Kōtoku had achieved most of the objectives he had set for his stay in the United States. There was, however, one item of unfinished business. It had always been his intention to leave behind a well-organized core of young Japanese radicals. This had been his goal in working with the young men of the Heiminsha. But many of these had been scattered by the earthquake. In his final weeks he devoted himself to salvaging the remnant of the movement. By concentrating on two radicals, Iwasa Sakutarō and Takeuchi Tetsugorō, Kōtoku molded what was left of his following into the Social Revolutionary Party of Oakland (Okurando no Shakai Kakumei tō). The party was officially inaugurated on June first with a declaration written by Kōtoku.

Four days later, to the well wishes of the members of this party, Albert Johnson, and other friends (including two government 'spies'),[2] Kōtoku sailed for Honolulu and home.

---

[1] This letter can be found in *Hikari*, no. 15 (June 20, 1906), p. 7; *Meiji Shakai Shugi shiryō shū* vol. II, p. 121.

[2] That Kōtoku's activities in San Francisco remained under government surveillance is clear from the compilation of *Zai Bei Shakai Shugi sha – Museifu Shugi sha enkaku*. The work was basically a 'top secret' history of Japanese radicals in San Francisco from 1906 to 1911. After World War II a mimeographed version of this work came into the possession of Suzuki Shigesaburō. It was recently published under the auspices of the Shakai Bunko (Tokyo, 1964). On the opening page of the published version of this history there is a picture showing Kōtoku's departure. Two of the men surrounding him are identified as government 'spies'.

CHAPTER 6

Direct action, 1906–07

KŌTOKU'S SHIP, the *Hong Kong Maru*, docked at Yokohama on June 23, 1906. Little more than six months had elapsed since his departure in November of the previous year. In the meantime much had changed, both within the Japanese socialist movement as well as in the mind of its leading theoretician. For most Japanese socialists the establishment of the Japanese Socialist Party paved the way for a new parliamentary struggle. For Kōtoku such a struggle was already confined to the rubbish heap of history. Only 'direct action' by workers which bypassed the quicksand of representative assemblies promised hope for the future. For him the tide of revolution was clear and distinct. It was a tide not only for the movement, but a personal tide as well. San Francisco had revived his personal quest for liberty. Despondency had transformed itself into a new feeling of confidence. Caught up in the surging tide of his own psychic fluctuations, Kōtoku was not content with minor tinkerings and readjustments, whether in the realm of parliamentary socialism or in the areas that governed his personal life. Again total in his demands, he was more concerned with freedom than with a gradual increase in material well-being.

In his last letter from San Francisco Kōtoku had written his friends in Tokyo requesting that they arrange a lecture meeting for him so that he might report on his trip to the United States. On June 28, to the 'thunderous applause' of an audience of seven hundred who gathered at the Kinkikan in Kanda, Kōtoku strode to the platform and delivered the summation of his experiences in San Francisco. The speech was aptly titled, 'The Tide of the World Revolutionary Movement'.[1]

Kōtoku began his speech by assuring his listeners that his 'ideals' had not altered in the year since his imprisonment. In essence he was still a socialist. It was only in the area of tactics, in the means to the realization of his ideals,

---

[1] 'The Tide of the World Revolutionary Movement' ('Sekai kakumei undō no chōryū') was first published in *Hikari*, no. 16 (July 5, 1906), p. 1, *Meiji Shakai Shugi shiryō shū*, vol. II, p. 123. Also *Senshū*, vol. III, pp. 66–71. The contents of this speech are also partially covered by Nobutaka Ike in 'Kōtoku: Advocate of Direct Action', *The Far Eastern Quarterly*, vol. III, no. 3 (May, 1944), pp. 222ff.

that he had undergone a transformation. He insisted, moreover, that this transformation was one in progress among revolutionaries the world over. 'The socialist party is a revolutionary party,' he hammered home, 'its movement is a revolutionary movement.'[1] He furthermore used Marx and Engels to show that such a party must be committed to 'support every revolutionary movement against the existing social and political order', and it must not shy away from the 'use of force' when necessary.[2]

Kōtoku tried to convince his audience that the trouble with the socialist movement lay in the fact that while socialism had originated as a revolutionary force in France, much of its revolutionary fervor had been destroyed by the current of reaction which swept Europe in the wake of the Franco-Prussian War. The defeat of the Paris Commune and the rise of Bismarck ushered in the new strategy of parliamentary struggle. The barricades were abandoned for the ballot. But this was a sop, a trick, a means of duping socialists. In many ways it represented the capitulation of the idealistic, progressive, and democratic traditions of France to the conservative, authoritarian, and military traditions of Germany. It was in these dark circumstances that socialism came to identify itself as a peaceful, lawful, parliamentary force. What it had in effect done was to sell out its revolutionary heritage for the lentils of parliamentary compromise. And what had it gained? To be certain, the German Social Democratic Party, upon which most Japanese had been willing to model the first Japanese socialist party in 1901, had been able to elect numerous representatives to parliament, but what had they achieved?

The German Socialist Party with its three million, five hundred thousand votes, the German Socialist Party with its ninety representatives in parliament! What after all has it accomplished? Is [Germany] not as much a militarist and dictatorial state as before? Is it not the same degenerate society as before? Is it not extremely insufficient to rely on votes?[3]

These, according to Kōtoku, were questions which socialists around the world were asking. Everywhere small groups of anarchists were beginning to awaken from the stupor of three decades of compromise, and were returning to the original revolutionary ideals of their movement.

Our comrades in Europe and America [he stated] have come to feel strongly of late that the so-called constitutional, peaceful, and lawful movement – the reliance on a majority of votes and seats in parliament – is worthless in the face of the financial, military, and police powers available to today's royalty and bourgeoisie.[4]

---

[1] *Meiji Shakai Shugi shiryō shū*, vol. II, p. 123.   [2] *Ibid.*   [3] *Ibid.*
[4] *Ibid.* The position taken here was, in fact, an extension of the arguments he had personally worked out at the time of the *Heimin Shimbun*'s demise in the winter of 1904-5. At that time he had

But how were socialists to achieve their goals without parliamentary tactics? Were they to arm themselves for the fight with daggers, spears, bombs, and straw flags?[1] Was this what he meant by 'direct action?' No, Kōtoku replied, these constituted the weapons of the past. The means which radical socialists would rely on in the future would have nothing to do with 'useless violence'. Instead, he continued, what was needed were strikes by the workers, leading eventually to one great 'General Strike':

It will be totally sufficient for the mass of the workers to join hands and do absolutely nothing for several days or several weeks, or perhaps even several months. If they stop all movement of the organs of production and communication in their society it would be sufficient. In short, the means of accomplishing the revolution lie in the execution of a General Strike.[2]

Throughout his speech Kōtoku made it clear that his sympathies lay with the 'idealistic, progressive, and popular' traditions of France, and not with the 'peaceful, lawful, and constitutional' traditions which had arisen under the influence of the German reaction. Thus, in many ways Kōtoku's earlier ideas on the continuing revolution towards liberty, equality, and fraternity, which he had gotten from Chōmin and which he had applied to the Meiji Restoration, were to be expanded and set into an international framework.

Japan, too, had undergone an original 'revolutionary' phase. The carriers of that phase had been the Restoration *shishi* and the members of the Popular Rights Movement, and yet these 'revolutionaries' had also allowed themselves to be duped into parliamentary action by an increasingly autocratic and authoritarian government which modeled itself on the Germany of Bismarck and the reaction. Under the corrosive influence of the *hanbatsu* government, the fire of the Japanese revolution had gone out, just as it had gone out in Europe.

The Japanese socialist movement had been born under the reaction. Few of its members possessed ties with the revolutionary past. What was

written: 'We confess here that we have little strength and are totally incapable of opposing such persecutions. We have neither financial power, schemes, nor influence. We have not a single mouth to serve as a dagger, nor a clod of earth to serve as a bomb. In fact, we possess nothing that might serve as a weapon with which to resist the government. We are truly individuals with nothing but our so-called bare hands. Therefore, if the government wants to suppress us by spending vast sums of money which it has received through taxes from the people, or by means of its police force or army, it is truly a simple matter. Furthermore, today, when parliament, the press, and general public opinion have all ceased to value liberty and people's rights, what illegal actions are there that the government cannot carry out?' 'Shakai Shugi ni okeru hakugai to sono kōka', *Heimin Shimbun*, no. 63 (January 22, 1905).

[1] Straw flags were traditional symbols of revolt used in Japanese peasant uprisings.
[2] *Meiji Shakai Shugi shiryō shū*, vol. II, p. 123.

necessary now was to purge the movement of its ideological desire for compromise with the forces of reaction which had already destroyed the original revolution. What was needed, therefore, was not the acceptance of parliamentary tactics, but a return to the true revolutionary spirit of 'direct action' which was to be incorporated in the new tactic of the General Strike. In league with their European and American comrades, Kōtoku believed, Japanese socialists should avoid the doldrums of parliamentary participation, and move directly to a new age. The Japanese worker would carry out his own revolution. What was important to the worker was the seizure of bread, not the seizure of parliament.

Having taken his stand for the 'direct action' of the working classes and the rejection of parliamentarianism, Kōtoku retired to the hospital of Katō Tokijirō. A few days later he withdrew to his native village in Tosa, hoping that the warm climate and familiar surroundings of Nakamura might benefit his lingering stomach ailment.[1]

While Kōtoku tried to regain his health in the south, the Japanese Socialist Party, led by Sakai, Nishikawa, and Katayama, maintained its propagation of socialism within the 'limits of the law', a policy which it had publicly expressed at the time of its founding in February. Despite Kōtoku's emphasis on 'direct action', the meetings and discussion groups of the party – as well as the speeches of most socialist leaders – continued to uphold the basic parliamentary strategy adopted early in 1906.

Moreover, the summer of 1906 found Japanese socialists much too busy to concern themselves with ideological disputes. The postwar recession had created considerable labor unrest. Taxes remained high because of Japan's war debts. And in the midst of growing public discontent, the municipal railway companies of Tokyo called for a fare hike that promised to double the cost of transportation for most of the city's inhabitants. Socialists were staunchly opposed to a fare increase and organized public opinion through rallies in Hibiya Park. After one such rally in April a crowd of over a thousand descended on the Tokyo municipal offices and the headquarters of the street car company. Before long the crowd had turned into an ugly mob which attacked government buildings and smashed streetcar windows. The police were called out and numerous socialists were arrested (including Nishikawa Kōjirō, Yamaguchi Kōken, and Ōsugi Sakae).[2] Further protest rallies were

[1] Soon after his return to Japan, Kōtoku's illness took a decided turn for the worse. It is not clear whether Katō Tokijirō's diagnosis at the time indicated tuberculosis of the intestines, but later it became quite clear that this was the disease from which Kōtoku was suffering.

[2] For the details of this episode see Akamatsu, *Nihon shakai undō shi*, pp. 137ff.

outlawed and the government temporarily suspended its approval of the fare increase. When, after a period of relative calm, the streetcar fares were increased, socialists organized a boycott. Under the circumstances, the spark of debate between social democrats and 'direct actionists', which Kōtoku had touched off with his speech in June, was allowed to smolder.

Despite his isolation in Tosa, Kōtoku did not hesitate to push for a truly 'revolutionary' party. Writing to Ishikawa Sanshirō from Nakamura he noted that there were always two types of political parties. One worked through parliaments and required a majority of votes to come into power, the other – the truly revolutionary party – never relied on parliaments. This, he pointed out, was true of the old Jiyūtō, the Russian Social Revolutionary Party, and the various anarchist parties of Europe. Echoing his earlier theme, he insisted that participation in parliamentary politics sounded the death-knell for any truly revolutionary party. 'I do not know the intricacies of the origins and histories of political parties' he wrote, 'but I was an eye witness to the way in which the power of the Jiyūtō originally destroyed our own autocratic regime. And yet, no sooner was a parliament established than the old Jiyūtō totally died.'[1]

In stating the reasons for the Jiyūtō's death, Kōtoku realized that he was repudiating a part of his own past. The Jiyūtō, he confessed, had been a party of brilliant and ambitious men of warrior origins. It was exactly for this reason that it had failed. 'The revolution does not depend on brilliance', he wrote. Instead, what it depends on is 'the little man'. It was to the little man that the socialist movement must address itself. For Kōtoku, who had admired Yoshida Shōin and Lassalle, and who for many years had chafed under the weight of his own political ambitions, such statements represented a new attempt to break with the past. Moreover, unlike earlier insights of a similar nature, his new convictions were backed up by concerted efforts to reach the common man.[2]

By the autumn of 1906, despite an incomplete recovery, Kōtoku decided to return to Tokyo. For weeks Sakai had been urging him to help with the badly-needed paper. Time was of the essence, and the summer months had already dragged by without a socialist mouthpiece. Once more in Tokyo,

---

[1] Letter to Ishikawa Sanshirō originally published in *Shin Kigen*, September 10, 1906. *Nikki to shokan*, pp. 240-2.

[2] Kōtoku's attempt to reach the workers and farmers of Japan after this period is usually underplayed by those who emphasize his aristocratic bearings. No doubt Kōtoku found it difficult to associate with the common man, but he did make the effort by travelling on extensive speaking tours in his own Hata district. He also wrote to Kinoshita that hereafter they would have to give up not only their 'ambitions for worldly fame' but also their 'literary talents' so that they might win over 'illiterate peasants and workers'. *Nikki to shokan*, p. 406.

Kōtoku addressed himself to the challenge of founding a new paper. By December, despite a serious relapse which virtually confined him to his bed, he was able to write to Albert Johnson: 'The preparation for the Socialist daily is almost completed. I hope the daily will have a success. The Japanese Socialist Party consists, as you know, of many different elements. Social-Democrats, Social Revolutionists, and even Christian Socialists. So the daily would be a very strange paper.'[1]

As Kōtoku pointed out, the new paper represented a variety of socialist positions. Inner tensions were present from the start, and with time, these, as much as government pressures, brought about the paper's downfall.[2] The second, or daily, *Heimin Shimbun* began on an auspicious note, however, and, despite the ideological misgivings of its editorial board, sold over 30,000 copies of its first edition. 'This fact proves', the editors stated in their English column, 'that the influence of socialism in Japan is on the increase.'[3] It was also a fact which substantially impressed the metropolitan police department – already alerted to increased socialist activities by the unrest of the previous summer. A conference of local police chiefs was immediately organized to consider the best means of dealing with the new socialist threat.[4]

There were additional reasons for the police and government authorities to become concerned with socialists in general, and the more radical 'direct actionists' who gathered around Kōtoku in particular.

On December 20 the group of young radicals, which Kōtoku had molded into the Social Revolutionary Party of Oakland a few days before his departure for Japan, published the first issue of their paper, *The Revolution (Kakumei)* in San Francisco. In a declaration more in line with Kōtoku's rejection of the parliamentary struggle, as well as his belief in 'direct action', the paper stated:

At the present time poverty increases at a terrific pace while the concentration of wealth in the institution of the Trust continues. We believe that such a thing as the trifling legislation which the capitalist class may from time to time fling to the workers will prove of no avail...Our policy is toward the overthrow of Mikado, King, President as representing the Capitalist Class as soon as possible, and we do not hesitate as to the means.[5]

---

[1] *Nikki to shokan*, p. 440.

[2] For an outline of the *Nikkan Heimin Shimbun*'s history, see Hosokawa Karoku, *et al.*, *Nihon Shakai Shugi bunken kaisetsu*, pp. 65ff.

[3] *Nikkan Heimin Shimbun*, no. 2 (January 20, 1907), p. 1. In *Meiji Shakai Shugi shiryō shū*, vol. IV, p. 13.

[4] *Ibid.*

[5] *Kakumei*, no. 1 (December 20, 1906), p. 1. In Shakai Bunko (ed.), *Zai Bei Shakai Shugi sha – Museifu Shugi sha enkaku*, p. 462.

During normal times this declaration written by a handful of radicals living in obscure poverty in a boarding house in Berkeley would no doubt have gone unnoticed. With time the Japanese government would have most likely received a report on the activities of the group through its 'spies' operating out of the San Francisco consulate. Such a report would have been filed away for future reference with the other materials being gathered on the activities of Japanese radicals abroad. Perhaps, in the end, it might have been forgotten like so much of the information gathered by the government.

But 1906 was hardly a normal year in Japanese–American relations. Tensions between the two countries had begun to mount. At the root of these tensions lay the immigration problem, which had resulted in widespread discrimination against Japanese settlers and laborers in California.[1] The already tense situation was aggravated further by the San Francisco School Board's decision in October to require Japanese children to attend segregated schools.

The School Board's decision elicited an immediate and strong protest from the Japanese government. Most Japanese considered the Board's action an affront to their national honor, an affront which Japan, still experiencing the elation of victory in her test of strength with Russia, was not willing to accept without retribution. For a time there was talk of war on both sides of the Pacific. But neither the American President nor the Japanese government favored such a drastic course of action. While Roosevelt set out to deal with the San Francisco School Board through his own brand of personal diplomacy, the Japanese government determined to preserve an atmosphere of calm in order to facilitate a negotiated settlement.

It was at this juncture that the first issue of *The Revolution* made its appearance. It took ten days for the editors of the *San Francisco Chronicle*, the paper which spearheaded the anti-Japanese drive, to hear about the publication, but when they did they made the most of their find. On December 30 the *Chronicle* ran a full banner headline reading, 'Secret Service Men on Trail of Japanese Publishers'. In a subtitle it went on to state, 'Japs Favor Killing of President Roosevelt', 'Anarchist Paper Advocates Assassination of All Rulers', 'Vicious Publication is Aimed at All Who Are in Authority'. In addition to the headline, much of the front page was taken up with pictures of the paper, including a portrait of Oka Shigeki to whom the article was falsely attributed and K. Ueno, the Japanese Consul.[2]

---

[1] For the details of this problem, see Thomas A. Bailey, *Theodore Roosevelt and the Japanese–American Crisis*, pp. 46ff.
[2] The article was written by Takeuchi Tetsugorō, not Oka. Oka did, however, publish the first

In the days that followed, the *Chronicle* made every effort to exploit the incident to show that Japanese immigrants represented a threat not only to West Coast labor and agriculture, but to Roosevelt and the American government as well. Federal authorities, for their part, played the matter down and wrote it off as a juvenile prank not worthy of the federal government's attention.

In the meantime, Japanese officials in Tokyo showed greater concern. While it soon became apparent that Washington was not going to allow the incident to interfere with negotiations on the immigration question, and that the matter was not going to affect foreign policy goals, the fact that a group of Japanese had openly threatened violence against the Emperor was a disturbing one for most government authorities. What was even more disturbing about the incident was the fact that the activities of the Social Revolutionary Party of Oakland appeared to be directly linked to the recently organized Japanese Socialist Party in Tokyo. Even the *Chronicle* had made it quite clear that the Japanese Socialist Party 'stands sponsor for *The Revolution (Kakumei)*'.[1]

Whether Kōtoku was directly responsible for the provocative language contained in the *The Revolution* remains a moot point. Certainly the position later adopted in the *The Revolution* (that the whole Imperial Institution represented nothing more than myth) was similar to the stand taken by Kōtoku after his imprisonment in 1905. Moreover, while in San Francisco Kōtoku's anti-imperial sentiments could be as extreme as anything which appeared in *The Revolution*. In a conversation with Oka, Kōtoku is recorded to have stated that in order to introduce new social ideas into Japan it would be necessary to destroy the traditional belief in the divinity of the Emperor, and that the most effective way of achieving this would be to assassinate him in order to demonstrate that he was mortal.[2] To what extent the government was aware of statements of this nature remains unknown, but it is clear that government authorities, quite naturally, linked him with the actions of the Social Revolutionary Party of Oakland which, after all, it was no secret he had founded.

If January 1907 found the government concerned about Japanese radical

issue of *The Revolution* on a press belonging to the San Francisco Heiminsha. Oka had obtained the press and type through Kōtoku's help – he had accompanied Kōtoku back to Japan for this purpose. Kōtoku may well have intended to set up a 'radical' printing office in San Francisco.

[1] *San Francisco Chronicle*, Sunday, December 30, 1906, p. 29.

[2] According to Oka, Kōtoku made this statement in a private conversation. The statement was told to Nobutaka Ike by Oka and appears in 'Kōtoku: Advocate of Direct Action', *The Far Eastern Quarterly*, vol. III, no. 3 (May, 1944), p. 225. Oka gave a similar account of Kōtoku's position to Arahata Kanson. See *Kanson jiden*, p. 191.

activities abroad, February returned the government's attention to domestic issues. In three days of spontaneous and uninterrupted violence thirty-six hundred outraged farmers and miners using dynamite and arson virtually destroyed the Furukawa copper mines at Ashio in Tochigi Prefecture. After troops were called in and martial law declared, the rioters were finally forced to surrender, but not before they had done several million dollars worth of damage.

Japanese socialists had long pointed to the Ashio mines as prime examples of heartless exploitation, not only of the mine workers, whose conditions were deplorable, but of the farmers of the area, whose lands were slowly being destroyed by the uncontrolled pollution of the surrounding streams and rivers by mine wastes. Although control measures had been annually suggested in the lower house of the Diet for nearly ten years, little action had been taken, and with no changes in sight desperation had exploded in a destructive rampage. Faced with the fruits of its own lack of social concern, the government was quick to blame socialists (especially the *Heimin Shimbun*) for fomenting the unrest.

The Ashio riots represented the first large-scale outbreak of violence in the history of the Japanese labor movement. This fact impressed Kōtoku as much as it did the Saionji Cabinet. It was probably no coincidence that he published on the fifth of February, in the midst of the rioting, his own 'Change of Thought' ('Yo ga shisō no henka'), which represented a clear-cut rejection of parliamentary tactics in favor of 'direct action' and the General Strike.

Kōtoku's 'Change of Thought' was an expansion of the ideas he had presented earlier in his speech on the tide of the world revolutionary movement. While much of his thought was based on theory acquired in the West, this theory now became united with ideas which he had been testing experientially for the past ten years.

'I will confess honestly', he wrote in the daily *Heimin Shimbun*, 'my views with regard to the policies of the socialist movement have changed a good deal after travel abroad last year, and when I look back a few years, I myself feel as if I were another person.'[1] His conclusions were clear-cut: 'We cannot by any means achieve a real revolution in society through universal suffrage, and by policies in the Diet. There is no other course but to depend on the "direct action" of the workers who are united in order to achieve the aims of socialism.'[2]

[1] *Nikkan Heimin Shimbun*, no. 16 (February 5, 1907), p. 1. In *Meiji Shakai Shugi shiryō shū*, vol. IV, p. 69.
[2] *Ibid.*

The reasons for this appeal to 'direct action' were much the same as those already elaborated in his earlier speech. Once again he traced the historical development of parliamentary socialism; once again he reiterated not only its failure to achieve the revolution, that is to say the abolition of the wage system and the fundamental reorganization of the social order, but went on to elaborate in detail the extent to which parliamentary participation and a dependence on universal suffrage corrupted the ideals of all revolutionary movements which allowed themselves to be pulled into the system.

Reaffirming the weakness of the individual to withstand the pressures of his environment, a weakness of which he was all too well aware personally, Kōtoku insisted that even the most idealistic of individuals was subject to corruption by the influence of parliamentary politics. Once elected, the social-ist candidate all too frequently turned against his own ideals. Instead of fighting for the interests of his fellow workers, all he cared for was his own fame, power, and profit. Look at Millerand in France! Dulled in fervor, aping the ways of the bourgeoisie, such individuals would be of no use to the socialist movement at the time of the revolution. This was true not only of those in parliament, but also of those who had elected them to their posts. 'Three million [Germans] who have been trained with elections as their objectives are of no use in a revolution,' he insisted, 'when they are told "It is the revolution! Rise!" they will say that this is not what they expected; that if voting is of no use they will have to think it over.'[1]

Somehow socialists would have to be able to maintain their purity, and this he felt could be accomplished best by refusing to participate in the parliamentary world which was the creation of the middle classes. Rather than spend their money on election campaigns and on the passage of a uni-versal suffrage bill, Kōtoku insisted it would be far wiser to educate and organ-ize the workers:

What the workers desire is not the conquest of political power, but the 'conquest of bread', not laws, but food and clothing...I, at least, as a socialist, and as a member of the Socialist Party, believe that as far as the accomplishment of our goal, which is the fundamental revolution of the economic order and the abolition of the wage system, it is far more important to arouse the self-consciousness of ten workers, than to gather a thousand signatures on a petition for universal suffrage. It is far better to spend ten yen organizing workers than a thousand yen on an election campaign. One simple conversation with workers, I am convinced, is worth more than ten lofty speeches in parliament.[2]

If workers were truly conscious and united, there would be nothing which

---

[1] *Nikkan Heimin Shimbun*, no. 16 (February 5, 1907), p. 1. In *Meiji Shakai Shugi shiryō shū*, vol. iv, p. 69.
[2] *Ibid.*

they could not achieve through their own 'direct action'. 'My friends,' he concluded, 'it is for these reasons that I hope our Japanese socialist movement will abandon its policy of working through the Diet, and will make the "direct action" of organized workers its only course of action.'[1]

For Kōtoku the break with parliamentarianism involved more than a mere rejection of one revolutionary tactic for another. In many ways parliamentarianism had become associated in his own life with years of ambivalence and compromise; perhaps it was this association which added a moralizing tone to his arguments. Kōtoku had never been able to accept compromise as anything other than moral degradation. Parliamentarianism's greatest fault lay in the fact that it destroyed the spirit; instead of lifting, it lowered the goals of its idealistic participants, whether these came from the socialist movement or from the old Jiyūtō made little difference, all were subject to the environmental pressures of the institution. In 'direct action', on the other hand, Kōtoku seems to have visualized new hopes for a totally pure existence. Here, at last, was the bridge between the ideals of his youth and his hopes for the future.

Kōtoku's 'Change of Thought' brought to flame the controversy between Social Democrats and Anarchists which had been smoldering since his arrival in Yokohama six months earlier. The ensuing battle came to be fought not only in the pages of the *Heimin Shimbun*, but also in the sessions of the first annual convention of the Japanese Socialist Party which met in the middle of February.

Kōtoku's principal opponent in his bid to sway the Socialist Party to adopt a platform more in keeping with his 'direct action' ideals was Tazoe Tetsuji, who, in Katayama Sen's absence,[2] became the chief spokesman for the social-democratic wing of the movement.

In an article appearing in the *Heimin Shimbun* Tazoe challenged Kōtoku's interpretation of the tide of the world-wide revolutionary movement.[3] Tazoe maintained that, contrary to Kōtoku's assertions, parliamentary action was not only still the prevalent socialist tactic in the West, but clearly offered the best means of assuring a bright future for the workers.

With the ideological lines clearly drawn the two sides gathered for a showdown battle before their fellow socialists at the Kinkikan in Kanda,

---

[1] *Ibid.*

[2] Katayama had left Japan for the United States in July 1906 and did not return until February 19, two days after the annual meeting of the *Nihon Shakai-tō*. See Kublin, *Asian Revolutionary*, pp. 193ff.

[3] 'Gikai seisaku ron', *Nikkan Heimin Shimbun*, no. 24 (February 14, 1907), p. 1. In *Meiji Shakai Shugi shiryō shū*, vol. IV, p. 101.

where the annual convention of the Japanese Socialist Party met. After two days of speeches by Kōtoku, Tazoe, Sakai, and others, the conflict finally hardened into a struggle over the official resolution to be adopted by the party.

Sakai, fully aware of the dangers inherent in the confrontation, made every effort to work out an acceptable compromise. As Chairman of the Executive Committee of the Party he had gone out of his way to draw up a draft resolution that might accommodate both Kōtoku and Tazoe. Skirting most of the major issues, the resolution declared simply that the Socialist Party stands for 'the fundamental reform of the social system' which is to be achieved through the 'public ownership of all the means of production, and their management for the happiness and well being of the public at large'.[1] Four specific means of achieving these goals under the 'existing circumstances' followed. The first of these stated, 'Our party endeavors to awaken the workers' class consciousness and exerts itself in their organization and training.' The second stated that the Socialist Party sympathized with the rioters at the Ashio Copper Mines, and disparaged the government's use of force to quell the miners' dissent. The third placed the Japanese Socialist Party squarely behind 'all the world's revolutionary movements' with whose 'aspirations' it 'sympathized deeply'. And finally, it suggested four areas of socialist activity – the reform of the Peace Police Law, the movement for universal suffrage, disarmament, and the movement against religion – in which socialists might wish to participate at their own discretion.

Sakai's hopes to prevent a split among the delegates by presenting a resolution acceptable to both social democrats and 'direct actionists' were quickly shattered. No sooner was the draft presented than Tazoe called for an amendment which was to add the clause, 'our party recognizes parliamentary participation as an effective means of action'. Kōtoku immediately countered with an amendment of his own which would have inserted the clause, 'our party recognizes the uselessness of parliamentary participation, and solely endeavors to awaken the class consciousness of the workers, making every effort to train and organize them'.[2]

Before a final vote was taken the opposing sides were allowed to speak in behalf of their positions. Kōtoku's plea for the adoption of his amendment was to prove one of the most impressive speeches of the convention. As Sakai

[1] The proceedings of the convention, as well as the resolution – in both its draft and final form – were published in the February 19, 1907, issue of the *Heimin Shimbun*. See *Meiji Shakai Shugi shiryō shū*, vol. IV, p. 119.
[2] *Ibid.*

later recalled: 'Contending in ill health with bitter cold, he fought for the adoption of his new position. Swept by waves of emotion, sparks flashing from his eyes and fire erupting from his mouth, ever stronger, ever swifter, he cast a spell over the entire audience for almost an hour.'[1]

By comparison with Kōtoku's emotionalism Tazoe's speech seemed cold and rational. When the voting came, it was clear which approach proved more appealing to the delegates. Tazoe's motion received two votes; Kōtoku's twenty-two. But even Kōtoku's twenty-two votes were not enough to carry the day, and the Executive Committee's draft was finally approved by an eight-vote margin.

While Kōtoku had not won an outright victory in his attempt to move the party towards a policy of 'direct action', his twenty-two votes were sufficient to prevent the inclusion of the clause 'within the limits of the law' in the party's platform. Moreover, in its emphasis on the organization and support of the radical activities of workers, in its support of world-wide revolutionary movements, and in its backing of strikes and labor violence along the lines of the Ashio riots, the program of the party had in effect followed his lead toward greater radicalism.

Needless to say, this new tone of the Socialist Party did not escape the watchful eyes of the government and police authorities. Already alerted to Kōtoku's influence on the Social Revolutionary Party of Oakland through the incident of the previous month, these authorities were not only concerned by the fact that the Socialist Party appeared to be throwing its weight behind labor violence at a time of intense economic unrest, but that having dropped the very pretense of operating 'within the limits of the law', the movement, under Kōtoku's leadership, might develop into one that threatened the Imperial Institution itself.

Unknown to Kōtoku, though sensed by Sakai and some of the less idealistic members of the movement, the question of socialism, and what was to be done with this potentially disruptive foreign ideology, had become one of the major points of dissension between Yamagata Aritomo and the Saionji government. Despite his increasing years, Yamagata was still one of the most powerful men in Japanese politics. Intensely loyal to the Throne, he looked with extreme suspicion on any group that questioned the position of the Emperor. Socialists, he was convinced, posed a subversive threat,

---

[1] Sakai Toshihiko, 'Shakai-tō Taikai no Ketsugi', in *Sakai Toshihiko zenshū*, vol. III, p. 274. I have used the Kublin translation found in *Asian Revolutionary*, p. 195. Kublin erroneously states that this description originally appeared in the *Heimin Shimbun* on February 17, 1907. A very abbreviated version, not under the above title, appears in the issue of February 19.

and he had made certain that Katsura, his protégé as Prime Minister from 1901 to 1906, had taken sufficiently strong measures to keep them in check.

Saionji's more liberal stance on the issue of socialism had done little to ingratiate him in the eyes of Yamagata. In fact, his decision to allow socialists to organize a legal party was interpreted by Yamagata as a personal affront.[1] Saionji, on the other hand, was convinced that as long as the Socialist Party continued to operate as a lawful body and was willing to comply with the 'limits of the law', socialism presented no threat to the Throne or the national polity.

The new policy of the Japanese Socialist Party, particularly its shunning of legal restrictions in favor of spontaneous violence, and the clandestine relationship of some of its members to anti-imperial extremism in San Francisco, left the Saionji Cabinet in a difficult position. In order to protect its political future against the Yamagata faction's mounting attack against its 'soft' policy on the 'socialist question', particularly after the Streetcar Incident and the Ashio riots, the Saionji Cabinet had little choice but to take a stiffer posture towards socialists.

On February 22, 1907, three days after the adjournment of its convention, Saionji ordered the dissolution of the Japanese Socialist Party. As under the Katsura regime, legal proceedings were once more initiated against the socialists' paper. By April the daily *Heimin Shimbun* was fighting four separate court actions.[2] Racked by internal dissent (which had grown after Katayama's return) and in financial difficulties as usual, the paper had in fact ceased to function as an effective voice for the 'unified' movement. With a good part of its staff already imprisoned, and many of those who remained destined for a similar fate, the paper voluntarily dissolved itself on April 14, 1907.

For most Japanese socialists looking on the events of early 1907 with historical hindsight, the Socialist Party's rejection of a clear-cut commitment to parliamentary action constituted a tactical error of gargantuan proportions. Arahata Kanson, later one of Japan's best known communists, was highly critical of Kōtoku's position. So too was Katayama Sen, who not only considered it a tactical blunder, but feared that Kōtoku's ideas, because of their novelty and complexity, might well serve to increase the gap between radical

---

[1] Shirayanagi Shūko, *Saionji Kimmochi den*, p. 528.

[2] The four cases involved: (1) the publication of the Socialist Party resolution; (2) an 'Insult to government officials'; (3) an article by Yamaguchi Kōken titled 'Kick Your Parents' (March 27, 1907); and (4) the publication of Kropotkin's 'Appeal to the Young'. For details see *Nikkan Heimin Shimbun*, no. 75 (April 14, 1907), pp. 2-3. *Meiji Shakai Shugi shiryō shū*, vol. IV, pp. 306-7.

intellectuals and the working class.[1] As Arahata later pointed out, it was extremely 'unrealistic' and 'idealistic' to imagine that Japanese workers could band together to carry out a General Strike in 1907.[2] Organized workers to whom Kōtoku directed his appeal were virtually nonexistent. Class consciousness among the working populace was underdeveloped. And the extent of workers' participation in the Socialist Party was reflected in the fact that of the twenty new councilors elected by the party at its convention in 1907 not one was a worker from a modern industry.[3] Under the circumstances, Arahata stated somewhat scornfully: 'Suppose that the Socialist Party had settled on a policy of "direct action". It would have been as if there were plenty of commanding generals without troops to move.'[4]

Arahata has furthermore pointed out that the socialists' only reasonable hope for success in the first decade of this century rested in their ability to revise the Peace Police Law (in order to facilitate unionism), and to gain freedom of speech, assembly, and the press for socialists in order to make effective agitation possible. All these, he insisted, required a political struggle, which like any political struggle would have necessitated compromise with those in power.[5]

But Kōtoku saw the situation in a different light. For him the government's destruction of the party and the paper confirmed what he had been predicting all along: namely, that when faced with ultimate government authority, any movement depending solely on the good will of a parliamentary regime could be struck down at any moment. In Kōtoku's eyes the loss of a party, or the loss of a paper, was of infinitesimal significance. What mattered was the loss of 'spirit', the will to revolution. As he wrote in the final issue of the daily *Heimin Shimbun*:

Now we have lost our political organization. We have lost our central organ. Our movement will be broken to pieces for the present. *But the spirit of revolution is now deeply implanted in the minds of people.* We may be sure that the day will come when we can raise our voice again so loudly that it will ring out from one end of the country to the other and will make the ruling class tremble under our feet.[6] [Italics added.]

One may well question the extent to which the 'spirit of revolution' had been 'implanted' in the minds of the Japanese 'people'. As in so many other cases, Kōtoku's declaration was more of a personal credo inductively extended

---

[1] Kublin, *Asian Revolutionary*, p. 196.
[2] Arahata Kanson, *Kanson jiden*, p. 143.
[3] *Ibid.*   [4] *Ibid.*   [5] *Ibid.*
[6] *Nikkan Heimin Shimbun*, no. 75 (April 14, 1907), p. 2. In *Meiji Shakai Shugi shiryō shū*, vol. IV, p. 306.

to the world at large than one deduced from the existing circumstances. What he in effect asserted was his own spiritual conversion to the revolution. As in other instances of spiritual transformation, Kōtoku's conversion was not complete until the effort had been made to convert others.

It is worth noting that much of Kōtoku's thought on revolution and the revolutionary involved a search for original purity. On the side of revolution as a whole this meant a return to the 'original' ideas of revolutionary activity, whether in the sense of the Japanese revolutionary of the *shishi* or *jiyū minken undō* type, or the French type, which had manned the barricades of the Commune. On the side of personal action there was a distinct sense of returning to the ideals of his youth. Both involved a strong longing for innocence, an unwillingness to accept compromise, and the desire for total, not piecemeal, solutions.

Perhaps the greatest failure of Kōtoku's conversion to 'direct action' involved his inability to see the revolution in a new light. Even as an Anarchist Communist, Kōtoku only momentarily visualized revolution as something other than an inevitable historical process, which man could do little to alter. In effect his basic attitudes towards the natural and the historical had not changed. While the debunking of myth had occupied his attention in such areas as religion, the state, and even the Imperial Institution, it had never extended itself to the basic natural order. Man was still dwarfed by forces beyond his control. One of these was the force of revolution itself. Given this belief, one can understand why Kōtoku was so lacking in a concrete theory of revolution and relied so heavily on what appears today at least as a highly mythical – if not apocalyptical – solution. It also explains why, despite his assertion that he was daily growing more 'agnostic, atheistic, and materialistic'[1] and that he 'loved liberty and not personal servitude',[2] the word 'fate' (*unmei*) with all its debilitating overtones once again reasserted its predominant role in the letters and conversations of his final years.

But in April 1907, despite renewed government harassment, which included the banning of his most recent book of essays, *Heimin Shugi*, he was still elated.[3] The government might suppress socialists, but the 'age of strikes', he was happy to declare, 'has at last come to Japan'.[4] With the paper closed and his comrades in prison, Kōtoku retired to his favorite hot spring

[1] *Nikki to shokan*, p. 262.

[2] *Ibid.* p. 405.

[3] Although *Heimin Shugi* was banned by the government, the 'clever' publisher, as Kōtoku noted, managed to sell 1,500 copies of the work before the officials could seize the rest. *Ibid.* p. 443.

[4] *Nikkan Heimin Shimbun*, no. 75 (April 14, 1907), p. 2. In *Meiji Shakai Shugi shiryō shū*, vol. IV, p. 306.

community, Yugawara, in order to rest and translate Arnold Roller's 'Social General Strike'.

Summer saw Kōtoku back in Tokyo. The battle there had evolved into one which pitted not only the government against socialists, but socialists against themselves. After Katayama's return, the split between social democrats and anarchists had taken a turn for the worse. Towards the end of June both sides made an attempt to patch up their differences. Their efforts were crowned with some success. In August both factions cooperated to run a joint socialist summer school, and later in the same month they worked together to give Keir Hardie, the veteran British labor leader, a warm welcome to Japan. But following the summer school and the Hardie visit, relations between the two groups once more deteriorated. By the close of the year, frustrated in all their efforts to rouse the public, the two camps resorted to a vindictive spree of name-calling.

Kōtoku had seen the storm coming. In July and August he supported the unified efforts his fellow socialists were making in Tokyo. At the same time he made efforts to extend his contacts among the young Chinese revolutionaries in the capital. He had already made contacts with Chang Chi and Liu Shih-p'ei, two Chinese students who had shown an interest in socialism and whom Kōtoku encouraged to organize a Society for the Study of Socialism among other Chinese students in Tokyo. On August 30 he attended the opening meeting of this society, and in his address to the assembled Chinese he urged them not only to pursue a study of socialism, but to practice anarchism.[1]

In September Kōtoku joined Sakai Toshihiko and Yamakawa Hitoshi in organizing the Kinyōkai, or Friday Association, through which they hoped to propagate Kōtoku's direct action position. The Kinyokai stood in direct opposition to a more moderate socialist group, the Doshikai, which Katayama Sen, Tazoe Tetsuji, and Nishikawa Kojirō had organized. Kōtoku regarded the in-fighting that soon developed between these two associations as a sad development.[2] Still plagued by illness, and a burden to his wife, who was herself ill with rheumatism, he decided to leave Tokyo for Tosa. In

---

[1] Kōtoku's influence on Chang Chi, Liu Shih-p'ei, and Liu's wife, Ho Chen, appears to have been considerable. All three later became well known figures in the Chinese anarchist movement. See Robert A. Scalapino and George T. Yu, *The Chinese Anarchist Movement* (Center for Chinese Studies, Berkeley, 1961), pp. 28ff.

[2] On November 17, 1907, the *Shakai Shimbun*, Katayama's paper which spoke for the Doshikai, went so far as to accuse Kōtoku, Sakai, and Morichika Unpei, the editor of the *Osaka Heimin Shimbun* which spoke for the Kinyōkai, of having accepted bribes from the Tokyo Streetcar Company to end the boycott of the previous year. *Shakai Shimbun*, no. 25 (November 17, 1907), p. 5. *Meiji Shakai Shugi shiryō shū*, vol. VI, p. 201.

Nakamura he could recover in peace, and devote himself to the translation of Kropotkin's works. These were his most important objectives. As he had written to Albert Johnson as early as December 1906: 'Most of our comrades are inclined to take the tactics of Parliamentalism [*sic*] rather than Syndicalism or Anarchism. But it is not because they are assuredly convinced which is true, but because of their ignorance of Anarchist Communism. Therefore our most important work at present is the translation and publication of Anarchist and Free-thought literature.'[1] Now, a year later, he was able to report: '[The] Japanese Socialist movement was split at last to two parties – Social Democrat and Anarchist Communist. It is a very natural development known in all countries. Japan, which had already produced Social Democrats and Anarchist Communists, shall now produce many Direct-Actionists, Anti-Militarists, General Strikers and even Terrorists.'[2]

Four months later, writing to Ishikawa Sanshirō, who was still serving a prison term, Kōtoku noted in the same matter-of-fact tone: 'The great fight rages in Tokyo. European history is repeating itself. The process is natural; the force inevitable. There is nothing we can do. I do not think the fault or responsibility belongs to anyone. More and more gods, prophets, and saints appear daily. It is a sad trend.'[3]

Kōtoku's response to the situation was to remain aloof from the in-fighting. When the members of the Kinyōkai asked him to openly defend himself against the charges of corruption leveled against him by Katayama and his group, he ignored the request, writing to a member of the association, 'Those who want to doubt, will doubt anyway!'[4]

While the battle raged in Tokyo, Kōtoku calmly proceeded to translate Kropotkin's *The Conquest of Bread*. At the same time, he traveled extensively through the villages of his native province. Having rededicated himself to the cause of revolution, he was struck by the extent to which the revolutionary fervor, which he identified with his youth in Nakamura, appeared to have died out among the young people of Tosa. 'What has happened to the Tosa of old?' he asked again and again. Addressing the youth of the region through the *Kōchi Shimbun* he wrote: 'The blood surging through your veins is the same blood of the revolutionaries who forty years ago destroyed feudalism and twenty years ago established the Diet. And yet, nowadays no one uses the word revolution anymore!'[5]

Like Kropotkin, Kōtoku directed his appeal to the young. In his call to

[1] Letter to Albert Johnson dated December 18, 1906. *Nikki to shokan*, p. 441.
[2] Letter to Albert Johnson dated December 6, 1907. *Ibid.* p. 449.
[3] Letter to Ishikawa Sanshirō dated April 20, 1908. *Ibid.* p. 273.
[4] Letter to Hayashi Sanjurokurō dated December 1, 1907. *Ibid.* p. 257.
[5] 'Byōkan Hōgo', *ibid.* p. 149.

revolution, he frequently relied on Bakunin's arguments from *God and the State*. There were three requisites for a progressive society, he insisted; the first two were 'production' and 'knowledge'. Of these Japan had acquired a surfeit in the last forty years. The third, he maintained, was the willingness to revolt, the 'spirit of resistance', in which the Japanese of the modern generation seemed to be entirely lacking. In urging on the young people of Tosa, he insisted that what they needed to nourish was the spiritual element of revolution. If progress were to continue they, themselves, would have to learn to resist and revolt.[1]

Kōtoku's conversion to 'direct action' was itself largely a spiritual experience belonging to the inner man, and not one depending on external organization. As such, it had strong moral overtones. Only the elect, the morally pure in the sense of revolutionary fervor, who were sustained by their refusal to compromise, would be privileged to see the revolution for what it was and march in its vanguard. In an age in which the young all too frequently looked upon their world as the finished product of their parents, Kōtoku inspired the restless to search for ways of going beyond the boredom of their new affluence through the path of revolt.

Unfortunately, in a society which by nature stressed conformity and compromise, the path of revolt could easily become both precarious and fruitless. Instead of providing the leaven for a rapidly transforming society, revolt all too often symbolized an unwillingness to comply with the established system. Rather than proving a source of productive exchange, it frequently led to complete ostracism, alienation, and frustration. Moreover, once embarked upon, it became a compelling course with few alternatives. In his final confrontation with the social system the rebel was left with but two choices – complete capitulation (*tenkō*) or ultimately self-destructive radicalization in which both he and society confronted one another with violence.

Through the proclamation of his personal revolt Kōtoku allowed himself to become the vortex for the 'gaseous passions' of a generation which shared neither his background nor his knowledge and experience. For them violence was not a part of the historical process to be enjoyed in a kind of vicarious communion with strikes and natural disasters. Instead, they pictured violence as an active tool of the political world, a tool which they fully intended to use against government authority and oppression. It was no doubt Kōtoku's inability to understand the scope and limitations of not only his own, but also his follower's, commitment to revolutionary violence that drew him ever more tightly into the web of the High Treason Incident from which there was to be no escape.

[1] *Ibid.* p. 150.

CHAPTER 7

High treason, 1907–10

U NKNOWN TO KŌTOKU, for whom the closing months of 1907 were occupied with the translation of Kropotkin's *The Conquest of Bread* and periodic speaking tours through his native province, events half-way around the world in San Francisco once more came to play a curious and decisive role in shaping his future.

On November 3, 1907, the birthday of the Meiji Emperor, there appeared pasted on the porch of the Japanese Consulate, as well as in other public places in San Francisco, an 'Open Letter to Mutsuhito, the Emperor of Japan from Anarchist Terrorists'.

Highly familiar and distinctly disrespectful in language, this letter went on to declare that the Emperor was a 'man' – a mere human being like anyone else – and consequently a product of the animal world – 'apes' – and not the descendant of 'mythical gods'. Not only was the Emperor human, far worse, he was an impure and imperfect human, a 'murderer' and 'butcher', whose ancestors had come to power through 'evil' and 'immoral' machinations which through the ages had served to enslave the Japanese people. Rather than an aid to the 'liberation' and 'enlightenment' of the nation, the Emperor was the chief drawback to 'progress', and an enemy of all who searched for 'liberty'.[1]

The letter called not only for the rejection of the 'sacred and inviolable' Throne, which had become the cornerstone of Meiji constitutional rule, but stressed the need for 'violence' in dealing with the Emperor. On this point it was unequivocal:

None of us are fond of violence, but when violence is used to suppress us, then we must resort to violence in reply. Moreover, we must resist the present order by shedding our last drops of blood in opposition to the Emperor. We must give up our slow and ineffective methods of talk and agitation and must by all means turn to assassination, willing to butcher without regard for rank or status anyone who suppresses or spies on us.[2]

Finally the letter concluded with the ominous lines: 'Your Excellency

---

[1] Itoya Toshio, *Kōtoku Shūsui kenkyū*, pp. 236–8.   [2] *Ibid.* p. 238.

152

Mutsuhito, old friend! Poor old friend, Mutsuhito! Your time is just about up. The bomb is right in your surroundings, just about to blow up. "Bye, your Excellency, old friend."[1]

As might have been expected, this strongly worded rejection of imperial authority was the product of the same group of radicals which had published *The Revolution* in the previous year. The two men principally responsible were Takeuchi Tetsugorō and Iwasa Sakutarō. These, needless to say, were the very individuals around whom Kōtoku had molded the Social Revolutionary Party of Oakland.

While Kōtoku later denied all knowledge of the letter's authorship or of the group responsible for it, he may not have been as innocent in this matter as he was subsequently to insist. Certainly the theme and tone of the letter – its emphasis on the Emperor as 'myth', and on the need for 'violence' to reveal him 'human' – involved sentiments which Kōtoku had already aired to Oka Shigeki in San Francisco. If he expressed such thoughts to Oka, it may not be going too far to presume that he discussed similar ideas with Takeuchi and Iwasa. Moreover, it was only natural for Kōtoku to remain in touch with the young men of whom he expected great things in the future.

Kōtoku's connections with *The Revolution* may well have been far deeper than hitherto surmised. The third issue of the paper (April 1, 1907) contained not only a full translation of his speech before the Socialist Convention, as well as a deferential bow to Shūsui as 'the organizer of our party', but in addition a curious letter, 'An Appeal to the Comrades', which, while unsigned, appears remarkably close to Kōtoku's position. In part, this letter stated:

I cannot express myself very well in English, but I must appeal to you, dear comrades, that we must take more practical action to overthrow the present system of capitalism...Yes, we men who have soul and heart, cannot look carelessly at it [the suffering and misery of the workers], like 'a fire on the other side of a river'... we must waste not even a minute to overthrow the present wolfish capitalists and under such terrible conditions there is neither wrong nor right, one uses any means...we must take direct action in desperation to advance the revolutionary general strike...Of course there is no one who likes bloodshed, but we cannot help it. We must acknowledge anyhow that 'social and political persecution is the mother of terrorism'... At the present time the capitalists over all the world are breeding terrible terrorists, especially in Japan. The Russian revolutionists showed us the successful results by using terrorism, opposed to the cruel persecution of the czar. I believe this policy will become necessary in every country that adopts the policy of persecution against us, and direct action is successful only if it

[1] *Ibid.*

is entire, desperate and positive...I think the greatest shame of revolutionists is to die safely in the warm bed [*sic*], while our fellow workers are crying and suffering.[1]

A month later Kōtoku wrote to Albert Johnson recommending that he exert himself in behalf of his youthful followers, noting: 'They are all clever and devoted libertarians. I hope the future revolution in Japan will be caused by their hands. Please teach them, educate them, instruct them.'[2]

From Kōtoku's conversation with Oka Shigeki and the foregoing letter to *The Revolution* – which under the circumstances could not have come from anyone else in Japan – one cannot help but conclude that some of Kōtoku's ideas were at least indirectly responsible for the Open Letter to the Emperor.

When one takes into consideration Kōtoku's new optimism and the expansive, aggressive, self-confidence which accompanied his own conversion to 'direct action', it is not surprising that he attempted to communicate something of the same mood to his youthful followers. For the moment even the revolution seemed to be within human grasp. For Takeuchi, Iwasa, and the other members of the Social Revolutionary Party, the Open Letter to the Emperor represented a logical extrapolation of their ideological leader's ideas.

What Kōtoku was unaware of was the extent to which the Open Letter incident was to become a part of the complicated backstage maneuverings of the Japanese political world. By once again playing into the hands of Yamagata Aritomo and his bureaucratic faction, Japanese radicals in San Francisco set in motion a historical chain reaction that led to increasingly violent and desperate confrontations between Japanese socialists and the government. This process eventually led to the High Treason Incident (Taigyaku Jiken) which cost Kōtoku his life in 1911.

For Yamagata Aritomo, whom a friend described as the 'pillar of the nation', the activities of Takeuchi and Iwasa's group confirmed earlier convictions that radical ideas were mushrooming in the social and economic unrest of the postwar years. He was convinced that if allowed to go unchecked such ideas would soon openly threaten the foundations of the Japanese state. Ever since the publication of *The Revolution* Yamagata had been keeping a wary eye on Japanese radical activities in San Francisco.

In the wake of the first shocking outbreak of anti-imperial agitation in

---

[1] From *Kakumei*, no. 3, in Shakai Bunko (ed.), *Zai Bei Shakai Shugi sha – Museifu Shugi sha enkaku*, p. 485.

[2] *Nikki to shokan*, p. 444.

San Francisco, the Saionji Cabinet had taken decisive measures against socialists at home. At the same time greater efforts were made through the San Francisco Consulate to keep the cabinet informed of radical activities in the Bay Area. In order to achieve the latter goal the Consulate hired two secret agents, Tatsumi Tetsuō and Kawasaki Minotarō, to infiltrate the Social Revolutionary Party.[1] The information that these men gathered was forwarded to Saionji through official channels.

By means of this process Saionji was kept fully informed on what had occurred in San Francisco on November 3, 1907. On the other hand, because the incident had not become a public issue, having been kept out of the hands of the press in the United States and in Japan, Saionji decided to bide his time, hoping that Matsubara Kazuo, his Consul in San Francisco, might negotiate with the United States District Attorney, Devlin, and the Commissioner of Immigration, North, for the deportation of the young men so that Japanese authorities could deal with the problem at home. The return of these radicals was doubly important, for all evidence coming from the Consulate seemed to indicate that the ring leader behind the incident was Kōtoku Shūsui. Meanwhile, the government was well aware – particularly after several legal defeats in 1907 involving socialists in which insufficient evidence had been presented – that if it hoped to indict Kōtoku on a serious charge involving the Throne, concrete evidence and testimony would be required. Such evidence and testimony could only come from his accomplices in San Francisco.

The Consulate's efforts to gain American cooperation remained fruitless. Inquiries merely revealed that United States authorities could do little to facilitate deportation. As North had already pointed out at the time of the Revolution incident – there had been a big clamor to deport Takeuchi Tetsugorō – Japanese radicals could not be deported under U.S. immigration law unless the American authorities could prove that these individuals had been anarchists at the time they entered the country.[2] Since this was virtually impossible in the case of Takeuchi and Iwasa, who told investigators that they had become radicals under the influence of Jack London, North maintained that the Americans' hands were tied. Moreover, when the Japanese tried to take their case to the United States Attorney General, Bonaparte, they were given the same reply.

[1] Tatsumi and Kawasaki were both secretaries of local Japanese Associations. Kawasaki was also a reporter for the *Shin Sekai* and for the Tokyo *Nichi Nichi*.

[2] North's position was reported in an article titled 'Says He Emulated Doctrine of London', *San Francisco Chronicle*, December 31, 1906.

At this juncture, while Consulate officials were debating what to do next, a Tokyo University professor named Takahashi Sakuei suddenly appeared in San Francisco. Takahashi's speciality was international law, and the alleged purpose of his visit to San Francisco was to investigate the immigration problem.

While the question of Japanese immigrants may well have constituted the primary reason for his trip to the United States, Takahashi soon involved himself in other matters. One of these was the question of the Open Letter and its authorship. In order to obtain more detailed information on the activities of Japanese radicals in the San Francisco area, as well as his own copy of the letter to the Emperor, Takahashi began to bribe the Consulate's spies, Tatsumi and Kawasaki. With their help he soon came into possession of names, dates, and other 'facts', including a copy of the letter and with it the interpretation that the person responsible for it was none other than Kōtoku Shūsui. Takahashi carefully bundled this information up and sent it to another Tokyo University professor, Hozumi Nobushige, who transmitted it to Yamagata Aritomo through his brother, Hozumi Yatsuka.[1]

One may well imagine Yamagata's reaction to the information Takahashi sent him. For Yamagata, who had made the defense of the Throne the central purpose of his life, an open threat to the Emperor was equivalent to a declaration of war. As he later noted in reaction to the High Treason Incident, 'To think that I should live to see the day when men openly advocate the destruction of the Imperial system!'[2] But Yamagata was also a man of action. His immediate fears about the effects of radical ideas on the fiber of Japanese society were no sooner reconfirmed than he determined to take counter measures.

Yamagata attributed the unstemmed growth of radical ideas to Saionji's laxness. The two men had never shown much fondness for one another. Party politics remained an area of modern Japanese political development that Yamagata found personally repugnant. Yamagata regarded Saionji as a tool of the Seiyūkai, but since Saionji had come to power with a clear-cut majority in the Diet, he was forced to bide his time, waiting for an opportunity to topple the cabinet. Takahashi's information provided new possibilities.

In order to bring maximum pressures to bear on the Saionji Cabinet, Yamagata took the Open Letter directly to the Emperor. The Emperor, who

---

[1] Takahashi's role as 'information gatherer' for Yamagata was first hinted at by Shirayanagi Shūko in *Saionji Kimmochi den*, pp. 520ff. Further confirmation has come from Ōhara Kei's article, 'Genro Yamagata Aritomo e no shokan – "Taigyaku Jiken" to kanrenshite', *Tokyo Keidai Gakkaishi*, no. 39 (June, 1963).

[2] Tokutomi Iichirō, *Kōshaku Yamagata Aritomo den*, vol. III, p. 767.

had not been informed of the incident by Saionji, naturally expressed concern and immediately had the Imperial Household Minister, Baron Tanaka Kōken, inquire of the Home Ministry what it knew about the case, and what actions, if any, had been taken. The Police Bureau of the Home Ministry and the Tokyo Metropolitan Police Department replied that they were aware of the incident, and that while they could do little about the activities of Japanese radicals in San Francisco they were taking appropriate measures to prevent the Open Letter from entering or being circulated in Japan. Finally, they maintained that, despite a lack of concrete evidence, the 'ringleader' behind the incident was Kōtoku Shūsui.[1]

Baron Tanaka reported the information he had been given by the Home Ministry to Yamagata. In effect, the information which had begun with Tatsumi and Kawasaki in San Francisco had now gone full circle. In the process both official and unofficial sources seemed to corroborate as 'fact' Kōtoku's relationship to the incident.

At this point Yamagata decided to press his advantage. Having already made an effort to shake the Emperor's confidence in Saionji, he now set out to create an impasse in the Cabinet which would make Saionji's future as Prime Minister dependent upon an Imperial decision. Yamagata hoped, of course, that the Emperor would side against Saionji under such circumstances. If this were the case, General Katsura Tarō, Yamagata's protégé, could once more assume the premiership. Under Katsura the anti-socialist measures, which Yamagata was convinced were needed for the preservation of the Imperial Institution, might soon be put into effect.

In order to bring about the downfall of the Saionji Cabinet, Yamagata had his adopted son, Yamagata Isaburō, who served as Minister of Communications, involve himself in an open conflict with the Minister of the Treasury over railway construction funds. The outcome of this confrontation was the resignation of both ministers; at the same time, Saionji, incapable of drawing up an acceptable budget without their cooperation, tendered his resignation as well.

For the moment it appeared that Yamagata had gained his objectives. Saionji had presented the Emperor with his resignation, and the way seemed cleared for Katsura Tarō. But at this juncture the Emperor balked. While he accepted the resignations of the Minister of Communications and the Minister of the Treasury, he refused to accept Saionji's resignation. With the Emperor's help Saionji successfully withstood Yamagata's challenge.[2]

[1] For the details for Yamagata's efforts see Itoya Toshio, *Kōtoku Shūsui kenkyū*, pp. 242–3.
[2] The struggle between Yamagata and Saionji is discussed in Itoya Toshio, *Kōtoku Shūsui kenkyū*, pp. 236–49. For the role of the Emperor see p. 243.

The main effects of Yamagata's criticism and the Emperor's concern was a hardening of Saionji's posture towards socialism and socialists. Yamagata's attempt to destroy the cabinet had occurred early in January 1908. By the latter half of the same month, Saionji's new hard line towards socialists – particularly towards Kōtoku's followers – became increasingly apparent.

On January 17, 1908, the members of the Kinyōkai met for their usual Friday night lecture and discussion. Sakai Toshihiko and Ōsugi Sakae were both present. So were the police. Shortly after the meeting commenced, the authorities ordered the gathering to dissolve and insisted that the audience disperse. While many of those present left the building peaceably, Sakai, Ōsugi, and some of the other members of the association decided to remain behind to carry on a 'private' discussion. The police refused to permit this, and during the ensuing argument the lights suddenly went out and a fight between the two sides erupted. While the struggle was in progress, Sakai opened a second story window and began to address a rapidly gathering crowd on 'police brutality'. When the authorities dragged him from his perch, others took his place. So one after another six members of the Kinyōkai were forcibly arrested and ushered to police headquarters through an ugly mob which openly revealed its hostility to the officers of the law and tried to prevent the arrest of Sakai and the others.[1]

No doubt Kōtoku was not far from the truth when he observed from Nakamura in a letter to Albert Johnson: 'I would have been arrested also had I been there.'[2]

The Kinyōkai disturbance represented but the beginning of increased government pressures on Kōtoku's followers. Far more serious and far-reaching in its consequences was the Red Flag Incident which erupted on June 22, 1908.

On June 18 Yamaguchi Kōken was released from prison in Sendai after serving a fourteen months' sentence for various infringements of the Press Laws in connection with articles that appeared in the former daily *Heimin Shimbun* and *Hikari*. When Yamaguchi arrived in Tokyo early on the morning of June 19, he was met at Ueno Station by a large delegation of socialists that included representatives of Kōtoku and Katayama's factions. Those who came to the station brought with them large red flags inscribed with the words 'socialism' and 'revolution'. After Yamaguchi had been placed in a rickshaw and sent off to the offices of the *Shakai Shimbun*, the members of the welcoming delegation proceeded to demonstrate through the streets of the

---

[1] Nishio Yōtarō, *Kōtoku Shūsui*, p. 201.
[2] Letter to Albert Johnson dated February 3, 1908. *Nikki to shokan*, p. 451.

neighborhood waving their huge red flags and singing a revolutionary song. Finally, after several skirmishes with the police, who tried to seize the flags, the delegates reached the offices of the *Shakai Shimbun*, where, following several cheers for Yamaguchi, they dispersed.

Three days later many of the same individuals reassembled at the Kinkikan in Kanda to honor Yamaguchi. While in theory a 'united effort', the gathering proved as much a confrontation between direct actionists and parliamentarians as a welcome for Yamaguchi. This time it was Kōtoku's followers who came armed with red flags. The slogans inscribed on them were no longer the comparatively innocuous 'socialism' and 'revolution', but the far more provocative 'anarchism' and 'anarchist communism'. Shortly after the meeting adjourned Ōsugi and his compatriots burst out of the hall shouting, 'anar . . . anar . . . anarchy', and started waving their red flags. No sooner had they begun to proceed up the street outside of the hall singing 'The Revolution is at hand', than they were set upon by policemen from the Kanda Police Station. What resulted was an hour-long public melee in which Ōsugi, Sakai, and a dozen of Kōtoku's followers were arrested and charged with violating the Peace Police Law.[1]

By all rights the Red Flag Incident should have gone down in the records of the times as a minor clash between socialists and police officials hardly worthy of historical attention. This was not to be the case. What had been a minor scuffle gradually came to play a decisive role in shaping Kōtoku Shūsui's future.

If the long run effects of the Red Flag Incident were to tie Kōtoku more closely into the net of events that was to lead to the High Treason Incident, the immediate effects of the incident helped bring about the downfall of the Saionji government.

Although Kōtoku interpreted the Red Flag Incident as a new extreme in government repression which called for an all-out effort of resistance, Yamagata viewed it as an extreme of something quite different. For him the incident once more indicated the need for firm and decisive measures against rapidly deteriorating social and intellectual conditions that served to further the growth of socialist ideas. At the same time, Yamagata was concerned that Saionji's extreme laxness prevented such measures from being taken. For Yamagata, who had become increasingly preoccupied with the whole question of 'dangerous thoughts' early in 1908, the only solution lay in Saionji's

[1] For the above details of the Red Flag Incident see Itoya Toshio, *Kōtoku Shūsui kenkyū*, p. 246. The incident is also described in Akamatsu, *Nihon Shakai undō shi*, pp. 149–51, and Kublin, *Asian Revolutionary*, pp. 203–4.

resignation. Consequently, he once more directed himself to the task of bringing about Saionji's demise.

In keeping with his previous efforts, Yamagata went directly to the Emperor. Again he reported his own misgivings about the Saionji Cabinet's insufficient exertions on the socialist question. The Emperor was not without his own concern and, after hearing Yamagata's report, inquired whether stronger measures could not be taken. Yamagata indicated that this would be difficult as long as Saionji remained in office as Prime Minister.[1]

On June 25, 1908, Hara Kei, the Home Minister in the Saionji Cabinet was called before the Emperor and questioned in detail regarding the whole socialist problem. The Emperor wanted to know what measures had been taken against socialists since Katsura left office; what policy the Cabinet proposed for the future; what steps it had taken in dealing with the 'Socialist Party in America'; and what attitude the Cabinet intended to adopt towards the possible formation of a new Socialist Party in Japan.[2]

While Hara Kei's answers appear to have alleviated some of the Emperor's doubts, Yamagata had already begun to set in motion his scheme for a new Cabinet crisis. This time he urged Terauchi, the War Minister, to resign. Terauchi, who was not in favor of having the army shoulder the responsibility for bringing about the downfall of the Cabinet, informed Saionji of Yamagata's intentions. Ill and disappointed in the House of Peer's rejection of some of his most important Seiyukai policy, Saionji was neither physically nor psychologically prepared to meet Yamagata in an open confrontation. Adopting the course of least resistance he resigned from the Premiership on July 4, 1908. This time the Emperor accepted his resignation, and on July 14 General Katsura Tarō once more came to power.

As might have been expected of Yamagata's protégé, Katsura determined to make up for Saionji's lack of zeal. Katsura was to make certain that no one would be able to accuse him – as Yamagata had accused Saionji – of being deficient in loyalty and devotion to the Throne. The new cabinet's posture towards socialists was clearly spelled out in its opening policy declaration in which Katsura wrote:

Although socialists at the moment are said to constitute little more than a thin

---

[1] Yamagata's accusations of laxness were not totally correct. The Saionji Cabinet was hardly as liberal as Yamagata tried to insist. As early as March 1907 Saionji had sent Hiranuma Kiichirō to Europe to study what measures the German, French, and English governments were adopting towards the problems of socialism, anarchism, and strikes. Hiranuma spent much of his time talking to the Paris police about measures that could be applied against anarchists. Later Hiranuma was to become the Chief Prosecutor in the High Treason Trial. See Itoya Toshio, *Taigyaku jiken*, pp. 72ff. For Yamagata's maneuvering see *Hara Kei nikki*, vol. III (Naisō Jidai no. 1), pp. 203ff.

[2] *Hara Kei nikki*, vol. III (Naisō Jidai no. 1), p. 204.

thread of smoke, if we overlook this thread of smoke, it will someday develop the force of a wildfire, and then it would be too late for anything but regrets. Consequently, it goes without saying that while we must nourish the morality of the people through education, increase their production, restore their steadfastness, and always guard against harmful words, we must also control socialist meetings and publications in order to prevent them from spreading throughout the land.[1]

The Red Flag Incident provided Katsura with an excellent opportunity to reveal his true colors.

In January, when Kōtoku's followers fought with officers of the law, Sakai, Ōsugi, and the others arrested had been sentenced to moderate terms of thirty to sixty days imprisonment. No doubt Yamagata considered this an example of Saionji's laxness. Katsura, on the other hand, was aware that Yamagata considered the new criminal code far too lenient in dealing with those who showed disrespect for the Emperor, or openly opposed the national polity. Katsura considered it his responsibility to see that the courts should come to the defense of the Imperial Institution. The sentences handed down in the Red Flag Incident – two and a half years of imprisonment for Ōsugi, two years for Sakai, Yamakawa, Morioka, and at least a year for most of the other defendants – were designed to leave few doubts in the minds of Japanese socialists what the future of their movement would be like under the Katsura administration. Katsura was provided with a further opportunity of showing his devotion to the Throne when one of the defendants allegedly scribbled a few lines of anti-Imperial poetry on the wall of his cell. For such 'disrespect' he was sentenced to an additional three years.[2]

The harsh sentences which concluded the Red Flag Incident served as a start for an all-out drive against radicalism. In the months that followed, virtually all the remaining socialist papers were suppressed by the government. Socialist meetings of any kind were harassed by police officials. In addition, socialists soon discovered their rights of assembly and expression seriously restricted. Speakers were not allowed to use the words 'labor strikes', 'labor organizations', 'boycott', 'socialism', or 'revolution'.[3] Words such as 'anarchism', 'anarchist communism', and 'the General Strike' were anathema. Police surveillance was carried to unprecedented extremes. In October 1908 the weight of the Imperial House was thrown behind the government's efforts through the Boshin Rescript which stated that 'the

[1] Shiota Shōbei, 'Taigyaku jiken no haikei' in Shiota Shōbei and Watanabe Junzō (eds.), *Hiroku taigyaku jiken*, vol. I, p. 37.
[2] The defendant was Satō Satori and the incident may well have been a frameup. See Kanzaki Kiyoshi, *Taigyaku jiken*, pp. 152–5.
[3] Hyman Kublin, *Asian Revolutionary*, p. 206.

teachings of Our revered Ancestors and the records of Our glorious history are clear beyond all misapprehension' and called upon all Japanese to be 'faithful', 'frugal', 'submissive', and 'sincere' in order to assure 'the growing prosperity of Our Empire'.[1] Katsura in commenting on the Rescript made it clear that Socialism constituted one of the 'frivolities' against which the Emperor's letter inveighed.[2]

Needless to say the effects of the government's actions served to drive much of the socialist movement underground. Given such circumstances the arguments favoring violence as a means of countering government oppression became increasingly appealing. When all other methods of propagating socialism had fallen under the blows of the government, the need for 'propaganda by deed' became imperative. Confronted with the harsh realities of a hostile environment Kōtoku Shūsui's highly spiritual position on 'direct action' was to be transformed into a program for assassination.

While much of the stage on which Kōtoku was to play his final dramatic chapter was being set in Tokyo, he became increasingly aware that even the isolation of his home town was not sufficient to protect him from the authority of the state.

In the wake of the Open Letter Incident Kōtoku was placed under continuous surveillance. Wherever he went there was the inevitable 'tail'. By the summer of 1908 surveillance turned into open harassment. Police detectives were now continuously posted outside of the Kōtoku home and sake shop. Customers who did not care for the indignities of police interrogation ceased coming; overnight the shop's trade virtually ceased. Kōtoku dashed off indignant letters to the Kōchi papers, but all to no avail.

Placed under the mounting pressures of police authority, and aware that his stay in Nakamura was jeopardizing the family's livelihood, Kōtoku's frustrations mounted. Then on June 23 he received a one-line telegram from Tokyo which announced: 'Sakai struck down, return at once.'[3] When the full details of the Red Flag Incident reached Nakamura, Kōtoku decided to return to the capital.

All evidence suggests that Kōtoku was seriously disturbed by the arrest of his friends and followers in Tokyo. At the same time he was aware that the burden of leading the anti-government movement had once more fallen on his shoulders. With Sakai's demise his own return to what he regarded the

---

[1] *Taiyō*, vol. XIV, no. 14 (November 1, 1908), p. 1. English translation of the Boshin Rescript is in the same issue of *Taiyō* (English Section) p. 11.
[2] *Ibid.* p. 12.
[3] Kōtoku Tomiji, 'Oji Kōtoku Shūsui', *Chūō Kōron*, vol. LXX, no. 4 (April, 1955), p. 216.

front lines of the struggle became a foredrawn conclusion. But there was still the question of his health and his unfinished translation of the *Conquest of Bread*. As he wrote in a letter to a friend, 'The only one up and around in the family is the dog, Chiyame.'[1] He himself was 'so awfully weak' that he was afraid he might be of little use to friends and the movement. Hoping that a few additional weeks of rest might restore his health to the point where he could safely undertake the arduous trip to the capital, he delayed his departure from Nakamura. Finally, having completed his translation of the *Conquest of Bread*, he started for Tokyo towards the end of July.

At a farewell meeting held in his behalf by the members of his family on the evening before his departure, Kōtoku was once more moody. The latest word from Tokyo, particularly news of the fall of the Saionji Cabinet and Katsura's strong anti-socialist statements, did not bode well. Sharing a parting cup of sake with his guests he remarked that he was not 'destined to die in bed' and asked his relatives to take care of his mother should he fail to return.[2]

Although one cannot totally discount the possibility that Kōtoku might have entertained the idea of violence against the Throne at this juncture, any assertion that he did – which in essence is what the government prosecutors later claimed – is totally based on conjecture. The finality of his departure seems more attributable to the state of his health, and to the realization that given the present conditions a return to Nakamura would be impossible in the future, than to any clear-cut assassination scheme.

Certainly the whole question of his failing health troubled him more than ever. Despite all efforts to remain optimistic, Shūsui could not deny the gradual signs of decline. It was for these reasons that he decided to visit Ōishi Seinosuke, a doctor and fellow socialist, on his way to Tokyo.

In the absence of Katō Tokijirō, who was away in Europe, Ōishi had come to serve as Kōtoku's physician. Kōtoku's visit to Ōishi's home in Shingu, a small town in Wakayama Prefecture, was for the purpose of extensive tests and consultations. Ōishi, who was startled by Kōtoku's condition, prescribed at least a month of complete rest. Kōtoku considered a month out of the question, but agreed to stay for a lesser period while Ōishi made further tests. During the two weeks he spent under Ōishi's care Kōtoku came to know many of Ōishi's socialist friends; discussions on the future of socialism in Japan became common occurrences.

One day Ōishi suggested a boating excursion on the Kumano River.

---

[1] Letter to Morichika Unpei dated July 15, 1908. *Nikki to shokan*, p. 278.
[2] Kōtoku Tomiji, 'Oji Kōtoku Shūsui', *Chūō Kōron*, vol. LXX, no. 4 (April, 1955), p. 217.

During the day's outing the conversation ranged to include a variety of subjects including the current socialist dilemma. At one point, as the boatman later recalled, Kōtoku quite casually asked Ōishi if he 'knew how to make bombs'. Ōishi replied that he did not. But on the following day he made a special effort to consult an English encyclopedia on the subject of 'bombs', and reported his findings to Shūsui.[1]

While the above episode took place in broad daylight on what appears from all descriptions to have been nothing more than a picnic with Ōishi and some of his friends and relatives, the prosecution subsequently insisted that the incident marked the beginning of a plot against the life of the Emperor. According to the court, the episode had taken place at 'night' and constituted a rapidly maturing conspiracy, first to construct bombs, and then to use them to bring harm to the Throne.[2]

Given the fact that Kōtoku was aware – as his letters from Shingu indicate[3] – that he was under constant 'observation' by police officials, one can hardly imagine him plotting against the life of the Emperor in the presence of strangers in a small boat where every word could be overheard. At the same time, his inquiry into the construction of bombs tends to suggest that violence – perhaps not, as the government insisted, against the Throne, but in an effort at strikes and the hoped-for General Strike – was becoming increasingly attractive to Kōtoku.

What seems clear about Kōtoku's month-long journey to Tokyo is that 'direct action', which prior to the Red Flag Incident had concerned him largely on a personal and theoretical level, now began to take on an aura of concrete and violent measures. While there was still no plot or conspiracy in the formal – and one must insist legal – sense at this time, it becomes equally difficult to maintain that Kōtoku excluded the possibility of anti-Imperial violence as one of the uses of the bombs in which he showed himself interested.[4]

By the time Kōtoku reached Hakone, where he paid a visit to the Buddhist priest, Uchiyama Gudō, he stated quite frankly that the time was 'no longer one for talk'.[5] This is perhaps the best description of his position at the time of his arrival in the capital. In the wake of the government's repressive action

---

[1] Itoya Toshio, Kōtoku Shūsui kenkyū, p. 253.
[2] Shiota Shōbei and Watanabe Junzō (eds.), Hiroku taigyaku jiken, vol. II, p. 119.
[3] Nikki to shokan, p. 279.
[4] It is possible to document, for example, that Kōtoku was interested in the subject of 'high treason' at this time. On his way to Tokyo he stopped at the home of Chiyoko's sister, Matsumoto Sugako, and questioned her husband, a judge by profession, on the details of what constituted 'high treason'. Whatever his intentions might have been, Kōtoku was certainly aware of what the new Criminal Code regarded as crimes against the Throne. Itoya Toshio, Kōtoku Shūsui kenkyū, p. 254.
[5] Ibid. p. 255.

something would have to be done; this 'something' went under the category of 'direct action', but what 'direct action' implied remained vague and ambiguous.

The full implications of the Red Flag Incident did not strike Kōtoku until August 29, 1908, when sentence was passed on Ōsugi, Sakai, and the other defendants. It was only then that he realized, as he wrote in the *Kumamoto Hyōron*, that the movement's activities had been brought to a 'full stop'.[1] Such a situation called for counter measures. For those who escaped Ōsugi and Sakai's fate Kōtoku's new Heiminsha in Sugamo served as a rallying point. In September 1908, after word of the outcome of the trial spread throughout the country, radicals slowly began to drift into Tokyo in order to consult with Kōtoku on what steps might be taken in the future.

One of the steps which became increasingly imperative in the wake of the Katsura Cabinet's all-out attack on socialist papers and magazines was the establishment of small, clandestine printing offices that could continue to publish radical pamphlets and tracts. Such centers were not new. Kōtoku's translation of Roller's 'Social General Strike' had been secretly published through one such office in the previous year, but with the fall of the *Osaka Heimin Shimbun* and the *Kumamoto Hyōron* the number of these establishments began to mushroom.

Perhaps the most curious of the underground printing offices involved the Zen priest, Uchiyama Gudō, whom Kōtoku had visited in Hakone on his return to Tokyo. Uchiyama was a member of the Sōtō Sect attached to the Rinsenji Temple. Concerned with the welfare of the impoverished peasants of the mountainous region in which he served, he had developed an early interest in socialism after reading Yano Fumio's *Shin Sekai* (*New World*). In 1905 he met Kōtoku at Katō Tokijirō's hospital in Odawara, and thereafter Uchiyama became seriously interested in revolutionary activity.

In September 1908 Uchiyama came to Tokyo to consult with Kōtoku. The purpose of his visit was to inquire into Kropotkin's teachings and to acquire the equipment necessary to start an underground press in Hakone. Much impressed by Roller's 'Social General Strike', from which Kōtoku orally translated passages in reply to Uchiyama's questions on how Kropotkin hoped to achieve the revolution, and by Kōtoku's ability to procure the equipment he desired, Uchiyama returned to Hakone to run off not only additional copies of the 'Social General Strike', but other strongly worded anti-Imperial statements as well.[2]

---

[1] Nishio Yōtarō, *Kōtoku Shūsui*, p. 215. *Kumamoto Hyōron*, September 20, 1908.
[2] For the scope of Uchiyama's activities see Itoya Toshio, *Kōtoku Shūsui kenkyū*, p. 257. The whole issue of underground publishing is discussed in Kanzaki Kiyoshi, *Taigyaku jiken*, pp. 166ff.

Meanwhile the late summer heat began to tell on Kōtoku's health. Constant visitors, police interference, and the frustrations of mundane household chores inflicted on him by Chiyoko's absence,[1] combined to sap what little strength remained. Virtually disabled by his illness, he was only too grateful for the kindness and attention of Kanno Sugako, the woman who entered his life at this point.

Kanno Sugako contrasted sharply with the other women in Kōtoku's life. Neither Asako nor Chiyoko, the products of a traditional upbringing, possessed the intellectual and emotional daring necessary to earn Kōtoku's respect, and consequently neither was capable of providing him with the psychological support he required. Since his return from the United States Kōtoku's relationship with Chiyoko had become increasingly strained. With each new sign of her husband's extremism Chiyoko had withdrawn further into what Kōtoku considered her 'fearfulness'. Supported by her older sister, she had even made several efforts to dissuade him from his 'direct action' stand. Kōtoku regarded these attempts as meddlesome and wrote indignant letters to his in-laws criticizing their efforts to scare his wife and set her against him. In one of these letters he noted:

If I cannot have a wife who will sympathize with the things I do, understand my position, and constantly support me in my quest to offer up my life at the right moment, it may be difficult to achieve this. It may be bad enough for me to have a wife who lacks a sense of determination, and whose fears shackle my every move, but if on top of this she is frightened by others who speak of the many dangers of the revolution, and is alarmed by them through arguments of misery and loss, she may lose all determination, and constantly resist her husband's efforts, finally causing him to lose his own commitment. If this were the case it would be better not to have a wife at all.[2]

The foregoing letter reveals both what Kōtoku hoped for in a wife and what Chiyoko lacked. At the same time, written as it was a few months after he had come to know Kanno Sugako, one is struck by Kōtoku's subconscious comparison of the two women.

Sugako was not the daughter of a former warrior; consequently she possessed nothing of the demure obedience and passivity which characterized the well-bred Japanese woman. A born activist, her childhood had instilled in her a deep-seated distrust for others, and for society in general. As a young woman she determined to liberate herself from her social environment by striking out against the constricting authorities of her age.

---

[1] Chiyoko had not been able to accompany him to Tokyo because of her arthritis.
[2] *Nikki to shokan*, pp. 288–9.

Sugako was born in Osaka in 1881.[1] Her father was a mine operator. Her mother, about whom little is known, died at an early age, leaving Sugako to be brought up by a stepmother. When Sugako matured into a handsome young lady of sixteen, her stepmother, by nature jealous and insecure, had her seduced by one of the mine workers and then used the incident to break up the close relationship which had developed between father and daughter.

At the age of twenty Sugako was married to a man from Tokyo, but the marriage soon ended in divorce. Meanwhile her father's mine had gone bankrupt, and she was left to fend for herself. Still young and dazzled by the dream of literary fame, she apprenticed herself to a second-rate Osaka novelist, but lacking the ability and contacts necessary for success in what remained largely an all-male profession, her hopes were soon shattered. Overcome with despair she allowed herself to sink into a life of prostitution.

Several years of poverty and prostitution were brought to a close by a timely conversion to Christianity, which provided not only a measure of stability but a badly needed job tutoring one of the English missionary ladies who taught at Doshisha University in Kyoto.

In 1904 Sugako visited the Heiminsha in Tokyo, where she met Sakai Toshihiko. Through Sakai's help she came to know a number of journalists active in the Osaka area. These proved more interested in her physical charms than her journalistic talents, but Sukago had long ago learned to use her natural gifts to personal advantage; 'affairs' became a means of advancing her literary career. Fully convinced that her conduct was in keeping with the ideals of the modern emancipated woman, she became an open advocate of 'free love', a position which had aroused considerable debate in socialist circles since the days of the first *Heimin Shimbun*. After several liaisons with other men, she was introduced to Arahata Kanson by Sakai. In 1906 Arahata brought her to Tokyo and found her a minor position with a small paper. For two years Sugako lived with Arahata, who considered her his 'wife', although Sugako appears to have retained her own opinions on the subject.[2]

Under the influence of Sakai, Arahata, and their radical friends, Kanno Sugako became an outspoken socialist. Inclined to extreme solutions, she had no use for Katayama and his social democratic position. Kōtoku's 'direct action' stand was far more appealing. At the same time, impressed by the deeds of Russian revolutionaries, Sugako had developed an active

---

[1] For the following biographical details, I have relied on Setouchi Harumi, 'Kanno Sugako', *Chūō Kōron*, vol. LXXX, no. 9 (September, 1965), pp. 291–301. Also Itoya Toshio, *Kōtoku Shūsui kenkyū*, pp. 267–9.

[2] See Arahata Kanson, *Kanson jiden*, p. 177, where Arahata speaks of Sugako as his 'common-law wife'; Sugako, for her part, thought there was nothing lasting between them.

interest in violence. This culminated in her participation and arrest in the Red Flåg Incident. Police brutality, which she both witnessed and experienced on this occasion, merely served to harden her determination to resist. Unfortunately, the Red Flag Incident resulted in Arahata's imprisonment, while she herself was released. Having nowhere to go, she began to turn to Kōtoku. By October 1908 her relations with Kōtoku were such that he invited her to come to live at the Heiminsha.

Kōtoku had every reason to find Sugako attractive. Beautiful, clever, and talented, on the one hand; bitter, indignant, and fearless on the other, Sugako lived up to his image of the ideal wife and revolutionary. Here was the woman he had always sought. With Sugako's support he might even be able to 'offer up his life at the right moment'. Unknown to Kōtoku, Sugako's extremism was to channel his growing interest in violence in new directions.

Despite Sugako's care, Kōtoku's health did not improve substantially. In the middle of November (1908) Ōishi Seinosuke, the doctor from Shingu, visited Tokyo and gave him another careful physical examination. Ōishi's findings confirmed his earlier suspicions that Kōtoku was ill with intestinal tuberculosis, a disease still largely fatal. Only complete rest, Ōishi told a friend, held any hope for Kōtoku. Without it he would have but 'two or three years left at the most'.[1] Ōishi also examined Kanno Sugako. She too proved to be ill with consumption and her chances for recovery did not look bright either.

On the day that Ōishi administered the physicals, Kōtoku brought up the subject of 'violent revolution'. According to Ōishi's subsequent testimony, the conversation ran as follows:

In addition to discussing the French Commune, Kōtoku stated that given the fact that the government's actions against socialists had become extremely repressive of late, there was absolutely no hope of winning the struggle against the government through the power of the written and spoken word. He moreover asked me to be on the lookout for determined individuals, intimating that because of the condition of his illness and impending death he would like to arm a band of fifty 'death-defying men' and with them close in on Nijūbashi [the Imperial Palace] after gathering together the poor, setting them to pillaging, and putting the torch to courts, prisons, city offices, and all government buildings. I told him I would discuss the matter with the comrades in Kishu after my return, and left things as they stood.[2]

[1] Itoya Toshio, *Kōtoku Shūsui kenkyū*, p. 258.
[2] Shiota Shōbei and Watanabe Junzō (eds.), *Hiroku taigayaku jiken*, vol. II, p. 74. This testimony comes from the preliminary interrogation in the High Treason Trial.

Testimony of this nature was later to prove highly incriminating for Kōtoku, and while those attempting to vindicate him have gone out of their way to show that his interest in 'violence' involved nothing more than a theoretical exploitation of public unrest – strikes, riots, and the like – and consequently ought not to have been judged as 'conspiracy', passages like the foregoing tend to jeopardize such an argument. It seems equally reasonable to assume – following the logic of the court – that having been informed of the true nature of his illness, Kōtoku began to bank on one last decisive act, and that this included the destruction of the Emperor.[1]

Ōishi Seinosuke certainly appears to have taken Kōtoku seriously. Returning to Shingu he began to look over his own group to see who might join him in such a venture.[2]

Meanwhile, unknown to Kōtoku and Ōishi, a factory hand by the name of Miyashita Daikichi came to Morichika Unpei in Osaka. Miyashita was seriously troubled by doubts about the Imperial Institution.

Miyashita was born in Yamanashi Prefecture in 1875.[3] After an elementary education he moved around the country working in various machine shops. In 1902 he became employed in a factory producing steam engines in Aichi Prefecture. At the same time he developed an interest in socialism. Under the influence of the first Japanese treatise on modern anarchism, Kemuriyama Sentarō's *Kinsei museifu shugi*, Miyashita began to doubt the divinity of the Emperor. In 1907 Miyashita was transferred to Osaka, which gave him the opportunity to visit Morichika Unpei, the former editor of the *Osaka Heimin Shimbun*. Morichika began to lecture Miyashita on the Japanese Throne, stating that the first Emperors were mere human beings who fought their way to power in Kyushu and subsequently invented the myth of divine origins in order to legitimatize their rule.[4] Morichika's lecture on the Emperor

---

[1] The fact that conversations of this nature had become almost daily occurrences at the Heimin-sha can only lead one to conclude that either Shūsui was seriously looking for dedicated extremists or he was completely lacking in discretion. For he must have known the danger inherent in such talk, given the government's repressive measures.

[2] On New Year's Day 1909 Ōishi invited to his home a number of young men, including Nariishi Heishirō, Nariishi Kanzaburō, Sakikubo Seiichi, Takagi Kenmei, and Mineo Setsudō. Over numerous cups of sake Ōishi presented these young men with Kōtoku's ideas on violent revolution. At least one of these young men, Nariishi Kanzaburō was impressed enough by what he heard to begin to experiment with the construction of bombs and had in his possession four sticks of dynamite when police authorities arrested him in 1910. Later all of these young men were implicated in the High Treason Incident. Ōishi and Nariishi Heishirō joined Kōtoku on the gallows, and the others were sentenced to life imprisonment. For a discussion of the Kishu group's relationship to the plot against the Emperor see Itoya Toshio, *Taigyaku jiken*, pp. 169ff.

[3] The following biographical details are mentioned in Itoya Toshio, *Kōtoku Shūsui kenkyū*, pp. 264ff.

[4] *Ibid.* p. 265.

took place a month after the Open Letter was published in San Francisco. The tone of the letter and what Morichika told Miyashita are remarkably similar and one cannot help but suspect that one of the copies of the letter had been sent to Morichika.[1] As a result of Morichika's lecture, Miyashita later told the court he lost all 'respect' for the Throne.[2]

On November 3, 1908, Miyashita received a small parcel through the mails which contained a number of copies of a tract secretly printed by Uchiyama Gudō in Hakone.[3] Written in commemoration of those who had been imprisoned as a result of the Red Flag Incident, Uchiyama's tract was both an indictment of the present government, including the Emperor, and a call for renewed resistance. One sentence read: 'When we get rid of the present government, we will have a free nation without an Emperor.'[4] Miyashita shared Uchiyama's sentiments and conclusions; on November 13 he wrote to Morichika expressing his personal conviction that if socialism were to make any gains in Japan the myth of the Emperor's divinity would have to be destroyed. The best way of achieving this, Miyashita wrote, was by showing that the Emperor could be killed like any other man.[5] Morichika took Miyashita's letter and showed it to Kōtoku.[6]

The more Miyashita concerned himself with the problems of socialism and the national polity, the more he became convinced of the need to do away with the Throne. On February 13, 1909, Miyashita visited Kōtoku in Tokyo. During his stay at the Heiminsha he reiterated much of what he had written to Morichika. Again he insisted that the chief impediment to the propagation of socialism was the Imperial myth. In order to destroy that myth the Emperor would have to be killed The best way to do this, he insisted, was to 'make bombs' and 'throw them at the Imperial carriage'.[7] After listening to Miyashita's arguments Kōtoku agreed that 'such measures will no doubt be necessary; hereafter there will arise individuals who will see that such measures are carried out'.[8]

---

[1] Of course, there is also the possibility that Morichika's interpretation came directly from Kōtoku.

[2] Shiota Shōbei and Watanabe Junzō (eds.), *Hiroku taigyaku jiken*, vol. I, p. 159.

[3] The tract was titled 'Nyūgoku Kinen', and constituted one of Uchiyama's first printing attempts. Proud of his success, Uchiyama had transported most of the copies to Tokyo, hoping to distribute them through the Heiminsha, but Kōtoku disapproved. Instead, Morichika Unpei offered him a list of the addresses of the former subscribers of the *Heimin Shimbun*. As a result, Uchiyama mailed out numerous small packages of his tract. No doubt the extreme language of the document can be surmised from the fact that Ōishi Seinosuke considered it so radical that he immediately burned the ten copies he received.

[4] Itoya Toshio, *Kōtoku Shūsui kenkyū*, p. 266.

[5] *Ibid.*   [6] *Ibid.*

[7] Shiota Shōbei and Watanabe Junzō (eds.), *Hiroku taigyaku jiken*, vol. I, p. 126.

[8] *Ibid.* p. 127.

Kōtoku's response to Miyashita's proposal sounds a great deal like the comment he made to Albert Johnson in a letter in 1907 that 'Japan which has already produced Social-Democrats and Anarchist-Communists, shall now produce many Direct-Actionists, Anti-Militarists, General Strikers, and even Terrorists.' Kōtoku's rejoinder to Miyashita's suggestion was more that of an academic who had just witnessed the confirmation of a theory than that of a revolutionary concerned with action. His unwillingness to involve himself immediately in a 'plot' with Miyashita, who would have been quite happy to accept Kōtoku's support, has sometimes been interpreted as a personal reluctance to take part in an actual conspiracy against the Throne.[1] On the other hand, given the fact that Miyashita was a virtual stranger at a time when government 'spies' were becoming increasingly active, Kōtoku's reluctance to side actively with Miyashita's proposal could easily have been the result of caution rather than disinterest.

In contrast to the argument that Kōtoku's interest in violence was purely theoretical and that he wished to play no part in a conspiracy against the Imperial House, there is considerable evidence that he was in fact making the transition from dispassionate observer to active participant.

Writing to Matsumoto Sugako in January 1909 Kōtoku noted that he was fully aware of his physical condition; that he realized that he had only a few years left; and that given this state of affairs he was determined to do his 'utmost' for the revolution. As he symbolically described it, he was now 'entering the field of battle', and was fully prepared to die either of 'illness' or the 'death sentence' in the next few years.[2]

Although it remains difficult to establish the extent to which Kōtoku made his views known to those who looked to him for leadership, the fact that Uchiyama Gudō went around Osaka in April 1909 telling others that Kōtoku and Kanno Sugako were incurably ill and had decided on 'one last measure' to achieve the revolution, certainly tends to suggest that others beside Matsumoto Sugako were informed of his determination.[3]

Perhaps it would not be unfair to attribute Kōtoku's eventual demise to his own lack of clear and decisive leadership. His unwillingness to affirm or contradict the ideas of his followers – a quality which is exploited by many current scholars in his defense – tended to be interpreted by extremists of the day like Uchiyama and Miyashita as signs of tacit approval. Certainly

---

[1] A number of Japanese scholars, including Itoya Toshio, Shiota Shōbei, and others have attempted to vindicate Kōtoku by emphasizing his reluctance to join Miyashita at this time. Even if true at the time, Kōtoku's so-called 'reluctance' appears to have totally disappeared by the autumn of 1909.

[2] *Nikki to shokan*, pp. 287–9.   [3] Itoya Toshio, *Kōtoku Shūsui kenkyū*, p. 270.

the majority of those who discussed their radical ideas with Kōtoku in the spring and summer of 1909 came away convinced that he sympathized with their schemes. At the same time, most of his followers were totally lacking in prudence and discretion. Thus, at a time when police surveillance called for utmost caution, strict organization, and unusual discipline, Kōtoku refused to provide any of these. Without such leadership, Kōtoku's passionate followers were no match for the authorities. The problem was all too clearly illustrated by Uchiyama Gudō's arrest.

Uchiyama's lack of prudence expressed itself not only in his tracts and pamphlets, but in his conversations with virtual strangers.[1] His admiration for Kōtoku was echoed in his own effort to make bombs and recruit a band of five or six 'death-defying men' to assassinate the Crown Prince. No doubt he considered himself a participant in what he described as Kōtoku's 'one last measure', but unknown to him police detectives had already singled him out as the source of several seditious pamphlets, and late in May they raided the Rinsenji Temple in Hakone and discovered his secret workshop. In addition to a cache of anarchist materials, the police uncovered twelve sticks of dynamite, four packages of explosive gelatin, and a supply of fuses.[2] Six days later, on May 29, 1909, Uchiyama was arrested on his return to Hakone. Charged with illegal possession of explosives and violations of the press and publication laws, he was subsequently found guilty and sentenced to twelve years of imprisonment. Needless to say, the police investigation into Uchiyama's activities served to increase suspicions that an anti-Imperial plot was in the hatching and that Kōtoku Shūsui was involved in its formation.

At the time of Uchiyama's arrest Miyashita Daikichi was in the process of being transferred from his job near Osaka to a new post in Nagano Ken. The months since his visit to the Heiminsha had merely confirmed his conviction that the Emperor would have to be killed. Fully convinced that such an act required 'bombs', he began to investigate their construction in earnest. On May 25 he wrote to Kōtoku informing him of the state of his research, and reiterated his stand that as soon as he mastered the construction of bombs he was ready to 'die for the cause'.[3] Early in June, Miyashita stopped over at the Heiminsha on his way to Nagano and discussed his ideas on the assassination of the Emperor with Kōtoku and Kanno Sugako.[4] While Kōtoku's response to Miyashita's proposal remained ambiguous, he

---

[1] Itoya Toshio, *Kōtoku Shūsui kenkyū*, p. 270.   [2] *Ibid.*
[3] Shiota Shōbei and Watanabe Junzō (eds.), *Hiroku taigyaku jiken*, vol. I, p. 127.
[4] *Ibid.* pp. 127-8.

nevertheless recommended to Miyashita Niimura Tadao and Furukawa Rikisaku, two young men whom he described as possessing 'firm ideas', and whom he stated could be thoroughly 'trusted'.[1]

Miyashita had met Niimura at the Heiminsha in February 1909. At that time Niimura had just finished serving a two-month sentence in the Maebashi jail for violations of the press laws in connection with a small socialist journal, the *Tohoku Hyōron*. An ardent supporter of Kōtoku's 'direct action' position, Niimura decided to visit Kōtoku in Tokyo after his release. Out of work, he extended his stay at the Heiminsha to several months. Finally Kōtoku talked to Ōishi Seinosuke and got Niimura a position in Ōishi's pharmacy in Shingu. At their February meeting Miyashita told Niimura of the need to assassinate the Emperor. Niimura voiced agreement.[2] In June of 1909 Miyashita wrote Niimura in Shingu that he had begun to experiment with the construction of bombs.[3]

Despite his technical experience Miyashita soon discovered that the construction of bombs was not as easy as he had originally imagined. After consulting various encyclopedias and talking to a friend who worked in a fireworks plant, Miyashita became aware that a mixture of ten parts potassium chlorate with five parts realgar (arsenic monosulfide) could cause a powerful explosion. But these chemicals were not easily acquired. After exhausting what he regarded as the limit of a safely purchasable supply without success, he wrote to Niimura asking him to provide him with the necessary raw materials.[4]

As the summer months of 1909 passed, Miyashita's research made progress much more slowly than anticipated. Meanwhile Kōtoku Shūsui's position in Tokyo grew increasingly desperate.

One of the reasons for Kōtoku's difficulties stemmed from his relationship to Kanno Sugako. When Chiyoko returned to Tokyo early in 1909 still ailing and fearful, Kōtoku proved less sympathetic than earlier. Chiyoko's emphasis on caution contrasted all too distinctly with Sugako's careless abandon. In the light of this contrast Chiyoko appeared less and less ideal as the wife of a revolutionary. Meanwhile tensions mounted between her and Sugako. Kōtoku, faced with the need to choose between the two, concluded that Chiyoko could never become a revolutionary. Early in March he divorced her and sent her to live with her sister in Nagoya.[5] Thereafter he began to

[1] Itoya Toshio, *Kōtoku Shūsui kenkyū*, p. 270.
[2] Shiota Shōbei and Watanabe Junzō (eds.), *Hiroku taigyaku jiken*, vol. I, p. 174.
[3] Itoya Toshio, *Kōtoku Shūsui kenkyū*, p. 171.   [4] *Ibid.* p. 271.
[5] In explaining the divorce to his mother, Shūsui noted that the reasons for it were not merely government persecution and the opposition of her sister. More important was the fact that both

live openly in what was described as a 'free love' relationship with Sugako.

The Tokyo press made much of Kōtoku's new 'love' match. Many of the newspapers went out of their way to berate him, and opposition began to mount from all sides, including his wing of the socialist movement. What added to the dramatic effect of the controversy was the fact that Arahata Kanson, still incarcerated in prison for his involvement in the Red Flag Incident, was built into a maligned hero. Kōtoku, for his part, was accused of total disrespect for a friend, and what was worse, extreme callousness towards an imprisoned comrade. As the scandal grew, Kōtoku found himself increasingly isolated from his former friends.

There were other reasons for Kōtoku's isolation. Ever since the arrest of Uchiyama Gudō, police suspicions had mounted. The materials seized at the Rinsenji confirmed the possibility of violence against the Imperial House. Gudō's ties with Kōtoku were no secret, police surveillance at the Heiminsha was doubled,[1] and a persistent rumor circulated that Kōtoku was contemplating anti-Imperial violence.[2] Such conditions did not contribute to his popularity.

Publishing too had become a virtual impossibility. No one wanted to handle Kōtoku's books and articles, knowing that they were almost guaranteed to be prohibited. His effort to establish a new journal, *Jiyu Shiso* (*Free Thought*), with the aid of Kanno Sugako, immediately ran into a stone wall of government opposition. After only two issues the journal was banned, Kōtoku and Kanno were fined and before the case was concluded their fines had jumped to the unprecedented sum of one thousand yen.

Kōtoku was well aware that another prison term would be difficult to endure physically and might well mean his death. In an effort to shield him from such a fate Kanno Sugako had taken over official responsibility of the magazine and when the fines were levied most of the financial burden was cast on her shoulders. At the same time her own physical condition remained precarious. The constant pressures of life at the Heiminsha had

were bored with one another and had come to the conclusion that they would never be capable of loving one another. Kōtoku saw the fault for his unsuccessful marriage in the whole system of arranged marriage which did not take into consideration the personalities of the participants. With Sugako, he wrote home, there was no flattery or covering up. Sugako was a woman who understood him and his ideas; consequently, he was 'very happy' living with her. *Nikki to shokan*, pp. 315–16.

[1] Early in June of 1909 police officials set up a tent in a field across from the Heiminsha and anyone coming to visit Kōtoku was ushered behind its red and white curtain and interrogated. Four policemen constantly watched the exits of the building and anyone coming out was followed.

[2] In an interview with Sugimura Sōjinkan published in the newspaper *Asahi* on June 7, 1909, Kōtoku ridiculed this rumor, 'How can anyone', he told Sōjinkan, 'be foolish enough to contemplate such an act.'

begun to tell on her nerves. Overwork and exhaustion had served to aggravate her consumptive condition. The result was a state of hypertension in which the extreme pitch of her revolutionary fervor constantly teetered on the brink of hysteria and emotional collapse. Kōtoku soon became aware of this condition and realized that Sugako was hardly capable of enduring a prison sentence herself. On the other hand, his lack of financial resources once more towered as an insurmountable obstacle. With each passing day the thousand yen which stood between imprisonment and freedom grew in proportions. 'I am now fighting against the whole of Japan', he wrote home, 'the government is trying to destroy me through financial torture; how sad it would be to go down for the lack of a mere five to seven hundred yen!'[1] As a last resort, he asked Komatarō to sell the family land.

By the autumn of 1909 Kōtoku considered himself in a final struggle with the government. To meet the government's onslaught he was prepared to sacrifice everything he had. If he was to go under, he was determined to go under fighting.

With his back to the wall, Kōtoku began to take an active part in the plotting against the Emperor. During the first weeks of September 1909, Kōtoku, Kanno Sugako, and Niimura Tadao agreed upon tactics, which Niimura described in the preliminary interrogation of the High Treason Trial as follows: 'First of all we discussed the matter of bombing the Imperial Procession in the autumn of 1910, and then we conferred about simultaneously assembling twenty or thirty comrades, each armed with his own bomb, and setting out to start riots, destroy prisons, release prisoners, kill ministers, and attack government offices.'[2]

Kōtoku's active participation in the conspiracy against the Throne, vague and 'theoretical' as it may have been given the fact that weapons for its implementation were as yet nonexistent, remained highly incriminating. In the eyes of the Supreme Court the early September discussions in which Kōtoku openly revealed his approval of Miyashita, Niimura, Kanno, and Furukawa's plan to assassinate the Emperor irrevocably linked him to the crime contemplated by the others. What his subsequent attitudes were made little difference. As far as the court was concerned the die had been cast.

Niimura was pleased by Kōtoku's support. He immediately made a trip to Nagano Ken to inform Miyashita of the latest developments. At the time of this visit Miyashita reported to Niimura that his experiments remained unsuccessful; that he required more chemicals; and that if possible he would

---

[1] *Nikki to shokan*, p. 319.
[2] Shiota Shōbei and Watanabe Junzō (eds.), *Hiroku taigyaku jiken*, vol. I, p. 188.

like to consult with someone who had actually produced a successful proto-
type. Niimura related this conversation to Kōtoku upon his return to the
capital.

Miyashita's request for additional information on the construction of
bombs, hopefully from someone who had actually engaged in their production, was to be met by a curious historical coincidence which served to
implicate Kōtoku more deeply in the conspiracy against the Throne.

Early in October 1909 Kanno Sugako suffered a nervous breakdown. The
immediate influence of Sugako's emotional collapse was a sobering effect on
Kōtoku, who suddenly became more concerned with the woman with whom
he had grown intimate than with the plotting in which she had played such a
central role. The shift of emotional dependence once again emphasized
direct personal responsibility which had always weighed heavily on Kōtoku's
shoulders. This was precisely the area of his psychological nature which his
revolutionary ideology had failed to pierce on previous occasions. Again the
bonds of the past were to shackle him. Without Sugako's constant encourage-
ment, and what is perhaps more important, without the need to compete
with her brand of extreme radicalism in an effort to assert his own mascu-
linity, Kōtoku's ardor for the plot against the Emperor appears to have
waned.

Meanwhile Sugako's illness provided him with a chance to help Miyashita.
At the time of Miyashita's request for more information Kōtoku had been
at a loss for a reply. Preoccupied with Sugako's problems he had found
little time to do further research on the subject. Moreover, his gradually
shifting attitude towards the conspiracy did not aid such efforts. All this
changed when Okumiya Tateyuki came to the Heiminsha in the middle of
October to pay a call on Sugako. Okumiya had been a member of the
Popular Rights Movement as a young man. Deeply involved in the movement's most radical phase in the mid-1880s, a period during which bombs
had been resorted to on several occasions, Kōtoku concluded that Okumiya
must know something about their construction, and put the question to his
visitor. While Okumiya admitted that he had never personally constructed
a bomb, he indicated that he knew the man who had constructed the bombs
for the Osaka Incident and might be able to acquire the information needed
by Miyashita. After consulting with his friend, Okumiya presented Kōtoku
with a new chemical formula, as well as with the details for its use; Kōtoku
saw to it that this information was relayed to Miyashita through Niimura.[1]

[1] The details of the Okumiya episode are given in Kanzaki Kiyoshi, *Taigyaku jiken kiroku*,
vol. I, p. 321. Also Itoya Toshio, *Kōtoku Shūsui kenkyū*, p. 277.

Using his newly acquired formula, Miyashita succeeded in exploding his first bomb on November 3, 1909, in the mountains not far from the city of Matsumoto. His own explosion blended in neatly with the fireworks being set off by the city in celebration of the Emperor's birthday. Within a matter of days word of Miyashita's achievement reached the Heiminsha in Tokyo.

Although Kōtoku was partly responsible for Miyashita's success, the new possibilities that it opened did not elicit an enthusiastic response from him. In the month since his open approval of the assassination plot, Kōtoku's desire to pull out of the conspiracy had grown. As he later described his attitude to the Court:

At the time I thought that the intellectual propagation of socialism was most important. Moreover, I thought I would like to expound Nakae Chōmin's philosophy, and gathered various materials for this purpose. Under the circumstances I thought it would be of no benefit for the cause if I were to be laid low by taking part in Miyashita's efforts. In addition Tadaō encouraged me to withdraw from the plan, saying that it was better for a person like myself to devote my efforts to the propagation of knowledge. At the same time I wanted to provide Kanno, whose childhood had been spent under the most adverse conditions, and whose life had been nothing more than one long battle, with a few years of peace, and thought she ought to withdraw from the plan as well. I talked things over with her, and thereafter my attitude [towards the plot] became vague and indistinct.[1]

One of the reasons for Kōtoku's loss of ardor may well have stemmed from the behind-the-scenes efforts of Koizumi Sanshin and Matsui Hakken.[2]

Koizumi and Matsui were convinced that the cause of Kōtoku's extremism and plotting was excessive government pressure. Koizumi felt certain that if he could get the Home Ministry to ease up on Kōtoku, and at the same time provide him with a way out of his financial difficulties, he might still extricate his friend from what he considered a fatal position. At the same time, Koizumi was aware that if his negotiations with the Home Ministry were to succeed, he would have to have at his disposal some show of Kōtoku's good faith.

Unfortunately, records do not indicate the exact moment when Koizumi first warned Kōtoku that the situation was growing extremely dangerous and suggested an alternative through which he might free himself from the dilemma. Subsequent events tend to suggest, however, that this occurred almost simultaneously with his loss of enthusiasm for the assassination of the Emperor.

[1] Shiota Shōbei and Watanabe Junzō (eds.), *Hiroku taigyaku jiken*, vol. II, p. 19.
[2] For a recent discussion of Koizumi and Matsui's efforts see Itō Sei, 'Kōtoku Shūsui no taiho', *Gunzō*, vol. 22, no. 4 (April, 1967).

By March of 1910 Koizumi had formulated a plan that he was prepared to set in motion. First of all, he went to Hosono Jirō, a member of the lower house of the Diet, who was independently wealthy and knew Kōtoku personally. Koizumi got Hosono to agree to finance Kōtoku for the next few years if he were to give up his radical activities and turn to legitimate writing. Next, Hosono and Matsui paid a call on Hirata Tōsuke, the Home Minister in the Katsura Cabinet. Hosono and Matsui told Hirata that Kōtoku had recently undergone a change of heart, and that they, his friends, were willing to sacrifice anything to remove him from his present environment, and restore him to a position where his talents might be used for the good of the nation. They suggested to the Home Minister that the government could help them by easing up its restrictions on Kōtoku.[1]

Hosono was also a good friend of the Commissioner of Police, Kamei Eizaburō, and Koizumi and he paid a number of calls on Kamei to discuss the problem. Kamei assured them that he would make every effort to cooperate with their plan. It was decided that if Kōtoku showed himself willing to compromise, the police would ease up on their repressive measures.[2]

Having secured a promise for cooperation from government and police officials, Koizume decided it was time to try to work out an agreement between Kōtoku and the authorities. In the middle of March he arranged a meeting between Kōtoku, Hosono, and a representative of the Home Ministry at a house of assignation in Kōjimachi.[3] At this meeting Hosono openly urged Kōtoku to 'recant', and Koizumi suggested that given the present state of affairs it might be best to withdraw from the socialist movement for two or three years. If Kōtoku were willing to take up writing something like a 'history of the *Sengoku* (late Ashikaga) period', Koizumi hinted that several thousand yen could be made available through his and Hosono's efforts. Koizumi moreover indicated that should Kōtoku agree to his plan, it would be wise for him to get out of Tokyo for a while. Koizumi recommended that he retire to his favorite retreat, the Tennoya, an inn in Yugawara.

Although Kōtoku revealed himself interested in Koizumi's proposal, Koizumi was well aware that final agreement would depend on Kanno Sugako's attitude towards the plan. Rather than trusting Kōtoku to convince her of the advantages of such a solution, Koizumi went out of his way to discuss the whole issue with her at his home. Finally, having convinced her

---

[1] Itoya Toshio, *Kōtoku Shūsui kenkyū*, p. 281. [2] *Ibid.*

[3] The meeting is discussed in Itō Sei, 'Kōtoku Shūsui no taiho', *Gunzō*, vol. 22, no. 4 (April, 1967), p. 208.

to join Kōtoku in Yugawara, Koizumi felt that he had succeeded in rescuing his friend.

On March 22, 1910, Kōtoku and Kanno packed up their possessions, closed the Sendagaya Heiminsha, and moved to the Tennoya in Yugawara. In the weeks that followed, Kōtoku began working on a history of the Sengoku period. The government, true to its side of the bargain, saw to it that police harassment ceased.

For Kōtoku the cost of making peace with the authorities was extremely high. Since his trip to the United States he had become convinced of a new sense of freedom; he had returned to Japan fully prepared to reject compromise as degrading and had emphasized the need for spiritual resistance as the only means of retaining revolutionary purity. Under the influence of his conversion to 'direct action' he once more saw himself as a figure capable of resisting the pressures of the environment. But in the wake of subsequent experiences this too proved to be nothing more than an idle dream. Once more the environment had proved stronger than the spirit; once again his picture of the ideal had refused to conform to reality. In many ways Yugawara represented a final psychological low point in Kōtoku's life.

There were additional reasons for Kōtoku's renewed depression. In his years since his return from San Francisco Kōtoku had attempted to break emotionally with parts of the tradition which he had long ago rejected intellectually. His efforts to identify with the common man,[1] his willingness to break with accepted social mores in his relationship with Kanno Sugako, his willingness to move from a theoretical rejection of the Japanese Emperor to an actual assassination plot – all these testify to an effort to regulate his life by the principles of the doctrine to which he had come to adhere since his imprisonment. And yet, if these efforts taught him anything it was a new awareness of the powerful emotional forces that tied him to the past. Again he was faced with the dilemma that what his intellectual commitment required and what his emotional heritage permitted were irreconcilable. Perhaps this is what he had in mind when he told Hiranuma Kiichirō, the chief prosecutor at the High Treason Trial, that he had become involved in the conspiracy against the Throne because he was convinced that the

---

[1] George Elison in his article, 'Kōtoku Shūsui: "The Change in Thought"', *Monumenta Nipponica*, vol. XXII, no. 3–4, p. 466, echoes Hayashi Shigeru's criticism (*Kindai Nihon no shisōka tachi*, p. 96) that Kōtoku's principal failure was his inability to organize workers and peasants. Elison, like Hayashi, attributes this failure to Kōtoku's elitism, rather than to his concept of a spontaneous revolution which could not be affected by 'organization'. Certainly Kōtoku did attempt to go to the people in his final years, but his object remained to 'educate', and not to 'organize' them.

doctrine to which he adhered required such an act, but that, while he knew that such an act was necessary, he somehow found himself incapable of going through with it when the time for implementation arrived.[1] As on previous occasions, self-knowledge did not result in self-respect. Forced to confront the truth of his personal weakness, Kōtoku once more submitted to the temptations of self-pity and irresponsibility. Moping and depression, on the other hand, led to a renewed emphasis on man's lack of freedom. In the end the human being remained a victim of 'fate'.

Despite the external tranquility of the small hot spring resort and the absence of police interference, Kōtoku's despair seems to have mounted. Rumors of his defection rapidly spread throughout the movement. Even his few remaining friends were not willing to defend him against the charge that he had sold out to the government. Worse, the agreement with Koizumi and Hosono did not produce the necessary funds as soon as expected.[2] Time was running out on Kōtoku's attempts for a final appeal in connection with the fines of the previous year. By the middle of May the court sided against the appeal; unable to raise the necessary funds, Sugako had no choice but to enter prison for a three-and-a-half months term on May 18, 1910.

Sugako's return to Tokyo symbolized more than a temporary defeat at the hands of the government. One of the reasons for Kōtoku's acceptance of Koizumi's compromise was the possibility it offered for a few years of tranquility which he might share with Sugako. Sugako, for her part, found Yugawara dull and boring. Gone was the bustle of Tokyo; gone too was the excitement of conspiracy. As the weeks passed, Yugawara became a prison of its own. Under the circumstances even Kōtoku lost his appeal. Quarrels became common, and when Sugako boarded the train for Tokyo on May 17 both knew that the break was permanent.[3]

What had made Yugawara even more intolerable for Sugako was the fact that the conspiracy against the Throne had not collapsed with Kōtoku's defection. Kōtoku's reluctance to participate made little difference to Miyashita and Niimura. Late in January, after once more sounding him out on his position, Miyashita and Niimura decided to carry out the assassination without out his help. Until her departure for Yugawara, Sugako remained one of the participants in their discussions; her return to Tokyo on May 17 symbolized

[1] Hiranuma Kiichirō, *Hiranuma Kiichirō kaikoroku*, p. 60.
[2] Kōtoku subsequently wrote to Chiyoko that he was able to get food and lodging in Yugawara through Koizumi Sanshin's good graces, but that some arrangement on which Koizumi was working (the implication being that this was a financial arrangement for Kōtoku's support) would probably not come through until August or September. *Nikki to shokan*, p. 337.
[3] Setouchi Harumi, 'Kanno Sugako', *Chūō Kōron*, vol. LXXX, no. 9 (September, 1965), pp. 300–1.

her return to the conspiracy. That same evening she met with Miyashita, Niimura, and Furukawa to discuss and make plans for the assassination of the Emperor. At one point during this meeting straws were drawn to decide who would throw the first bomb. Sugako won, and it was decided to let matters rest until her release from prison in August.[1]

Meanwhile Kōtoku's despair continued. On the morning of May 20 he received an emotion-filled letter from Arahata Kanson.[2] Arahata wrote of the anger, disappointment, and despair that had overcome him after his discovery of Kōtoku's affair with Sugako. He related how he had been driven to come to Yugawara on May 9 to kill the two of them only to discover that they were both on a visit to Tokyo. Broke and unable to pay for the train fare to Tokyo, he had spent the night on a cold bleak beach near Atami. There in the rain he had contemplated ending his own life. And yet, each time he brought the pistol to his head he observed the desire for revenge proved stronger than the urge for self-destruction. 'No, I shall never be able to die', Arahata wrote, 'while you, my hated enemy, remain alive.' After berating Kōtoku for his failure to live up to the ideals he espoused, he accused Kōtoku not only of stabbing a fellow comrade in the back while that comrade was unable to defend himself in prison, but also of having finally sold out to the police. In conclusion Arahata wrote, 'I am telling you quite openly that I shall kill you.'

In contrast to the anger, frustration, and emotional crisis which bristles from every line of Arahata's letter, Kōtoku's reply suggests a certain air of resignation.[3] While the purpose of Kōtoku's letter was no doubt to placate Arahata, the content of the letter also tells us a good deal about Kōtoku's emotional state during his final days in Yugawara:

There is not much I can say [Kōtoku wrote]; rereading your letter I could not help but sympathize with you. When I read about your sitting in the rain on the cold, bleak strand of Sōshu holding the pistol to your head, tears unexpectedly came to my eyes. The wrath, indignation, and hatred you bear me are not without foundation. Good. In order to satisfy you I have determined to become a victim of your pistol. But I did not try to conceal as much from you, or bear you as much of a grudge, as your letter suggests. I certainly did not intend to ridicule and insult you. If I could have you read some of the letters I wrote at that time you would understand. When you were released from prison I had a great desire to see you. On any

[1] Itoya Toshio, *Kōtoku Shūsui kenkyū*, p. 285.

[2] The circumstances under which this letter was written are given in Arahata Kanson, *Kanson jiden*, pp. 176ff. A portion of Arahata's letter is reproduced in Asukai Masamichi, 'Kōtoku Shūsui', in *Hangyakusha no shōzō*, pp. 246–7.

[3] Kōtoku's letter to Arahata from which the following quotations are taken can be found in *Nikki to shokan*, pp. 333–6.

number of occasions I thought it best for the two of us to confront each other, but each time I was deterred by other people who said that seeing you would only serve to hurt and aggravate you further. Under the circumstances all I could do was sorrowfully accept this state of affairs as fate. Even today while you follow me around with a lethal weapon seeking revenge my desire to see you has not diminished in the least. I am convinced that I will be able to die by your hands with no ill feelings of any kind.

Kōtoku continued the letter by trying to trace for Arahata the process through which he had been forced to withdraw to Yugawara:

My love affair with Kanno has been censured by today's society as a great evil. I regret that it was the result of my weak nature and the fact that I was born without discretion. In any case, I find it difficult to bear the burden of knowing that because of this I have caused you to lose all hope, despair, and become desperate. Sinner or criminal, weakling or fool, I have no choice but to await your punishment with resignation. My life, at this time, is not something I particularly treasure. Ever since last summer I have been hated, abandoned by most of my comrades, and scathingly denounced for my love affair. Finally my reputation has been marred with rumors that I sold out. On the other hand, the authorities ceaselessly singled me out for their unscrupulous persecution. In the end, completely unable to make a living, I was forced to borrow money, and when this source was depleted I had to sell my library, my swords, my grandmother's gold and silver coins which she had left me as a memento, and even the house in which my old mother resided. Having exhausted all my resources I had no other choice but to board here. To make matters worse, ever since her release from prison last year Kanno has had attacks of extreme hysteria. For a while I thought that she had gone quite mad, and even now her condition is still one of extreme nervous prostration.

The pressures of the last six months, Kōtoku wrote, had brought him to the verge of suicide himself:

At present I can no longer endure the persecution and poverty. Despairing of the dark future that confronts me I have on more than one occasion secretly contemplated suicide. And yet, I have an old mother of seventy who depends on me. I also have a few books and proposals that I want to leave behind for posterity. And then there are still some areas in which I would like to help direct a movement. Drawn by these various circumstances I was a coward and procrastinated unable to make a clear decision.

Finally Kōtoku admitted that his efforts to liberate himself from the ties of his society in the name of freedom had ended in failure. Rather than a sense of liberation such an effort had led to personal anguish and to the realization that he could not discard his emotional ties in the name of his foreign ideology. 'When I look back and think of how my weakness and lack of discretion has brought great suffering to Chiyoko, for one, and you, for another, while at the same time forcing Sugako to pay the price of cruel sacrifice,' Kōtoku wrote, 'I think that I may well be a man who deserves even greater suffering in retribution.' 'To be frank,' he added, 'I have been worn out by life's battles. Life is no longer dear to me. At present I live on a frontier of anguish that few foreigners can imagine.' In his final paragraphs Kōtoku made it quite clear to Arahata that his relationship with Sugako was finished. Two days later, in keeping with his reply to Arahata, Kōtoku sent an apologetic letter to his former wife, Chiyoko, in which he admitted that he had wronged her and hinted at the possibility of a reconciliation.[1]

On May 20, while Kōtoku was writing his reply to Arahata's letter, Nagano Ken police authorities searched Miyashita's room in Akashina. The search was part of a local investigation begun when police officials became suspicious of Miyashita's activities, which included numerous orders for copper containers from a local tinsmith. The search of his quarters revealed several of the canisters under question. A further search of the shop where he worked brought to light the chemicals he had used in earlier experiments. Within a matter of days Nagano Ken detectives were able to piece together sufficient evidence for Miyashita's and Niimura's arrest. On May 25, 1910, both men were taken into custody. Questioning and further investigation soon uncovered not only the main conspiracy, but the complex nationwide tangle that tied other radicals to the plotters.

Cut off from developments in Nagano Ken, Kōtoku spent the last few weeks in May working on his anti-Christian treatise, *Kirisuto massatsu ron*.[2] Towards the end of the month he was joined by Taoka Reiun and Ōoka Ikuzō, the man who had originally discovered his literary talents on the staff of the *Chūō Shimbun*. Taoka reported unusual police activity in Tokyo, but things remained quiet in Yugawara, and Kōtoku's spirits improved under the influence of his old friends. On June 1, 1910, he felt optimistic enough to venture a trip to Tokyo in order to find a publisher for his new book. As he was about to board a train for the capital he was arrested and taken into custody.

[1] *Ibid.* pp. 337–8.
[2] Kōtoku soon lost interest in the history of the Sengoku period which he started to write in April. Instead, he once more turned to the subject of Christianity which had fascinated him for nearly a decade. Using the materials he collected in San Francisco and other anti-Christian works sent to him by Albert Johnson, he constructed a strongly-worded rejection of Christ as a historical figure, and of Christianity as a viable religion in the modern world. In its rejection of authority based on 'myth', the work had obvious implications for the Japanese Imperial system.

CHAPTER 8

The trial, 1910–11

KŌTOKU SHŪSUI'S ARREST was followed by a series of nationwide arrests that brought into custody many of the individuals discussed in the foregoing chapter. In the months that followed, literally hundreds of men and women were investigated and interrogated. At the end of six months of questioning, during which the strictest secrecy was enforced,[1] government prosecutors had in their possession most of the details outlined in the previous narrative. On the basis of this information the Court of Cassation concluded its preliminary investigation[2] with an indictment against Kōtoku that included the following points:

(1) Kōtoku Shūsui became an anarchist in the United States; organized the Social Revolutionary Party; and formulated a plan whereby those in America would work in concert with those in Japan.

(2) After his return in June 1906 he corresponded with Kropotkin and propagated a new hard line through the *Heimin Shimbun*.

(3) On his way to the capital [in 1908] he spoke in Osaka of the need for a 'spirit of rebellion' and was determined to revenge the Red Flag Incident.

(4) In 1908 he came to know Miyashita, and being aware of the limited time left to him decided to carry out a violent revolution by recruiting a band of fifty death-defying men with whom he hoped to seize the property of the wealthy, burn down all government offices, assassinate various officials, and bring harm to the Emperor in order to establish anarchism.

(5) Sharing Sugako's revolutionary fervor he joined her, Miyashita, Furukawa, and Niimura in conspiring against the Throne as well as in studying the construction of bombs until Miyashita produced a successful proto-

---

[1] From the first of June to the first of November, 1910, Kōtoku was not allowed to communicate with anyone outside of the Ichigaya Prison. During these months each of the defendants was questioned repeatedly and their stories were compared and corroborated. Only after the preliminary investigation had been completed (November 1, 1910) was Kōtoku permitted to have visitors and write letters.

[2] The preliminary investigation was conducted by the Tokyo District Court for the Court of Cassation. It concluded early in November that sufficient evidence was available to formulate the charge of 'High Treason' and prepared the way for the trial by the highest court in December.

type. Then, after conferring on how to put the plot into action, he retired to Yugawara to wait for the proper moment.[1]

Points four and five constituted the heart of the government's case against Kōtoku. Both fell under the jurisdiction of Article 73 of the new Criminal Code, i.e., 'Crimes against the Throne'; conviction under this article called for the death penalty.[2]

Because the trial, which commenced on December 10, 1910, has become the subject of considerable historical controversy it merits a scope of treatment which cannot be given here. Moreover, since much of the current Japanese criticism of the case involves Kōtoku's co-defendants, a full treatment of whom would seem to me to lie beyond the scope of this work, I shall focus my discussion of the trial largely around Kōtoku's involvement in the incident. In the process, as will become apparent, the present debate over Kōtoku and his fellow defendants' innocence cannot be avoided.

It would be pointless to deny the element of mystery that continues to surround the trial through which Kōtoku Shūsui lost his life. Whether this is the fault of government design or historical accident remains a further issue of debate. There is, for example, the whole question of records.[3] What became of the Court of Cassation documents in the years that followed? If the records of the trial are still extant, why has the postwar government

---

[1] These five points, abbreviated by Nishio Yōtarō in *Kōtoku Shūsui*, pp. 276–7, represent the essence of the government's charges against Shūsui, which are presented in full in the opinion of the preliminary investigation delivered by the Tokyo District Court which is cited in Shiota Shōbei and Watanabe Junzō (eds.), *Hiroku taigyaku jiken*, vol. II, pp. 116ff.

[2] A translation of Article 73 of the Criminal Code reads as follows: 'Every person who has committed, or has attempted to commit, a dangerous (or injurious) act against (the person of) the Emperor, the Emperor's Grandmother, the Empress Dowager, the Empress, the Emperor's Son, the Emperor's Grandson and the Heir to the Throne shall be condemned to death.' William J. Sebald, *The Criminal Code of Japan* (Kobe, Japan, 1936), p. 64.

[3] Perhaps nothing presents greater problems for the student of the High Treason Trial of 1910–11 than the existing documentation. What is available has been collected by Shiota Shōbei and Watanabe Junzō in their two-volume *Hiroku taigyaku jiken* and by Kanzaki Kiyoshi in his three-volume *Taigyaku jiken kiroku*. The documents in these volumes include the testimony of Kōtoku and the other principals before the preliminary investigation judges, records of the original investigation by Nagano Ken authorities, the opinions of the judges in the preliminary investigation, police documents, some of the defendants' prison letters and other prison writings, and a variety of other materials, including what appears to be a good part of the documentary evidence that came to light in the preliminary investigation and a complete version of the final decision rendered by the Court of Cassation. Unfortunately the materials available deal largely with the preliminary investigation and not with the subsequent trial; moreover, even the testimony available is not complete, for it consists primarily of those parts of the original records which Hirade Osamu, one of the lawyers assigned to defend Kōtoku and the others, considered useful for his defense. For a discussion of the records of the trial see Shiota and Watanabe, *Hiroku taigyaku jiken*, pp. 69ff; also Itoya Toshio, 'Taigyaku jiken kenkyū no rekishi', *Rōdō undō shi kenkyū*, no. 22 (July, 1960). The latter volume of *Rōdō undō shi kenkyū* also contains an extensive bibliography on the High Treason Incident which includes over 230 items.

failed to make them public? If they were lost, as may well have been the case in the Great Earthquake of 1923 or in the bombing raids of World War II, why have the authorities refused to acknowledge their loss? Until such questions are answered – that is to say, until the gap in documentation which now exists between the records of the preliminary investigation and the final decision rendered on January 18, 1911, is overcome – a considerable cloud of uncertainty cannot help but contribute to the accusations of 'frameup', 'government plot', etc., which are all too often used to describe the trial by current Japanese scholars.

The critical attitude towards the closed trial which many contemporary scholars have adopted should perhaps be judged more precisely within the historical context in which the trial was held. There was certainly nothing illegal about the decision of the court to hold the trial *in camera*.[1] More important, public opinion solidly backed the adoption of such procedure. As early as November 19, 1910, *The Japan Weekly Mail* noted:

We cannot find any Japanese newspaper now advocating a public trial. The universal belief appears to be that to place such desperate men before a public bar would be to provide for them precisely the opportunity they desire. They would certainly use it to pose as martyrs; to proclaim their mischievous doctrines to an audience such as they could not otherwise command, and in circumstances calculated to impart spurious weight to their words. Thus the conviction in journalistic circles is that they should be dealt with secretly and conclusively. This is a question which offers much room for discussion, but on the whole we are inclined to agree with our Tokyo contemporaries.[2]

The only argument to the contrary, an argument that might today be regarded as prophetic, was aired by the *Niroku Shimpō*. This paper observed:

The wisest course is to let the public hear with their own ears the evidence upon which these men are arraigned, and thus everybody will be convinced that the miscreants are as criminal as the Authorities allege. If that course be followed no dissentient voice will be raised, no matter how severe the penalty exacted, but if

[1] Chapter V, Article LIX of the Meiji Constitution stated: 'Trials and judgements of a Court shall be conducted publicly. When, however, there exists any fear, that such publicity may be prejudicial to peace and order, or to the maintenance of public morality, the public trial may be suspended by provision of law or by the decision of the Court of Law.' In his commentary on the Meiji Constitution, Itō Hirobumi noted in reference to this Article: 'The cases in which public trial may be "prejudicial to peace and order", are, for instance, those relating to offences connected with a state of internal commotion or with foreign trouble or those relating to the assembling of mobs, or to instigation to crime, thereby agitating and exciting people's minds. The cases in which public trial may be "prejudicial to the maintenance of public morality", are, such, for instance, as relate to private matters causing scandal and shocking public morality, when exposed to the knowledge of the community.' Itō Hirobumi, *Commentaries on the Constitution of the Empire of Japan* (tr. Itō Miyoji, Tokyo, 1889) pp. 106–7.

[2] *The Japan Weekly Mail*, November 19, 1910, p. 631.

the punishment be drastic and the procedure secret, false ideas will certainly be engendered.[1]

Therefore, it seems clear that, except for a small minority adhering to the *Niroku*'s position, the public at large favored a secret trial on the same grounds that were announced by Tsuru Jōichiro, the Chief Judge, on the opening day of the trial, namely that a public airing of the case would prove 'prejudicial to peace and order'.[2]

No doubt Tsuru was not alone in this opinion. Yamagata and Katsura had good cause to be concerned about the effects of a public trial on the nation's attitude towards the Imperial Institution. Ever since Miyashita's arrest and the discovery of the alleged conspiracy, Yamagata had become deeply concerned.[3] There were ample reasons for his anxiety. One thing the testimony of nearly all the defendants revealed at the preliminary examination was a loss of faith in the divinity of the Emperor. Yamagata considered this loss of respect for the core of the national polity a threat to the future of the nation. For him the mere airing of such views represented 'social destructionism', the odious synonym he coined for socialism. To place witnesses like Morichika and Miyashita, not to mention Kōtoku, before a nationwide audience would represent an insult to the Throne and would merely serve to spread the poison of 'social destructionism' more extensively among the people.

Katsura was as much concerned as Yamagata. While the trial was in progress Katsura insisted that he be kept in daily contact with developments through Hiranuma Kiichirō, the Chief Prosecutor (who was later to become Prime Minister in 1939). At one of these six-a.m. sessions Katsura expressed concern about the outcome of the trial. Hiranuma assured him that things

---

[1] The *Niroku*'s position was summarized in an article titled 'The Socialists', in *The Japan Weekly Mail*, November 19, 1910.

[2] Itoya Toshio, *Kōtoku Shūsui kenkyū*, p. 299.

[3] The actual extent of Yamagata's behind-the-scenes maneuverings at the time of the preliminary examination and the trial deserves further research. It is clear that Yamagata was shocked by the discovery of the conspiracy against the Throne. We know that he was sufficiently disturbed by these events to spend much of the summer months of 1910 drawing up, with Hozumi Yatsuka's help, a lengthy document titled, 'Shakai hakai shugi ron', in which he presented his thoughts on the 'social destructionism' of left-wing thought. This document shows that Yamagata determined to meet the socialist threat to the Throne with an even more vigorous response. In his written opinion, which was circulated among top government officials and presented to the Emperor, Yamagata argued, no doubt in response to the testimony presented at the preliminary examination, that the rise of socialism was attributable to the failure of the educational system and to economic unrest. Yamagata suggested that counter measures should include stepped-up government controls and stricter anti-socialist legislation (the implications for the trial were clear) as well as a revamping of the educational system to instill greater loyalty to the Throne and measures to relieve economic distress. For Yamagata's views see Ōyama Azusa (ed.), *Yamagata Aritomo iken sho*, pp. 315ff.

were going well, and that if he should be wrong in his prediction, he would be prepared to commit suicide. To which Katsura replied that if things turned out badly they might both have to commit suicide. While Hiranuma kept Katsura informed, Katsura reported directly to the Emperor.[1]

If the public held any doubts about the seriousness with which the government approached the trial these were soon dispelled by the events of the opening day. On the morning of December 10, as the horse-drawn carriages carrying Kōtoku and his fellow defendants slowly made their way from the Ichigaya Prison to the court at Hibiya, policemen could be seen everywhere. Hundreds of them guarded the major intersections along the route, and more stood guard at the entrances of the court building. Not only were Kōtoku and the others placed under the strictest guard, but each of the hundred and fifty spectators, many of whom had waited through much of the previous night, were individually searched before being admitted to the galleries. Even the members of the press found themselves subjected to similar indignities, which led at least one paper, the *Asahi*, to caricature the proceedings and question the need for such precautions.[2]

While the ritual of extreme caution was designed to add an air of graveness to the Court proceedings and justify the need for a closed trial, such measures also led to a growing sense of uneasiness and suspicion on the part of the public.[3] This was particularly true of the intelligentsia which, while far from supporting Kōtoku's position against the Throne, had itself become increasingly estranged from those in power. Perhaps it was only natural that many Japanese intellectuals, who were growing wary about the increasing power of an impersonal state which seemed to diverge from their original goals, should express anxiety over the outcome of the trial.

The intellectuals had good reason to be concerned. What many of them sensed quite correctly, and what was readily perceivable from the public statement issued by the Court at the close of the preliminary examination, was that the real issues of the trial were to focus not on concrete acts, but on the question of 'intent'. What was on trial, therefore, were ideas, not facts. This was certainly the position adopted by the prosecution; and Hiranuma Ki-ichirō later declared quite openly that in presenting the government's case

---

[1] *Hiranuma Kiichirō kaikoroku*, pp. 60–1.

[2] On December 11, 1910, the *Asahi Shimbun* devoted a full page to the opening session of the trial. The paper's cartoonist included several sketches lampooning the precautions of the Court.

[3] The closed proceedings made the trial a subject of considerable debate among intellectual circles. Because exact knowledge of the case's content remained unavailable except to a small minority which maintained personal contacts with the lawyers in the case, the reactions of individuals and groups were often more indicative of their personal fears about the future relationship of the government to the individual than deep personal sympathy for Kōtoku and the other defendants.

he emphasized the role of the defendant's 'beliefs' as the motive force behind the crime.[1]

The question of 'intent' upon which the case was decided has remained one of the most controversial features of the trial. What is more important, the debate over the interpretation of 'intent' predated the trial itself. In 1907, when the lower house of the Diet reviewed the proposed Criminal Code, Hatoyama Kazuo, who held a Doctorate in Law from Yale University, seriously questioned the wording of Article 73 of the new Code.[2] His objections were that while the first part of the Article clearly stated that anyone who 'has committed' a 'harmful' act against the Emperor should be 'condemned to death', the supplementary phrase, 'or who has intended to commit', was ambiguous and would allow the courts to punish individuals for their private thoughts. Although Kuratomi Yūsaburō, the public procurator of the Tokyo Court of Appeals, assured the lower house on this occasion that the law was not designed to convict anyone on the basis of their 'innermost intentions',[3] the law went into effect as written, and in the final analysis its interpretation was left to the judges of the Court of Cassation.

Since no actual attempt had been made on the life of the Emperor, the prosecution naturally constructed its case around the principle of 'intent'. Moreover, the freedom with which most of the defendants discussed their ideological positions during the preliminary examination now played into the hands of the prosecution. Even Kōtoku, who had been far from cooperative in the preliminary examination,[4] provided a considerable amount of useful testimony as can be seen from the following exchanges:

Question: Did Ōishi Seinosuke come to Tokyo in November 1908 and stay at the Heiminsha for three days?

[1] *Hiranuma Kiichirō kaikoroku*, p. 59.

[2] For a brief discussion of the Diet debate see Morinaga Eisaburō, 'Taigyaku jiken no hōritsu men', *Rōdō undō shi kenkyū*, no. 22 (July, 1960), p. 13. The law as proposed read as follows in Japanese: 'Tennō, Kōgōtaikō, Kōtaikō, Kōgō, Kōtaishi, mata wa Kōtaison ni taishi kigai o kuwae mata wa kuwaen to shitaru mono wa shikei ni sho su.' 'Kigai o kuwae' (literally, 'has brought harm to') clearly implied a completed act, but 'kuwaen' (which Sebald translated as 'attempt') does not necessarily imply a completed act, thus it lies closer to the English word 'intent', which suggests an act of volition which need not transform itself into a physical expression. The ambiguity of 'kuwaen', and its retention in the law allowed the Court to try Kōtoku and the others on the basis of 'volition' rather than physical 'attempt'. [3] *Ibid.* p. 13.

[4] While Kōtoku did not openly refuse to answer the questions of the presiding judge at the preliminary examination, he often made a point of being vague in his replies. This was particularly true when the questions put to him involved other members of the alleged conspiracy. On matters of no importance his memory could be infinitely detailed. Since the Court had at its disposal a considerable body of detailed testimony from the other defendants, Kōtoku's efforts, well intended as they may have been, simply served to give the impression that he was divulging only part of the truth and had something to hide.

Answer : He did.

Question : At that time did the defendant tell Ōishi that government persecutions had become so extreme of late that it was impossible to counter them through the spoken or written word, and that because the defendant was ill and did not expect to live long he thought he should like to enlist fifty 'death-defying' men, arm them with bombs, and carry out a violent revolution, asking Ōishi to recruit such 'death-defying' men in Kishu?

Answer : As I have stated previously, socialists were greatly angered by the measures adopted by the government at the time of the Red Flag Incident. Such a response was unavoidable given the fact that comrades were thrown into prison and accorded the cruelest of treatment for merely marching about carrying flags inscribed with the word 'Anarchy'. As a result I thought that our attitude of resistance should be expressed through more effective means. But while I talked about fomenting a revolution, I was also aware that it would be difficult to gather a large number of 'death-defying' individuals and raise the requisite finance, and thought I would have to make preparations slowly, one step at a time. Then, when Ōishi came I discussed my ideas with him, saying that if fifty 'death-defying' men were available and these were armed with bombs, I should like to attack with them the homes of the wealthy, open up the rice granaries to save the poor, and if sufficient power were available, burn to the ground all government offices. When I asked him whether he would join me in being on the lookout for determined comrades and accompany me in such a venture, Ōishi indicated his approval.

Question : Did the defendant state that he wanted to burn down all government offices in order to give rise to a state of anarchy?

Answer : I believe I stated that.

Question : Did the defendant also state that he would close in on Nijūbashi, drive away the sentries, and bring harm to the Throne?

Answer : I may have also said something to that effect. But the way I saw it was that this would take place three to five years hence, and could not be carried out in less than three or four years.[1]

At another point the judge at the preliminary examination questioned Kōtoku on his attitudes towards Miyashita's proposal to assassinate the Emperor. The interrogation took the following course:

Question : Did Miyashita stay at the home of the defendant for two nights on his way from Kamezaki to Akashina in June of the same year [1909]?

---

[1] Shiota Shōbei and Watanabe Junzō (eds.), *Hiroku taigyaku jiken*, vol. II, pp. 21–2.

Answer: He did.

Question: Did Miyashita confer with the defendant and Kanno on this occasion about making bombs and bringing harm to the Throne?

Answer: I believe we had a discussion of that nature.

Question: Did the defendant consent to such a proposal?

Answer: At the time I did.[1]

Kōtoku's agreement with the plan to assassinate the Emperor, theoretical and temporary though his assent may have been, was made even more explicit through his answers to the following questions:

Question: In September of the same year [1909] did the defendant confer with Kanno, Niimura, and the others on the use of bombs to bring harm to the Throne during the Imperial Procession?

Answer: While we did not make a point of conferring on the matter again, it did become the topic of conversation on several occasions.

Question: Were these conversations concerned with the implementation of the plan in the autumn of 1910?

Answer: Something of this nature was discussed, but no firm decisions were made.

Question: Did the defendant agree with the intention to put the plan into action, or not?

Answer: At the time I agreed.[2]

As the foregoing testimony reveals, Kōtoku made almost no attempt to deny his involvement in the conspiracy against the Emperor in the autumn of 1909. At the same time he made every effort to point out that his participation in the conspiracy had been temporary, and that he had parted company with the plan towards the close of the same year. This is the one major point of disagreement between Kōtoku's testimony and the government's indictment. Moreover, in going over the case this becomes a point of some significance, for despite the relative certainty with which the prosecution could show 'intent', on the basis of Kōtoku's testimony, the admission of a conscious act of withdrawal from the conspiracy, should have brought into play another section of the Criminal Code, namely, Article 43, which stated that 'if preparation (for a crime) has been voluntarily stopped, punishment shall be mitigated or remitted'.[3]

[1] *Ibid.* p. 8.   [2] *Ibid* p. 9.
[3] William J. Sebald (trans.), *The Criminal Code of Japan*, p. 24.

Despite the fact that the three lawyers assigned to Kōtoku, Hanai Tokuzō, Isobe Shirō, and Imamura Rikisaburō, based the defense's case on a hope for mitigation, arguing that the government through its persecution of socialists was itself responsible for the conspiracy,[1] nowhere in the records now available is there any indication that an effort was made to use Article 43 in Kōtoku's behalf.

Although Article 43 may well have presented the most cogent line of reasoning in Kōtoku's defense, there was good reason for Kōtoku to resist its use on his behalf. While it is clear that Kōtoku was not the 'ringleader' of the conspiracy, as the prosecution insisted, the testimony of the other defendants, as well as his own letters from prison, show that he considered himself, and was looked up to by the others, as the ideological leader of the group. This was a position of which he was proud, and given the fact that he had suffered considerably under the cloud of suspicion that surrounded his retreat to Yugawara, he was not in favor of adding a few years to his already doomed existence at the cost of discrediting himself in the eyes of his followers.

The government, for its part, was quite willing to discard Kōtoku, Niimura, and Kanno's testimony regarding his withdrawal from the conspiracy, for Kōtoku's conviction was vital if the prosecution's case against the other defendants was to hold. Moreover, in discarding such testimony the judges of the preliminary examination did not act as arbitrarily as it would appear, for the judges did have to evaluate some contradictory testimony delivered by Miyashita Daikichi. In this testimony Miyashita stated:

When I told Kōtoku and Kanno that I now understood the preparation of blasting powder and that I would soon construct bombs and kill the Emperor, both Kōtoku and Kanno agreed with my ideas. Naturally Kōtoku did not openly state that he would himself join me in such a venture, but he did tell me that since I lived in the country it would not be difficult, but since they lived in Tokyo where they were well known they would have to disappear into the countryside at least three months before the actual implementation of the plan. Moreover, he stated that in carrying out such a thing one would have to leave behind a written statement declaring one's reasons, otherwise the public might consider the act the work of lunatics. As a result, I naturally thought that he and the others would join me in carrying out the scheme.[2]

The indictment brought against Kōtoku included Miyashita's interpretation of Kōtoku's retreat to Yugawara. To counter Miyashita's testimony

---

[1] *Hiranuma Kiichirō kaikoroku*, p. 59. Hiranuma states that this was the position around which Hanai constructed the defense.

[2] Shiota Shōbei and Watanabe Junzō (eds.), *Hiroku taigyaku jiken*, vol. I, p. 164.

Kōtoku would have had to disclose his negotiations with the Home Ministry through Koizumi Sanshin. This he was not prepared to do. The trial provided Kōtoku with a final opportunity of proving his commitment to the cause and to his followers. Whatever their fate he was prepared to share it.

For Kōtoku the final months in prison were spent largely in finishing *Kirisuto massatsu ron*, which constituted not only a clear-cut rejection of Christianity, but also a call for the re-examination of 'myth' in all areas of human experience. Unfortunately, few of his contemporaries were willing to explore the subtle implications of his study for the Japanese Imperial Institution.[1]

Although Kōtoku clearly saw the handwriting on the wall, many of his young followers remained totally oblivious to the seriousness of the charges facing them until the final stages of the trial. If Kōtoku had any regrets, they involved the many young lives that had become entangled in the trial with him. In an effort to save his followers Kōtoku wrote a lengthy statement in his own and their behalf titled, 'A Discussion of Violent Revolution from a Jail Cell.'[2]

In this essay Kōtoku tried to deny that he or his followers backed 'violent revolution' or proposed the assassination of the Emperor. He disparaged the government's simplistic logic that tried to convict the defendants on the syllogism: 'The anarchist revolution is concerned with the destruction of the Imperial Family. Kōtoku's plan was to carry out a revolution by violence. Therefore, all who joined him in this plan intended to commit High Treason.'[3]

One of the most interesting features of Kōtoku's statement in his own defense is the extent to which the questions of human 'freedom' and 'responsibility', questions which had been of uppermost importance for the young student, reasserted themselves. The switch from viewing man as an active creator and molder of his environment, to viewing him as a passive victim of impersonal forces, a switch which was always indicative of a psychological low point in his spiritual existence, was clearly present in his essay. The tide of optimism which had billowed in San Francisco and crested with his 'direct action' stand after his return, now lay dissipated in his own failure

[1] One of those who did was Kinoshita Naoe. Kinoshita considered this work more directed against the Japanese Imperial tradition than against Christianity. See *Yajingo*, pp. 104ff.

[2] This statement was dated December 18, 1910, and was addressed to Mr Hanai, Mr Isobe, and Mr Imamura. The work has recently been translated by George Elison. For the full text see *Monumenta Nipponica*, vol. XXII, no. 3-4, pp. 468ff.

[3] *Nikki to shokan*, p. 176. Also Elison, *Monumenta Nipponica*, vol. XXII, no. 3-4, p. 480.

to act. Under the circumstances, the role of 'fate' once more assumed its dominant position.[1]

Revolutions, Kōtoku reiterated, were not man-made; they were part of a natural historical process which men could not affect, and which ought to be distinguished from 'uprisings' or 'disturbances'. The revolutionary's task lay in understanding the historical process and preparing men's minds for the new order which was to follow. Consequently, his chief responsibility lay in the realm of knowledge and not in the realm of action. Under the circumstances it was foolish to accuse any individual (or group of individuals) of fomenting 'violent revolution'; to do so was to misunderstand the nature of historical change.

Kōtoku's theoretical position on revolution stated here differed markedly from his testimony before the preliminary examination, where he openly admitted having talked about 'fomenting a revolution'. The contradictory nature of these positions must be seen not only within the framework of his attempt to save his followers, but also within the light of his psychological fluctuations.

Kōtoku's arguments in his own and his followers' behalf was basically that adopted by the defense lawyers, i.e., that the government must itself shoulder the responsibility for creating the conditions that led to the rise of such desperate men. And that in the ultimate analysis it was the suppressive measures of the authorities, and not the ideas of the defendants, that served as primary causes for the conspiracy. As he wrote to his lawyers:

The making of an assassin is not relative to the school of thought of his adherence. Special conditions of the time tied to special characteristics of the person lead to the act of assassination. Picture the following circumstances: a group of comrades in thought becomes the target of extreme governmental oppression; their rights are wrested away, and their freedom of speech, of assembly, of publication is, of course, destroyed; they are even robbed of the means to live...lawful, peaceful methods seem to be ineffectual; in short, there appears to be no way out. Under the circumstances excitable, passion-driven youths might well resort to violence and assassination, and the action might well be termed legitimate self-defense.[2]

One cannot help but detect in Kōtoku's arguments a remnant of a fundamentally Mencian attitude towards government. The premise that good government was by nature benevolent government, and that social unrest was indicative of a government's failure to meet the needs of the people, a

---

[1] It should be pointed out that the change in Shūsui's attitude predated the discovery of the plot and can be traced back at least as far as the closing months of 1909.

[2] *Nikki to shokan*, p. 164. The translation is from Elison, *Monumenta Nipponica*, vol. XXII, no. 3–4, pp. 470–1.

failure which threatened its legitimacy, and provided the citizen with the right of rebellion, reveals the extent to which his roots remained in the Mencian tradition. While Kōtoku's appeal may well have elicited a favorable emotional response from those towards whom it was directed, this response was of temporary duration. In the end the case had to be decided on the cold, clear, and one might add 'Western', logic of the new Criminal Code.

Given the nature of the evidence available to the Court, Kōtoku's attempt to draw subtle distinctions between assassins and revolutionaries, on the one hand, and his efforts, curiously contradictory as they were, to deny the existence of a conspiracy at one point and to condone it as government-inspired, on the other, were futile and meaningless gestures.

On December 28, the day before the trial was officially concluded, Hanai Tokuzō asked Kōtoku to remain behind after the other defendants had been cleared from the courtroom. In the silence of the empty chamber Hanai informed him of the death of his mother in Tosa. On December 6, after Tajiko had made the long and difficult trip to Tokyo to pay a final visit on her son in the Ichigaya Prison, Kōtoku had written to Sakai about his mother noting that there was something truly great about the old woman and wondering how she could have produced such a foolish child.[1] At the time of her visit both had been struck by the premonition that they were seeing one another for the last time. As a result, her death, he admitted in a letter to Sakai on New Year's Day, did not come as a complete surprise.[2] And yet, he added, this did not make her passing any less painful. It was his 'foolishness' and not his 'selfishness', he insisted, that had led to the trial. His mother understood and had forgiven him for this. Finally he could not help but wonder if his mother had committed suicide. Not out of 'shame', he was quick to add, but so that he might face his end 'as a man'.[3]

By the middle of January, 1911, the Court of Cassation was ready to render its verdict in the case. With the partial lifting of press restrictions on January 15, the incident was once again open to public speculation. Many Japanese felt that the defendants would be found guilty, but at the same time they were also convinced that punishment would be mitigated. Only a minority believed the persistent rumors that Kōtoku and the others would be found guilty and executed.

Greater concern for the welfare of Kōtoku and the other defendants was

[1] *Ibid.* p. 359.
[2] *Ibid.* p. 371.
[3] His mother did not commit suicide. Weakened by her trip to Tokyo she died of acute pneumonia.

expressed abroad where news of the closed trial aroused a storm of protest.[1] The Japanese embassies in London and Paris and the Consulate in New York were besieged by socialists and anarchists who expressed concern that Kōtoku and the others would be 'condemned to death practically without a trial'.[2] Fuel was added to such arguments by Robert Young, editor of the *Japan Chronicle*. In a letter to *The Times*, published in London on January 6, he accused the Japanese Court of being 'unjust in the extreme',[3] in its handling of the case. What particularly disturbed the editor of the *Chronicle* was the Japanese government's treatment of the press:

The procedure adopted by the authorities throughout in this case has been extremely unjust. When the arrests were originally made, the editor of every newspaper in Japan – myself included – received a notification couched in peremptory terms to the effect that any statement regarding the reasons for the arrest would render the offending editor liable to prosecution...Thus while the police have been able to publish the most serious charges against the accused and to assert their guilt before trial, the mouths of the accused have been shut, and any newspaper which dared to give publicity to their defence would have been prosecuted under the Press Law.[4]

Young's letter to *The Times* was picked up by the Tokyo *Asahi* which added to the domestic controversy. The Japanese government's response was to divulge more details to foreign correspondents. Whether this was done to prepare Westerners for the verdict, or to shore up the national image remains unclear; what is clear is that such procedures clearly violated the 'limits of

[1] The plot was first mentioned in the Western press on September 22, 1910, in a Reuter's dispatch from Tokyo. This dispatch presented the mere outlines of the incident, stating only that a conspiracy against the Imperial House had been uncovered; that those involved were now being tried in a 'secret' trial; and that due to restrictions placed on the press the full details of the case could not be discussed. Western ignorance of Japanese legal procedures (there was nothing illegal about the closed proceedings of the preliminary examination) added to the confusion, and censorship of of the press to distrust, on the part of many Westerners. Left-wing papers like Emma Goldman's *Mother Earth*, *Humanité*, *Die Neue Zeit*, and the *International Socialist Review* strongly protested the secret proceedings. Moreover, such protests mounted significantly with the actual trial in December. Quick to take advantage of foreign criticism against the Japanese government, some Japanese papers like the *Nippon* insisted that the decision of the Court to hold the trial *in camera* was dissipating the international good-will that the nation had taken such care to preserve at the time of the Russo-Japanese War. The government was quick to respond to the arguments of foreign and domestic critics by making every effort to show that the conduct of the trial was in keeping with the Code of Criminal Procedure and the Constitution. It also went out of its way to allow representatives of the various foreign embassies to attend the Court sessions – although few of them seem to have availed themselves of these privileges. See *The Times* (London), January 5, 1911, p. 5, for a typical Japanese government communiqué on the case. For an excellent discussion of the international repercussions of the High Treason Trial see Ōhara Kei, 'Taigyaku jiken no kokusai teki eikyō', *Shisō*, no. 471 (September, 1963), pp. 1236–47; also the continuation of the same article, *Shisō*, no. 475 (January, 1964), pp. 111–22.
[2] 'The Japanese Anarchists', *The Japan Weekly Mail*, December 17, 1910, p. 759.
[3] 'The Alleged Plot against the Emperor of Japan', *The Times* (London), January 6, 1911, p. 6.
[4] *Ibid.*

the law' within which the government repeatedly insisted its actions fell. In a final attempt to clarify its position, the Japanese government provided foreign correspondents with a news brief on January 16, two days before the rendering of the verdict by the Court of Cassation, which read in part:

Many of the accused are believers in anarchism and communism. As a means of diffusing their principles, they planned to make an attempt on the life of the Emperor, to assassinate Ministers of the Crown, and excite an incendiary movement on the occasion of the grand military maneuvers last autumn. This fact is clearly established by confessions made by many of the anarchists, and the discovery of explosives, and other evidence.[1]

The remainder of the statement once more spelled out in detail the legal course pursued by the authorities.

Although Hiranuma Kiichirō was later to go to great length to show that no one, not even the Emperor, was informed of the decision in the case before the public session of the Court on January 18,[2] it seems strange that the correspondent for *The North China Herald* could forward a cable to Shanghai on January 17 in which he stated quite conclusively: 'Sentence of death will be passed tomorrow on the anarchists alleged to have been concerned in a plot directed against the Emperor of Japan, but many of them will be specially pardoned afterwards.'[3] Where such information came from remains a mystery. On the other hand, the conviction with which it is rendered hardly serves to convince the reader that the reporter's information was based on sheer conjecture.

If the authorities went out of their way to prepare Westerners for the Court's decision, they were also intent on making the rendering of judgment an event that would continue to live in the memory of the public at home. It was no accident that the events of January 18, 1911, were to remain etched on many Japanese minds.[4]

Shortly before noon on the eighteenth the black-lacquered prison carts, each drawn by two horses and guarded by four men, slowly made their final trip through Yotsuya and Kasumigaseki carrying Kōtoku and the other defendants to the Court in Hibiya. As on the occasion of the opening session

---

[1] *The North China Herald*, January 27, 1911, p. 205. The dispatch is dated Tokyo, January 16. This may well be the statement referred to in the *Jiji Shimpō* of the same date which was presented to the various embassies.

[2] Hiranuma tells us that Katsura wanted to see to it that the Emperor was informed of the Court's decision before anyone else, but that the Court's procedures forbade this. It was therefore decided that as soon as the decision was read by the judge the palace should be informed by telephone. *Hiranuma Kiichirō kaikoroku*, p. 61.

[3] *The North China Herald*, January 20, 1911, p. 117. The dispatch is dated Tokyo, January 17.

[4] For the following descriptive details of the events of January 18, I am indebted to Itoya Toshio, *Kōtoku Shūsui kenkyū*, pp. 311ff., and Kanzaki Kiyoshi, *Taigyaku jiken*, pp. 7ff.

of the trial, the procession was imbued with ritual significance that was not lost on the throngs of silent spectators. Everywhere there were the dark-uniformed police. Thousands of these flanked both sides of the route from Ichigaya to Hibiya at twenty-yard intervals, a procedure that was almost unknown except during Imperial Processions. At the Court House there were more officials of all descriptions who guarded the exits of the building and the courtyards. Visitors, who had stood through much of the freezing night in hopes of being admitted to the galleries, were once more subjected to questioning and personal searches, and plainclothesmen walked up and down the lines of those waiting, picking out socialists who were summarily refused admission. Under the circumstances, even the casual observer could readily deduce the message about to be delivered within the precincts of the Court.

For Kōtoku, who had prepared himself for the worst, the sonorous tones of the Chief Judge's rendering of the Court's arguments, a performance that took up most of the hour between one and two, held few surprises. Members of the press who knew something of the explosive potential of the former editor of the *Heimin Shimbun* were struck by the air of calm and well-being that surrounded him. Dressed in the formal *haori* and *hakama*, Kōtoku looked more like a man of learning listening to a scholarly treatise than an anarchist on trial for his life. Perhaps he had once more discovered the meaning of what he had written to a friend years earlier when he had observed that 'prison becomes a place where one cultivates the spirit. The normally passionate man who calms himself by grappling with Zen in his cell will naturally establish new means of appreciating heaven and become content with life.'[1] Kōtoku's composure suggests that he had somehow made peace with his environment.

As the Chief Judge, Tsuru, confirmed point after point of the original indictment against Kōtoku and the other defendants, the outcome of the trial was no longer in doubt.

The representatives of the press, anxious to get the verdict to their papers whose extra editions were ready to flood the Tokyo streets, began to fidget and eye the doors of the chamber. A few miles away in a sideroom of the Imperial Palace, Katsura the Prime Minister, and Hiranuma Kiichirō the Chief Prosecutor, whose absence from the Court aroused considerable speculation, awaited a phone call from the Court telling them of the decision. With them was the Grand Chamberlain, Tokudaiji, whose job it was to relay the message to the Emperor.[2]

---

[1] *Nikki to shokan*, p. 263.
[2] Kanzaki Kiyoshi, *Taigyaku jiken*, p. 18.

At a few minutes after two the Judge ordered the defendants to stand for the actual sentencing. After Kōtoku and the others had risen to their feet, Tsuru delivered the verdict. Kōtoku and twenty-three of his fellow defendants were declared guilty of violating Article 73 of the Criminal Code and sentenced to death. The other two were found guilty of violations of the regulations governing the manufacture and possession of explosives and were sentenced to eight and eleven years imprisonment.

With the utterance of the Judge's final words, a hush fell over the courtroom. All eyes suddenly turned to the defendants. While Kōtoku retained his composure, some of his young followers were visibly unprepared for the verdict. Many had hoped to the last moment that the charges would be dismissed. The severity of the sentences left everyone momentarily stunned. Even the press, which had been anxious to leave earlier, now remained silently in place. The only sounds came from the judges' feet as they rapidly got up and left their elevated platform by a side door.

As the dulling effect of the finality of the Court's decision slowly began to wear off, Kanno Sugako was among the first of the defendants to react audibly. Turning to Kōtoku and the others she bid them farewell. Suddenly loud shouts of 'Long Live Anarchists!' and 'Long Live Anarchy!' filled the the air. Minutes later the courtroom was cleared by the guards.

Kōtoku's response to the outcome of the trial was expressed in a letter to Imamura Rikisaburō. 'With the passing of sentence today', he noted a few hours after returning to prison, 'I felt as if a burden had been lifted from my shoulders. While I feel sorry for those with children, and the many young men whose future still lay before them, I myself feel greatly relieved.'[1] A day later he wrote to Sakai Toshihiko, 'For me it is a happy ending; I feel as if a load were off my shoulders. Today I am physically and spiritually at ease.'[2]

It remains a curious paradox that the death sentence provided Kōtoku with a sense of emancipation that neither socialism nor anarchism had been able to provide. But the death sentence, as he was well aware, terminated his 'troublesome duties and responsibilities to the world of men'.[3] Thus, the ruling of the court had in effect achieved the destruction of the particularistic obligations that had done so much to shackle him as a revolutionary. As a condemned man he was at last free.

Kōtoku's final days in prison were devoted to reading and writing. Letters to his many friends assured them that his death would not be 'totally without significance',[4] and urged them to carry on the struggle. On January 21, two

---

[1] *Nikki to shokan*, p. 382. [2] *Ibid.* p. 384.
[3] *Ibid.* [4] *Ibid.* p. 385.

days after an Imperial rescript commuted the sentences of twelve of the convicted to life imprisonment, Kōtoku, now aware that the end was not far off, wrote to Koizumi Sanshin expressing his views on death. 'Death is like a cloud on a distant high hill,' he observed. 'Seen from afar it looms like a great specter, but when one approaches it, it is nothing at all. For a materialist it simply means that the hands on the clock have stopped moving.'[1]

At eight o'clock on the morning of January 24, 1911, Kōtoku climbed the stairs of the scaffold in the Ichigaya Prison compound. Perfectly calm and composed, he smoked a final cigarette. Six minutes later the trap door opened beneath him and brought to a close his turbulent career.

[1] *Nikki to shokan*, pp. 385–6.

Epilogue

In the wake of the High Treason Trial it soon became obvious that all radical activity, whether that of the socialists or anarchists, was to be firmly suppressed by the Japanese government. As socialists entered what came to be called the 'winter years' – a term which aptly described the standstill of left-wing activity which lasted from 1911 to the early 1920s – defections were numerous. Perhaps the most significant of these involved Katayama Sen, Kōtoku's moderate rival, who left Japan full of discouragement in 1914 never to return. Others, like Ishikawa Sanshirō, disassociated themselves entirely from active politics and labor agitation, and turned instead to the realm of abstract theory. A few, following Ōsugi Sakae's example, went underground. What little inner life the movement retained was all too frequently channeled into unproductive theoretical debates which further fragmented the remnant. As far as the public was concerned the socialist movement was dead. It was not until World War I and the Russian Revolution created new economic and ideological circumstances that the left succeeded in mounting a renewed bid for power.

One can easily argue that Kōtoku's tactics, 'direct action' and the 'General Strike', were ill-suited to the Japanese environment. It would not be wrong to insist, as Arahata Kanson and other have done, that any effective General Strike required a well-organized federation of unions and a level of labor solidarity that was not present in Japan during the Meiji period. To attempt a General Strike without such support was to invite disaster. Moreover, direct action, as the High Treason Trial showed all too clearly, was ultimately suicidal.

But it must also be pointed out that tactics were not Kōtoku's primary concern. For him the abstract questions of spirit and morality, of freedom and determinism, of individual responsibility and the coercive power of the environment, continued to take precedence over matters of economic and political strategy. In the end even direct action was transformed into a rejection of compromise with greater internal than external implications.

Like some of his European contemporaries, particularly the French syndicalist and fellow supporter of the General Strike, Georges Sorel, of whose writings he seems to have been unaware, Kōtoku was confronted with

2 Roads for a society

1

*

2

the problem of political separatism. Believing that his society was a society in crisis, Kōtoku was convinced that in the life of such a society there were only two alternatives. The first he pictured as degeneration and decline, in which the ruling class of politicians and property owners corrupted by self-seeking and the power of office manipulated a mass of indifferent individuals lost in their own hedonistic quest for self-aggrandizement and material well being; the second he saw as regeneration, in which those aspiring to power, refusing compromise and focusing constantly on the remote goals of the future, committed themselves to a morality of self-sacrifice and shunned the corrosive political process in favor of an apocalyptical solution.

Regeneration, as Kōtoku was personally conscious, was as much the the problem of the individual as it was the problem of the social body as a whole. For Kōtoku, the will to resist, which he had always attributed to the late Tokugawa *shishi* who served as his political model, constituted the spiritual side of revolution. Without the will to resist, even the best-laid plans and the most ingenious strategy would come to nothing.

It must also be pointed out in the Japanese political environment in which Kōtoku found himself, an environment in which the infant socialist movement possessed almost no hope for political success, and where the political 'outsider' was constantly confronted with the social pressures of conformity and compromise, not to mention the more invidious temptations of political and financial rewards for selling out to those in power, an emphasis on spiritual resistance and total separatism may well have been necessary to maintain the life of the group and the integrity of the individual.

It was therefore no accident that Kōtoku was to inspire more in death than he did in life. For the Japanese intellectual living in the first decade of this century, who was himself increasingly aware of his alienation from the political world, Kōtoku's message of resistance transcended his role as socialist and anarchist thinker. For him, Kōtoku, like Uchimura Kanzō, appears to have become something of a symbol of protest against an increasingly authoritarian and restrictive state. For many of his contemporaries Kōtoku's career projected ideals which had been common to early Meiji youth in general. Like him they had been convinced that the age of the Restoration *shishi* was over, but that in the new Japan about to emerge the educated man was himself a kind of *shishi* with a positive role to play in the creation of his new society.

In the years between 1900 and 1910 a number of Japanese thinkers had reached the frontiers of Western social and political thought only to find that they were now considered *persona non grata* by the Meiji government.

Many Meiji intellectuals, who were concerned about the superficial elements of Japan's Westernization, could not help but be influenced by the paradoxical situation in which a government and society emphasized becoming more like the West, and then suppressed those who carried this ideal to its logical conclusion. It was the gulf that had grown between the Japanese government and the intellectuals that imbued the High Treason Trial with its significance and led some of Japan's foremost thinkers and writers to mourn Kōtoku's death.

Kōtoku's legacy for his contemporaries, as well as for the generations that were to follow, was perhaps best summarized by Tokutomi Roka, the novelist, in his speech at the First Higher School in February 1911:

My friends [Tokutomi stated after outlining the dilemmas of a society which seemed to him to have lost its vision of change and progress], Kōtoku and the others have been labeled rebels and executed by the present government. But one should not be afraid of rebellion. One should not fear the rebel. One should not be afraid of becoming a rebel himself. To do something new has always been called rebellion. 'Do not fear those who destroy the flesh but cannot destroy the spirit.' The death of the flesh is unimportant. What is to be feared is the death of the spirit. To believe only what one is taught to believe, to say only what one is told to say, to do only what one is asked to do, to find security in life by existing formally like a doll poured from a mold, to lose completely the idea of self-confidence in one's independence and the belief in self-improvement – this is the death of the spirit. To live is to rebel. Kōtoku and the others died rebelling. They have passed away, but they have also come back to life again. And now their graves are empty.[1]

In the eyes of men like Tokutomi, Kōtoku symbolized rebellion against complacency and the *status quo*, the same shibboleths against which the Restoration *shishi* had fought fifty years earlier.

Finally one is reminded of Kōtoku's own words:

In a society with a perfect system of organization, the interests of the individual and those of society will be in complete harmony...but in a society organized along today's imperfect lines the individual member who wants to fulfill to the utmost his obligations to that society, must by all means determine to sacrifice himself for that society. Consequently, the higher one's morality, the greater the corresponding sacrifice. The greater the sacrifice, the greater is the honor one gains.[2]

And yet, it remained a long way from Yoshida Shōin and the *shishi* loyalist of the *bakumatsu* years who was prepared to sacrifice himself for the Imperial cause, to the twentieth-century *shishi* who was convinced that the only way

[1] Tokutomi Roka, 'Muhon ron', in *Hiyūmanizumu*, vol. 17 of *Gendai Nihon shisō taikei*, p. 133.
[2] 'Hiranuma Senzō', in *Kōtoku Shūsui hyōron to zuisō*, p. 184.

to preserve the *shishi* tradition was to do away with the Throne. While the tensions and complexities of this transition, as exemplified in Kōtoku Shūsui's career, continue to interest the historian of modern Japan, it is in the example of his life, rather than in his ideas, that the political 'outsider' and ideological visionary of contemporary Japan finds his inspiration.

Glossary

Abe Isoo 安部磯雄
Arahata Kanson 荒畑寒村
Asako 朝子
Asakusa Kōen 淺草公園

Bakin 馬琴
bakumatsu 幕末
bantō 番頭
Bunzō 文三

Chian keisatsu hō 治安警察法
Chikamatsu 近松
Chokugen 直言
Chūō shimbun 中央新聞
Chuseitō 中正党

dobyakushō 土百姓
Dōkyūsha 同求社
Dōshikai 同志社

Ebina Danjō 海老名彈正
Eiri jiyū shimbun 絵入自由新聞

Fuhei no rireki 不平の履歴
Fukao Shō 深尾韶
Fukuzawa Yukichi 福沢諭吉
Furukawa Ichibe 古河市兵衛
Furukawa Rikisaku 古河力作
Futabatei Shimei 二葉亭四迷

gō 号
Goda Fukutarō 合田福太郎
gōshi 郷士
Gotō Shōjirō 後藤象二郎

hakama 袴
Hakkan chō 八官町
Hanai Tokuzo 花井卓蔵
hanbatsu 藩閥
haori 羽織
Hara Kei 原敬
Hata 幡多

Hatoyama Kazuo 鳩山和夫
Hayashi Kaneaki 林包明
Hayashi Yūzō 林有造
Heike monogatari 平家物語
Heimin shimbun 平民新聞
Heimin shugi 平民主義
Heiminsha 平民社
Heiwa shugi 平和主義
Higuchi Shinkichi 樋口真吉
Hikari 光
Hirade Osamu 平出修
Hiranuma Kiichirō 平沼騏一郎
Hirata Tōsuke 平田東助
Hōan jōrei 保安条例
Honda Noboru 本田昇
Hōonji 法恩寺
Hoshi Tōru 星亨
Hosono Jirō 細野次郎
Hozumi Nobushige 穂積陳重
Hozumi Yatsuka 穂積八束

Imamura Rikisaburō 今村力三郎
Inoue Kowashi 井上馨
Inukai Tsuyoshi 犬養毅
Ishikawa Sanshirō 石川三四郎
Ishikawa Takuboku 石川啄木
Isobe Shirō 磯部四郎
isshin no kakumei 維新の革命
Itagaki Taisuke 板垣退助
Itō Ginsuke 伊藤銀月
Itō Hirobumi 伊藤博文
Iwagaki Gesshū 巖垣月洲
Iwasa Sakutarō 岩佐作太郎
Iwasaki Yatarō 岩崎弥太郎

Jijiroku 時至録
Jiji shimpō 時事新報
Jiyū minken undō 自由民権運動
Jiyū shimbun 自由新聞
Jiyū shisō 自由思想
Jiyū shugi 自由主義
Jiyūtō 自由党

205

Jizōji 地藏寺

Kaheiji 嘉平次
kaikoku shinshu 開国進取
Kaiseikan 開成館
Kaishin shugi 改進主義
Kakumei 革命
Kamei Eizaburō 亀井英三郎
Kanno Sugako 管野須賀子
Katayama Sen 片山潜
Katō Hiroyuki 加藤弘之
Katō Tokijirō 加藤時次郎
Katsura Tarō 桂太郎
Kawakami Kiyoshi 河上清
Kawasaki Minotarō 川崎己之太郎
Kawashima 川嶋
Kemuriyama Sentarō 煙山専太郎
ken 県
Kenseihontō 憲政本党
Kido Mei 木戸明
Kinkikan 錦輝館
Kinoshita Naoe 木下尚江
Kinsei museifu shugi 近世無政府主義
Kinyōkai 金曜会
Kirisuto massatsu ron 基督抹殺論
Kōchi shimbun 高知新聞
Koizumi Sakutarō (Sanshin) 小泉策太郎
　　(三申)
Kojima Tatsutarō 小島竜太郎
Kokugaku sha 国学者
kokumin 国民
Kokumin eigakkai 国民英学会
Kokumin no tomo 国民之友
Kōtoku Atsuaki 幸徳篤明
Kōtoku Atsuchika 幸徳篤親
Kōtoku Atsumichi 幸徳篤道
Kōtoku Denjirō (Shūsui) 幸徳伝次郎
　　(秋水)
Kōtoku Kachiyuemon 幸徳勝右衛門
Kōtoku Kakyūta 幸徳嘉久太
Kōtoku Kameji 幸徳亀治
Kōtoku Komatarō 幸徳駒太郎
Kudan 九段
Kuga Katsunan 陸羯南
Kumamoto hyōron 熊本評論
Kuratomi Yūsaburō 倉富勇三郎

Kuwabara Kaihei 桑原戒平

machi no ko 町の子
Machi otona 町大人
Mainichi shimbun 毎日新聞
Maru maru chinbun 団々珍聞
Matsubara Kazuo 松原一雄
Matsui Hakken 松井伯軒
Matsui Matsuba 松屋松葉
Matsumoto Sugako 松本須賀子
Meirokusha 明六社
miai 見合い
Mineo Setsudō 峰尾節堂
minken jiyū 民権自由
Minyūsha 民友社
Miyake Setsurei 三宅雪嶺
Miyashita Daikichi 宮下太吉
Miyazaki Fuyō (Muryū) 宮崎笑蓉
　　(夢柳)
Mori Arinori 森有礼
Morichika Unpei 森近運平
Morioka Eiji 森岡栄治
Morooka Chiyoko 師岡千代子
Morooka Masatane 師岡正胤
Murai Tomoyoshi (Chishi) 村井知至
museifuteki kyōsansei 無政府的共産制

Nagai Kafū 永井荷風
Nakae Chōmin 中江兆民
Nakamura 中村
Nakamura Masanao (Keiu) 中村正直
　　(敬宇)
Nakano Seigō 中野正剛
Nakaoka Shintarō 中岡慎太郎
Nariishi Heishirō 成石平四郎
Nariishi Kanzaburō 成石勘三郎
naruhodo 成程
Natsume Sōseki 夏目漱石
Nichi nichi 日日
Nihon shakai-tō 日本社会党
Nihonjin 日本人
Niimura Tadao 新村忠雄
Niroku shimpō 二六新報
Nishikawa Kōjirō 西川光二郎
Nishino Buntarō 西野文太郎
Nochi no katami 後の形見

Ōi Kentarō 大井憲太郎
Ōishi Seinosuke 大石誠之助
Oka Shigeki 岡繁樹
Okazaki Kunisuke 岡崎邦輔
Okumiya Tateyuki 奥宮健之
Okurando no shakai オクランドの社会
  kakumei-tō 革命党
Ōmiwa Chōbei 大三輪長兵衛
Ōno Ryōsuke 小野良輔
Ōno Teru 小野輝
Ōno Tōichi 小野道一
Ōoka Ikuzō 大岡育造
Ōsaka heimin shimbun 大阪平民新聞
Ōsugi Sakae 大杉栄

Rinsenji 林泉寺
Risōdan 理想団
Rōdō kumiai kiseikai 労働組合期成会
Rōdō sekai 労働世界
rōnin 浪人

Saionji Kimmochi 西園寺公望
Saitō Ryoku-u 齋藤緑雨
Saji Jitsunen 佐治実然
Sakai Toshihiko (Furukawa) 堺利彦
  (枯川)
Sakamoto Ryōma 坂本龍馬
Sakikubo Seiichi 崎久保誓一
San suijin keirin mondō 三酔人経綸問答
Sanjūsaiki 三十歳記
Satō Satori 佐藤悟
Seikyōsha 政教社
Seiri sōdan 政理叢談
Seisho no kenkyū 聖書の研究
seitai 政体
Seiyūkai 政友会
sengoku 戦国
Shakai minshu-tō 社会民主党
Shakai mondai kenkyū kai 社会問題研究会
Shakai shimbun 社会新聞
Shakai shugi 社会主義
Shakai shugi kenkyū kai 社会主義研究会
Shakai shugi kyokai 社会主義協会
Shikoku genso dōmekai 四国減租同盟会
Shimpuren ran 神風連乱
Shin kigen sha 新紀元社

Shin nippon no seinen 新日本の青年
Shin sekai 新世界
Shirayanagi Shūko 白柳秀湖
shishi 志士
shizoku 士族
sho 斗
Shōrai no nihon 将来之日本
shōya 庄屋
Shunai 春靄
Shūshin seika 修身政家
  chikoku heitenka 治国平天下
sonnō jōi 尊王攘夷
sōshi 壮士
Suematsu Kenchō 末松謙澄
Sugamo 巣鴨
Sugimura Sōjinkan 杉村楚人冠
Suzuki Shigesaburō 鈴木茂三郎
Suzuki Shōgo 鈴木省吾

Taigyaku jiken 大逆事件
Taiheiki 大平記
Tajiko 多治子
Takagi Kenmei 高木顕明
Takahashi Sakuei 高橋作衛
Takano Fusatarō 高野房太郎
Takeuchi Tetsugorō 竹内鉄五郎
Tanaka Kōken 田中光顕
Tanaka Shōzō 田中正造
Taneda Masaaki 種田政明
Tani Kanjō 谷干城
Taoka Reiun 田岡嶺雲
Tatsumi Tetsuō 巽鉄男
tawaraya 俵屋
Tazoe Tetsuji 田添鉄二
Teiseitō 帝政党
tenkō 転向
Tennoya 天野屋
Terauchi Masatake 寺内正毅
Tohoku hyōron 東北評論
Tokutomi Iichirō (Sohō) 徳富猪一郎
  (蘇峰)
Tokutomi Roka 徳富蘆花
Tokyo asahi 東京朝日
Tominaga Yūrin 富永有隣
Tosa ben 土佐弁
toshiyori 年寄

Tōyō jiyū shimbun 東洋自由新聞
Tsubouchi Shōyō 坪内逍遙
Tsuru Jōichirō 鶴丈一郎

Uchiyama Gudō 内山愚童
Ukigumo 浮雲
Ura-jimbochō 裏神保町

waka 和歌

Yamagata Aritomo 山県有朋
Yamagata Isaburō 山県伊三郎
Yamaguchi Kōken 山口孤剣

Yamaji Aizan 山路愛山
Yano Fumio 矢野文雄
Yasuoka Hideo (Nankyoku Rōsei)
　安岡秀夫 (南極老星)
Yasuoka Ryōsuke 安岡良亮
Yasuoka Yūkichi 安岡雄吉
Yokota Kinba 横田金馬
Yorozu chōhō 萬朝報
Yoshida Shōin 吉田松陰
Yoshiwara 吉原
Yoshiwara de 吉原で止って来た
　tomatte kita
Yuengijuku 遊焉義塾
Yūrakuchō eigakkan 猿樂町英学館

Bibliography

The following is a select list of books and articles consulted in the preparation of the book. Until recently the most widely available collection of Kōtoku's writings was the three-volume *Kōtoku Shūsui senshū* edited by Hirano Yoshitarō and published in Tokyo in 1949–50. Five volumes of a new *Kōtoku Shūsui zenshū*, which is scheduled to run to eleven volumes, have been published by the Meiji Bunken Sha as of January 1970. Since much of this study was completed before the later collection was published most of my references are to the earlier work. I have, however, indicated titles of Kōtoku's books and articles whenever possible so that these may be consulted in the new collected works.

I WORKS IN JAPANESE

Akamatsu Katsumarō (赤松克麿)
　Nihon shakai undō shi (日本社會運動史) Tokyo, 1949.
Akiyama Kiyoshi (秋山清)
　Nihon no hangyaku shisō (日本の反逆思想), Tokyo, 1960.
Arahata Kanson (荒畑寒村)
　Kanson jiden (寒村自伝), Tokyo, 1965.
　'Kōtoku Shūsui' (幸徳秋水), *Sandai genron jin shū* (三代言論人集), vol. VIII, Tokyo, 1963.
　Nihon Shakai Shugi undō shi (日本社会主義運動史), Tokyo, 1922.
Asahi Shimbun (朝日新聞)
Asukai Masamichi (飛鳥井雅道)
　'Kōtoku Shūsui' (幸徳秋水), *Hangyaku sha no shōzō* (反逆者の肖像), vol. XIII of *Nijū seiki o ugokashita hitobito* (20世紀を動かした人々), Tokyo, 1963.
Ebina Danjō (海老名弾正)
　Kirisuto kyō gairon: waga shinkyō no yurai to keika (基督教概論我が信教の由来と経過), Tokyo, 1937.
Hara Kei nikki (原敬日記), 9 vols, Tokyo, 1951.
Hayashi Shigeru (林茂)
　Kindai Nihon no shisōka tachi (近代日本の思想家たち), Tokyo, 1965.
　'Nihon ni okeru Shakai Shugi kenkyū soshiki no shōtai' (日本における社会主義研究組織の正体), *Shakai kagaku kenkyū* (社会科学研究), vol. I, no. I, February 1948.
Hijikata Kazuo (土方和雄)
　Nakae Chōmin (中江兆民), Tokyo, 1959.
Hiranuma Kiichirō (平沼騏一郎)
　Hiranuma Kiichirō kaikoroku (平沼騏一郎回顧録), Tokyo, 1955.
Hirao Michio (平尾道雄)
　Shishaku Tani Kanjō den (子爵谷干城伝), Tokyo, 1935.
Hosokawa Karoku, Watanabe Yoshimichi, and Shiota Shōbei (eds.) (塩田庄兵衛)
　Nihon Shakai Shugi bunken kaisetsu (日本社会主義文献解説), Tokyo, 1950.

Ichii Saburō (市井三郎)
  Tetsugaku teki bunseki (哲学的分析), Tokyo, 1963.
Imamura Rikisaburō (今村力三郎)
  Hōtei gojūnen (法廷五十年), Tokyo, 1948.
Ishida Takeshi (石田雄)
  Meiji seiji shisō shi kenkyū (明治政治思想史研究), Tokyo, 1964.
Ishikawa Sanshirō (石川三四郎) and Kōtoku Shūsui (幸徳秋水)
  Nihon shakai shugi shi (日本社会主義史), in *Meiji bunka zenshū*, (明治文化全集) vol.
    21, Shakai hen (社会篇), Tokyo, 1929.
Ishimoda Shō (石母田正)
  Zoku rekishi to minzoku no hakken (續歴史と民族の発見), Tokyo, 1963.
Itō Sei (伊藤整)
  'Kōtoku Shūsui no taiho' (幸徳秋水の逮捕), *Gunzō*, (群像), vol. 22, no. 4
    (April 1967).
Itoya Toshio (糸屋壽雄)
  Kōtoku Shūsui den (幸徳秋水伝), Tokyo, 1950.
  Kōtoku Shūsui kenkyū (幸徳秋水研究), Tokyo, 1967.
  Taigyaku jiken (大逆事件), Tokyo, 1960.
Iwaki Yukinori (岩城之德)
  Ishikawa Takuboku den (石川啄木伝), Tokyo, 1961.
Iwanami Kōza (岩波講座) (pub.)
  Nihon rekishi, Gendai I (日本歴史現代一), Tokyo
Jiji Shimpō (時事新報)
Kanzaki Kiyoshi (神崎清)
  Kakumei densetsu (革命伝説), Tokyo, 1960.
  Taigyaku jiken (大逆事件), Tokyo, 1964.
  (ed.) *Taigyaku jiken kiroku* (大逆事件記録), 3 vols, Tokyo, 1964.
Katayama Sen (片山潜)
  Katayama Sen chosaku shū (片山潜著作集), 3 vols, Tokyo, 1959–60.
Kawanami Hideo (川並秀雄)
  Takuboku no shakai shisō (啄木の社会思想), Kyoto, 1948.
Kida Junichirō (紀田順一郎)
  Meiji no risō (明治の理想.), Tokyo, 1965.
Kinoshita Naoe (木下尚江)
  'Hakaba' (墓場), *Gendai Nihon bungaku zenshū* (現代日本文学全集), vol. LIII,
    Tokyo, 1958.
  Kami ningen jiyū (神人間自由), Tokyo, 1934.
  'Katayama Sen to boku' (片山潜と僕), *Chūō Kōron* (中央公論), vol. XLVIII,
    no. 12, December 1933.
  Yajingo (野人語), Tokyo, 1911.
Kōchi Kenritsu Toshokan (高知県立図書館) (ed.)
  Kōchi han kyōiku enkaku torishirabe (高知藩教育沿革取調べ), Kōchi, 1932.
Koizumi Sakutarō (Sanshin) (小泉策太郎・三申)
  'Sakai kun to Kōtoku Shūsui o kataru' (堺君と幸徳秋水を語る), *Chūō Kōron*
    (中央公論), vol. XLVI, no. 10, October 1931.
Kōtoku Shūsui (幸徳秋水)

Kirisuto massatsu ron (基督抹殺論), Tokyo, 1911.

Kōtoku Shūsui hyōron to zuisō (幸徳秋水評論と随想), edited by Kawano Hiroshi (河野廣), Tokyo, 1950.

Kōtoku Shūsui no nikki to shokan (幸徳秋水の日記と書簡), edited by Shiota Shōbei (塩田庄兵), Tokyo, 1965.

Kōtoku Shūsui senshū (幸徳秋水選集), edited by Hirano Yoshitarō (平野義大郎), 3 vols, Tokyo, 1949–50.

Kōtoku Shūsui zenshū (幸徳秋水全集), published by Meiji Bunken Sha (明治文献社), to be 11 vols, Tokyo, 1968– .

Kōtoku Shūsui shisō ronshū (幸徳秋水思想論集), special edition of *Kaihō* (解放), vol. 19, no. 11, November 1929.

Shūsui bunshū (秋水文集), Tokyo, 1947.

Teikoku shugi (帝国主義), Tokyo, 1959.

Kōtoku Tomiji (幸徳富治)
   'Oji Kōtoku Shūsui' (伯父幸徳秋水), *Chūō Kōron* (中央公論), vol. LXX, no. 4, April, 1955.

Kōtoku Yukie (幸徳幸衛)
   'Oji Shūsui no omoide' (叔父秋水の思い出), *Chūō Kōron* (中央公論), vol. XLVIII, no. 4, April, 1933.

Kumamoto hyōron (熊本評論)

Maruyama Masao (丸山眞男)
   Gendai seiji no shisō to kōdō (現代政治の思想と行動), Tokyo, 1964.
   'Kuga Katsunan to kokumin shugi' (陸羯南と国民主義), *Minken ron kara nashi-yonarizumu e* (民権論からナショナリズムへ), Tokyo, 1957.
   Nihon seiji shisō shi kenkyū (日本政治思想史研究), Tokyo, 1963.

Matsuda Michio (松田道雄)
   Anakizumu (アナーキズム), *Gendai Nihon shisō taikei* (現代日本思想大系), vol. 16, Tokyo, 1963.

Matsui Hirokichi (松井広吉)
   Yonjūgonen kisha seikatsu (四十五年記者生活), Tokyo, 1929.

Matsushita Yoshio (松下芳男)
   Sandai hansen undō shi (三代反戦運動史), Tokyo, 1960.

Meiji Shakai Shugi shiryō shū (明治社会主義史料集), 12 vols., Tokyo, 1960–4.
   Vol. I   *Chokugen* (直言).
   Vol. II   *Hikari* (光).
   Vol. III   *Shin Kigen* (新紀元).
   Vol. IV   *Nikkan Heimin Shimbun* (日刊平民新聞).
   Vol. V   *Osaka Heimin Shimbun* (大阪平民新聞).
   Vols. VI–VII *Shūkan Shakai Shimbun* (週刊社会新聞).
   Sp. vol. I   *Sekai fujin* (世界婦人).
   Sp. vol. II   *Kumamoto Hyōron* (熊本評論).
   Sp. vols. III–IV *Shūkan Heimin Shimbun* (週刊平民新聞).

Miyake Setsurei (三宅雪嶺)
   Dōjidai shi (同時代史), vol. 4, Tokyo, 1952.

Miyatake Tohone (宮武外骨)
   Kōtoku ippa taigyaku jiken temmatsu (幸徳一派大逆事件顛末), Tokyo, 1946.

Morinaga Eisaburō (森長英三郎)
　'Taigyaku jiken no hōritsu men' (大逆事件の法律面), *Rōdō undō shi kenkyū* (労働運動史研究), no. 22, July, 1960.
Morito Tatsuo (森戸辰男)
　Nihon ni okeru kirisuto-kyō to shakai shugi (日本における キリスト教と社会主義運動), Tokyo, 1950.
Morooka Chiyoko (師岡千代子)
　Otto Kōtoku Shūsui no omoide (夫幸徳秋水の思出), Tokyo, 1946.
Nagai Kafū (永井荷風)
　'Hanabi' (花火), *Nagai Kafū zenshū* (永井荷風全集), Tokyo, 1949.
Nakae Chōmin (中江兆民)
　San suijin keirin mondō (三酔人経綸問答), Tokyo, 1965.
Nakamura Chō Yakuba (中村町 役場) (ed.)
　Nakamura chō shi (中村 町史), Kōchi, 1950.
Nakamura Katsunori (中村勝範)
　'Chokusetsu kōdō ron no taitō: Kōtoku Shūsui no riron o megutte' (直接行動論
　　の抬頭・幸德秋水の理論をめぐって), *Hōgaku Kenkyū* (法学研究), vol. 31, no. 10,
　　October 1958.
　'Heiminsha no kaisan to danatsu' (平民社の解散と弾圧), *Hōgaku Kenkyū*
　　(法学研究), vol. 33, no. 2, February 1960.
　'Heiminsha no zaisei jijō' (平民社の財政事情), *Hōgaku Kenkyū*, (法学研究),
　　vol. 32, no. 12, December 1958.
　'Kōtoku Shūsui no shōgai to shisō' (幸德秋水の生涯と思想), *Hōgaku Kenkyū*
　　(法学研究), vol. 30, no. 11, November 1957.
Nihon kindai shi jiten (日本近代史辞典), Tokyo, 1958.
Nishio Yōtarō (西尾陽太郎)
　Kōtoku Shūsui (幸德秋水), Tokyo, 1966.
Ōhara Kei (大原慧)
　'Genro Yamagata Aritomo e no shokan: "taigyaku jiken" to kanrenshite'
　　(元老山県有朋への書翰 大逆事件と関連して), *Tokyo Keidai Gakkaishi* (東京
　　経大学会誌), no. 39, June, 1963.
　'Taigyaku jiken no kokusai teki eikyō' (大逆事件の国際的影響), *Shisō* (思想),
　　no. 471, September 1963 and no. 475 January 1964.
Ōsugi Sakae (大杉栄)
　Jijoden (自叙伝), Tokyo, 1923.
Ōyama Azusa (大山梓) (ed.)
　Yamagata Aritomo iken sho (山県有朋意見書), Tokyo, 1966.
Rikugo Zasshi (六合雑誌)
Rōdō undō shi kenkyū (労働運動史研究), no. 22, July, 1960.
Sakai Toshihiko (堺利彦)
　Nihon Shakai Shugi undō shi (日本社会主義運動史), Tokyo, 1954.
　Sakai Toshihiko zenshū (堺利彦全集), 6 vols, Tokyo, 1933.
Sakata Yoshio (坂田吉雄)
　Meiji zenhanki no nashiyonarizumu (明治前半期のナショナリズム), Tokyo,
　　1958.
Setouchi Harumi (瀬戸内晴美)

'Kanno Sugako' (菅野須賀子), *Chūō Kōron* (中央公論), vol. LXXX, no. 9, September 1965.

Shakai Bunko (ed.)
Zai bei Shakai Shugi sha – Museifu Shugi sha enkaku (在米社会主義者無政府主義者沿革), Tokyo, 1964.

Shakai keizai rōdō kenkyūjo (社会経済労働研究所)
Kōtoku Shūsui hyōden (幸徳秋水評伝), Tokyo, 1948.

Shinobu Seizaburō and Nakayama Haruichi (信夫清三郎・中山治一) (eds)
Nichi-rō sensō shi no kenkyū (日露戦争史の研究), Tokyo, 1959.

Shiota Shōbei and Watanabe Junzō (塩田庄兵衛・渡辺順三) (eds)
Hiroku taigyaku jiken (秘録大逆事件), 2 vols, Tokso, 1959.

Shirayanagi Shūko (白柳秀湖)
Meiji Taishō kokumin shi: Meiji kōki (明治大正国民史・明治後期), Tokyo, 1937.
Saionji Kimmochi den (西園寺公望伝), Tokyo, 1929.

Shūkan Heimin Shimbun (週刊平民新聞), edited by Hattori Shisō (服部 之總) and Konishi Shirō (小西四郎), 4 vols, Tokyo, 1953–8.

Sumiya Mikio (隅谷三喜男)
Nihon shakai to kirisuto-kyō (日本社会とキリスト教), Tokyo, 1963.

Taiyo (太陽)

Tanaka Sōgorō (田中惣五郎)
Kōtoku Shūsui: ikkakumeika no shisō to shōgai (幸徳秋水・革命家の思想と生涯), Tokyo, 1955.
Nihon shakai undō shi (日本社会運動史), Tokyo, 1948.

Teradani Takeshi (寺谷 隆)
'Kōtoku Shūsui ron' (幸徳秋水論), *Kokugo to koku bungaku* (国語と国文学), vol. 37, no. 5, May 1960.

Tokutomi Iichirō (徳富猪一郎)
Kōshaku Yamagata Aritomo den (公爵山県有朋伝), 3 vols, Tokyo, 1935.

Tokutomi Roka (徳富蘆花)
'Muhon ron' (謀叛論), *Hiyūmanizumu* (ヒューマニズム), vol. 17 of *Gendai Nihon shisō taikei* (現代日本思想大系), Tokyo, 1964.

Uchimura Kanzō (内村鑑三)
Uchimura Kanzō shinkō chosaku zenshū (内村鑑三 信仰著作全集), 25 vols, Tokyo, 1961–6.

Watanabe Junzō (渡辺順三)
Kōtoku jiken no zembō (幸徳事件の全貌), Tokyo, 1947.

Yamagiwa Keiji (山極圭司)
Kinoshita Naoe (木下尚江), Tokyo, 1955.

Yamaji Aizan (山路愛山)
Genji no shakai mondai oyobi shakai shugi sha (現時の社会問題及び社会主義者), *Meiji bunka zenshū* (明治文化全集), vol. XXI, Tokyo, 1929.

Yamamoto Seibi (山本正美)
'Hito to shite no Kōtoku Shūsui' (人としての幸徳秋水), *Nihon Hyōron* (日本評論), February 1947.

Zai Bei Shakai Shugi sha – Museifu Shugi sha enkaku (在米社会主義者無政府主義者沿革), Tokyo, 1964.

2 WORKS IN ENGLISH

Bailey, Jackson H.
'Prince Saionji and the Popular Rights Movement of the 1880's', *Journal of Asian Studies*, vol. 21, no. 1, November, 1961.

Bailey, Thomas A.
Theodore Roosevelt and the Japanese – American Crisis: An Account of the International Complications Arising from the Race Problem on the Pacific Coast, Gloucester, Mass., 1964.

Beardsley, Richard K., Hall, John W., and Ward, Robert E.
Village Japan, Chicago, 1959.

Beasley, William G.
The Modern History of Japan, New York, 1963.

Bellah, Robert N.
Tokugawa Religion: the Values of Pre-Industrial Japan, Glencoe, Ill., 1957.
'Values and Social Change in Modern Japan', *Asian Cultural Studies* (International Christian University, Tokyo), vol. III, 1962.

Blacker, Carmen
The Japanese Enlightenment: a Study of the Writings of Fukuzawa Yukichi, Cambridge, 1964.

Borton, Hugh
Japan's Modern Century, New York, 1955.

Brissenden, Paul Frederick
The I.W.W.: A study of American Syndicalism, vol. 83 of *Studies in History, Economy, and Public Law* (Columbia University), New York, 1919.

Brown, Delmer M.
Nationalism in Japan: an Introductory Historical Analysis, Berkeley, 1955.

Buber, Martin
Paths in Utopia, translated by R. F. C. Hull, London, 1949.

Colbert, Evelyn S.
The Left Wing in Japanese Politics, New York, 1952.

Cole, George Douglas Howard
History of Socialist Thought, 2 vols., London, 1954.

Dore, Ronald P.
Education in Tokugawa Japan, Berkeley, 1965.

Elison, George
'Kōtoku Shūsui: "The Change in Thought"', *Monumenta Nipponica*, vol. XXII, no. 3–4, 1967.

Ely, Richard T.
Socialism and Social Reform, New York, 1894.

Fairbank, John K., Reischauer, Edwin O., and Craig, Albert M.
East Asia the Modern Transformation, Boston, 1965.

Fujii, Jintarō
Outline of Japanese History in the Meiji Era, translated and adapted by Hattie K. Colton and Kenneth E. Colton, Tokyo, 1958.

George, Henry
Progress and Poverty, New York, 1942.
Grave, Jean
Moribund Society and Anarchy, San Francisco, 1899.
Havel, Hyppolyte
'Kōtoku's Correspondence with Albert Johnson', *Mother Earth*, vol. IV, no. 6, August, 1911.
Iglehart, Charles W.
A Century of Protestant Christianity in Japan, Tokyo, 1959.
Ike, Nobutaka
The Beginnings of Political Democracy in Japan, Baltimore, 1950.
'Kōtoku: Advocate of Direct Action', *The Far Eastern Quarterly*, vol. III, no. 3, May, 1944.
Ishii, Ryosuke (ed.)
Japanese Legislation in the Meiji Era, translāted by William J. Chambliss, Tokyo, 1958.
Itō Hirobumi
Commentaries on the Constitution of the Empire of Japan, tr. Itō Miyoji, Tokyo, 1889.
Jansen, Marius B.
(ed.) *Changing Japanese Attitudes Towards Modernization*, Princeton, 1965.
'Ōi Kentarō: Radicalism and Chauvinism', *Far Eastern Quarterly*, vol. 11, no. 3, December 1959.
Sakamoto Ryōma and the Meiji Restoration, Princeton, 1961.
Joll, James
The Anarchists, New York, 1964.
Katayama, Sen
The Labor Movement in Japan, Chicago, 1918.
Kirkup, Thomas
An Inquiry into Socialism, New York, 1888.
Kosaka Masaaki (ed.)
Japanese Thought in the Meiji Era, translated and adapted by David Abosch, Tokyo, 1958.
Kropotkin, Peter
The Conquest of Bread, London, 1913.
Kublin, Hyman
Asian Revolutionary: the Life of Sen Katayama, Princeton, 1964.
'The Japanese Socialists and the Russo-Japanese War', *Journal of Modern History*, vol. XXII, no. 4, December, 1950.
'The Origins of the Japanese Socialist Tradition', *Journal of Politics*, vol. XIV, no. 2, May, 1952.
Lane, Michael A.
The Level of Social Motion, New York, 1902.
Lockwood, William W.
The Economic Development of Japan; Growth and Structural Change, 1868–1938, Princeton, 1954.

Maruyama, Masao
Thought and Behavior in Modern Japanese Politics, London, 1963.
Nitobe, Inazo
Western Influences in Modern Japan, Chicago, 1931.
Notehelfer, Fred G.
'Ebina Danjō: A Christian Samurai of the Meiji Period', *Papers on Japan* (East Asian Research Center, Harvard University), vol. II, 1963.
Powles, Cyril H.
'Abe Isoo and the Role of Christians in the Founding of the Japanese Socialist Movement: 1895–1905', *Papers on Japan* (East Asian Research Center, Harvard University), vol. I, 1961.
Pyle, Kenneth
The New Generation in Meiji Japan, Stanford, 1969.
Russell, Bertrand
Proposed Roads to Freedom: Socialism, Anarchism, and Syndicalism, New York, 1919.
Ryan, Marleigh Grayer
Japan's First Modern Novel: Ukigumo of Futabatei Shimei, New York, 1967.
San Francisco Chronicle
Sansom, George
A History of Japan, 3 vols., Stanford, 1958–63.
The Western World and Japan, New York, 1962.
Scalapino, Robert
Democracy and the Party Movement in Prewar Japan, the Failure of the First Attempt, Berkeley, 1953.
Schaffle, Albert
The Quintessence of Socialism, New York, 1898.
Sebald, William J.
The Criminal Code of Japan, Kobe, Japan, 1936.
Smith, Thomas C.
Political Change and Industrial Development in Japan: Government Enterprise, 1868–1880, Stanford, 1955.
The Agrarian Origins of Modern Japan, Stanford, 1959.
Smith, Warren W.
Confucianism in Modern Japan: a Study of Conservatism in Japanese Intellectual History, Tokyo, 1959.
Snow, Edgar
Red Star Over China, New York, 1961.
Sorel, Georges
Reflections on Violence, London, 1950.
Soviak, Eugene
'The Case of Baba Tatsui: Western Enlightenment, Social Change, and the Early Meiji Intellectual', *Monumenta Nipponica*, no. 18, 1963.
Takekoshi, Yosaburō
Prince Saionji, Kyoto, 1933.

BIBLIOGRAPHY

Takeuchi, Tatsuji
  War and Diplomacy in the Japanese Empire, New York, 1935.
  The Japan Weekly Mail
  The North China Herald
Totten, George Oakley III
  The Social Democratic Movement in Prewar Japan, New Haven, 1966.
Tsunoda, Ryusaku, *et al.*
  Sources of Japanese Tradition, New York, 1958.
Uyehara, Cecil H.
  Leftwing Social Movements in Japan: an Annotated Bibliography, Tokyo, 1959.
Ward, Robert E. (ed.)
  Political Development in Modern Japan, Princeton, 1968.
Wildes, Harry Emerson
  The Press and Social Currents in Japan, Philadelphia, 1927.
Woodcock, George
  Anarchism: a History of Libertarian Ideas and Movements, New York, 1963.
Yanaga, Chitoshi
  Japan Since Perry, New York, 1949.

Index

Abe Isoo, 39, 62, 67, 70n, 94, 103, 118
'Advice to the Teachers of Primary Schools' ('Shōgakkō kyōshi ni tsugu'), 104
Alaska, Oka Shigeki in, 121n
American Socialist Party, 127–8
Anarchism: in the ideology of Kōtoku, 1, 113, 116–17, 124, 126–8; advocated by Kōtoku, 149–50; of Kōtoku's followers, 159
Anarchist Communism: in Kōtoku's ideology, 126; in the Japanese socialist movement, 150, 159
Anarchists, controversy of, with the Social Democrats, 143, 149
Anglo-Japanese Alliance (1902), 89
Anthony, of the I.W.W., 128
'Appeal to the Young' (Kropotkin), 146n
Arahata Kanson, 95; ideological differences with Kōtoku, 146–7; relationship of, with Kanno Sugako, 167; imprisoned, 168; a maligned hero, 174; angry letter from, to Kōtoku, 181; letter to, from Kōtoku, 181–3
Arena, 98
Asahi Shimbun, 188, 196
Ashio Copper Mine problem, 65–6, 68n
Ashio riots, 141, 144, 146
Assassination: in Kōtoku's ideology, 26, 73–4, 81, 140, 194; of government leaders urged by Mrs Fritz, 127; of the Emperor desired by Miyashita Daikichi, 170–2; of the Crown Prince plotted, 172; of the Emperor plotted, 191; plot against the Emperor denied by Kōtoku, 193
'Attitude of the Educator Towards the War, The' ('Sensō ni tai-suru kyōiku-sha no taido'), 104

Bakin, Kōtoku's interest in the novels of, 25
Bakufu, destruction of the Nakamura fief by, 4
Bakumatsu loyalist movement, Morooka Masatane in, 47n
Bakunin, Mikhail, *God and the State*, 151
Baltic Fleet, of Russia, 104
Bebel, August, 111
Bellah, Robert, 2
'Bethink Yourselves!', 101, 103
Bible, 109
Blanc, Louis, 62
Bloody Sunday Massacre, 129n
Bombs: discussed by Kōtoku and Ōishi, 164; Nariishi Kanzaburō's interest in, 169n;

Miyashita Daikichi's interest in, 170, 172–3, 175–7; Uchiyama Gudō's interest in, 172; Kanno Sugako willing to use, 181; mentioned in Kōtoku's indictment, 184–5
Bonaparte, U.S. Attorney General, 155
Boshin Rescript, 161–2
Boxer Rebellion, 82, 89, 90

California, tension over Japanese immigrants in, 139–40
Chang Chi, 149
Chian Keisatsu Hō, *see* Peace Police Law
Chiba prefecture, pollution problem of, 65
Chikamatsu, read by Kōtoku, 25
China: Kōtoku's desire to visit, 20; after the Sino-Japanese War, 89; Japanese attitude toward, 91; *see also* Sino-Japanese War
Chinese students, in Tokyo, 149
Ch'ing government, 89; *see also* China; Sino-Japanese War
Chokugen (Plain Talk; monthly), 56n, 109
Christian missionaries in Japan, 70–1n
Christian Socialism, 71
Christianity: Kōtoku's opposition to, 68, 71, 75, 78–9, 95, 112, 116, 183n, 193; effect of, on traditional Japanese social structure, 71–2; appeal of, to the samurai class, 74–5; a progressive force in Japan, 95; identified with socialism, 102–3
'Christianity and Socialism' ('Kirisuto Kyō to Shakai Shugi'), 102
Christians, Japanese: and the socialist movement, 39, 62, 70–1, 86, 101, 118; and the Sino-Japanese War, 56,000; Western individualism of, 72; ideology of, 74–5, 78–9; pacificism of, 91; Kōtoku's differences with, 103; and the demise of the *Heimin Shimbun*, 107–8; in the United States, 124n
Chuang Tzu, 33n
Chūō Kōron, 102
Chūō Shimburn, 36, 38, 40–1, 43–4
Chūseitō, 13
'Clique of the Divine Wind' (Shinpūren), 9n
Commentaries on Hebrew and Christian Mythology, 112
Common man, Kōtoku's desire to reach, 137
Commoner's News, The, see *Heimin Shimbun*
Communist Manifesto, The, 105–7
Confucianism: in Kōtoku's education, 11; in Kōtoku's thought, 56–7, 60, 68–70, 74–5, 80, 82–4, 194; restructured in Japanese Christian

219

INDEX